VARÈSE

A Looking-Glass Diary

Louise Varèse

VARÈSE

A Looking-Glass Diary

VOLUME I: 1883-1928

W · W · NORTON & COMPANY · INC ·
NEW YORK

Library of Congress Cataloging in Publication Data

Varèse, Louis (McCutcheon) 1890–
    Varèse; a looking-glass diary.

    CONTENTS: v. 1. 1883–1928.
    1. Varèse, Edgard, 1883–1965.
ML410.V27V272   785'.0924 [B]   74-139392
ISBN 0-393-07461-7

Published simultaneously in Canada
by George J. McLeod Limited, Toronto
PRINTED IN THE UNITED STATES OF AMERICA

1 2 3 4 5 6 7 8 9 0

To my son, Michael Norton

CONTENTS

Photographs follow page 146

FOREWORD

I feel that I am in honor bound to warn musicians and musicologists that they will find nothing musical about the music of Varèse in this book by his nonmusical wife.

It is not really a biography either; it is a personal remembering with all that that entails of bias.

You write a diary so that you won't forget your life as it gallops by. It seemed to me that all those prodigal years with Varèse had been one long gallop. Could I remember all the things that had rushed backward away from me? I held up my memory to the mirror and I have written what I saw.

Its incentive and inception were very different and, for my part, more modest. I was to have written a brief caption-biography for a Varèse picture book composed by Thomas Bouchard and Diane Bouchard. It is a lifetime of photographs of Varèse (many of them by Bouchard, whom Varèse called "the poet of photographers"), of cartoons and of painted and sculptured portraits of Varèse, of his own paintings, of his scores; of programs; a lifetime of photographs of places in his life, friends, teachers, colleagues, patrons; of paintings and poems inspired by his music and dedicated to him.

Confidently Diane Bouchard showed their Varèse picture book to publishers; too wise, unfortunately, in the precarious ways of the life of books, after admiring, they rejected it as unprofitable.

What was to have been a short caption-biography grew into a long diary *à rebours*. This book is half of it.

ACKNOWLEDGMENTS

That is much too cool a word to convey the warmth of my gratitude to:

John Maurer—lifetime researcher, designer, inventor of photographic equipment—for the generous gift he made me of his expert knowledge restoring Varèse's unusable family pictures and old newspaper photographs that had been disintegrating for almost half a century.

Thomas Bouchard, Varèse's "poet of photographers," who worked with John Maurer on the old photographs and made most of the prints for this volume; also an advance thanks for his many photographs—the best of all those taken of Varèse in his later years—which he has so liberally put at my disposal for the volume to come.

Diane Bouchard, without whose encouragement, criticism, overpraise, researching energy, and never-lagging nagging I might well have faltered on the road to the publication of these notes on a life that encompassed so much more than one memory has treasured.

Mrs. Christina Zimmer, for her kindness in helping to make Varèse's letters to her father, Hugo van Hofmannstahl, available.

The MacDowell Colony for the many months spent working in the sumptuous surroundings of its green lawns, old trees, meadows, and endless woods, enjoying the privilege of perfect peace and privacy.

VARÈSE

A Looking-Glass Diary

If any one faculty of our nature may be called more wonderful than the rest, I do think it is memory. There seems something more speakingly incomprehensible in the powers, the failures, the inegalities of memory, than in any other of our intelligences. The memory is sometimes so retentive, so serviceable, so obedient; at others, so bewildered and so weak; at others again, so tyrannic, so beyond control!

Jane Austen, *Mansfield Park*

PART I

Early Years
1883–1915

Monsieur n'est pas comme tout le monde.
Varèse's father

V ARÈSE was born in Paris but for some reason that he never seems to have inquired into, when still a baby he was taken down to the little village of Le Villars, near Tournus in Burgundy, and entrusted to the care of Oncle Joseph (one of his grandfather's brothers) and Tante Marie.

All his life Varèse was to cherish the memory of this little village, which was the birthplace of his beloved grandfather, Claude Cortot, his mother's father. Varèse had a storyteller's gift for lifting everything out of the commonplace; as I listened to him telling me, with that warmth and eagerness that was peculiarly his, about Le Villars and Grandpère, the stories gradually took on for me the heightened reality of legend and still hold an emotional appeal that Varèse had the power to communicate.

When asked in 1961 for a biographical note for a cookbook to which he had contributed a recipe learned from his grandfather, Varèse wrote:

> I am a *Bourguignon*, even though I was born in Paris. Burgundy was the country of my mother's family, and I was still a baby when I was taken down to her people in the village of Le Villars, near Tournus. There I grew up to boyhood, and I remember how I hated to return to my family to go to school in Paris. But later, when a student at the Paris *Conservatoire* and afterwards when I was living in Berlin before the First World War, I would go back to Le Villars for vacations to stay with my grandfather. I often took friends with me, among others the Spanish sculptor Gonzales, who made a drawing of him. Not having any fixative, he used the juice of garlic as preservative. The portrait, a perfect likeness, still hangs in the room where I work, the only picture I have of my grandfather.
>
> At that time my grandfather was living alone in a little house which is a part of the 12th century Prieuré. There is a small Romanesque church connected with the Prieuré which is not unknown to anyone who has read Anatole France's *Rôtisserie de la Reine Pédauque*, for it is outside this little church that his Abbé Jérôme Coignard dies.
>
> My grandfather, like all the other peasants in our village, had a vineyard and made his own wine. He also did his own cooking and was an excellent cook. As a soldier he had visited several Eastern countries and knew many Oriental recipes. One I remember, and I have often made myself—Syrian, I think—consists of cucumbers sliced very thin and prepared with sour cream and mint. This, as well as old familiar French dishes such as *Boeuf Bourguignon, Potée Bourguignonne, Coq-au-vin, Veau* (or poulet) *Marengo,* I learned from him.
>
> One of my early scores, the first orchestral work I ever had performed (Berlin, 1910) I called *Bourgogne* in his honor and dedicated to him. And I have inherited only one thing of value, the memory of my Burgundian grandfather.

Equal to Varèse's own was the love of the grandfather for the boy and then for the headstrong, eager young man. One has only to read Claude Cortot's untutored letters to be touched by them. Varèse kept a packet of them dating from 1904 to November 1910, the year of Grandpère's death.

From babyhood to school age, Varèse lived in Le Villars with his great aunt and uncle and their little daughter, Marthe, a few years older than her baby cousin Gogo—the name he gave himself. He lived the life of a peasant boy and was happy. Like most villages in the Mâconnais, Le Villars was surrounded by vineyards and Oncle Joseph was the *forgeron,* the ironsmith of the village who made the iron bands for his neighbors' wine kegs. Even stronger than a taste for good wine, Varèse always kept a taste for the poetry of *la vigne.*

During his childhood in Burgundy, Varèse used to be taken occasionally to see his parents in Paris, but he remembered those trips only as one recalls dreams in vivid flashes surrounded by darkness: walking along a street with his grandmother, the sensation of his hand in hers, feeling very happy, being in his grandfather's arms, being lifted high in the air and laughing. Of his mother and father, nothing. His grandfather at that time had a little bistro in Paris in the rue de Lancry, between the boulevard de Magenta and the canal Saint-Martin. I can still hear Varèse repeating these names as though the mere sound of the words gave him pleasure.

When finally Varèse had to leave Le Villars to go to school in Paris and live with his parents in their apartment (probably at that time on the boulevard de Strasbourg), from being afraid of his brutal father, who indulged in corporal punishment for the slightest fault, Varèse soon began to hate him with a bitter hate that never abated to the end of his life. In fact, during the almost fifty years I knew him, I heard him say over and over again like a refrain, *"J'aurais du tuer ce salaud!"* or, sometimes in English, "I should have killed that bastard!" Of his mother all he would say was: "I pitied her; she was too unhappy." For Varèse pity seems always to have been a belittling emotion precluding any deep regard. In any case, after he left Le Villars it seems that Grandmère and Grandpère took the place of both mother and father in his affections. Varèse told me little of those school days in Paris except that he hated school, and, even more violently, his father, that he adored his grandmother and grandfather and remembered driving with the latter to *les Halles,* the central markets of Paris, behind an old piebald horse whose name was Frèrot.

Soon after the death of Varèse's grandmother in the summer of 1893, Varèse's father moved his family to Turin, Italy, where he had business interests, and not long afterward Grandpère sold his bistro, and, to his grandson's great joy, came to live with his daughter's family in Turin.

Varèse disliked Turin as much as he loved Le Villars. He used to say: "It's a dead city, bourgeois, *emmerdante comme la pluie.*" And when I, remembering pictures of the arcade of the Piazza San Carlo, suggested that it must be at least architecturally charming, he would deny it vehemently: *"Non, elle est moche."* Ugly from his point of view, lack of life being for him a synonym of ugliness. You have only to listen to Varèse's music to understand that he could never like "perfection at the expense of life," which is the way Lewis Mumford has characterized Turin's famous piazza, or if you happen to know that Varèse preferred living in New York because for him it was, in the words of Henry James about the city of *his* choice, "the particular spot that communicates the greatest sense of life." The Hoover Dam (Boulder Dam when Merle Armitage took him to see it in 1939) and bridges such as the George Washington Bridge and all the other masterpieces of bridge building excited his imagination, and those giant iron towers that stride across the Jersey marshes, inspiration of how many sculptors! They were the dynamic present. "Italy is the past," he would say. "I don't like looking over my shoulder." Italy was also his father.

After moving to Italy, the first summers were spent at Bergeggi, a little town on the Mediterranean near Savona where Varèse's father used to rent a house for his family. There was a little garden, there were olive trees, Varèse recalled, and the house perched high on the cliffs overlooking the sea. "In seconds I could be in the water by going down some steps, really nothing but slits in the rocks—safe for goats and boys only." Varèse's memories of Bergeggi were happy ones, his father being absent almost the whole summer. It was in Bergeggi that Varèse became acquainted with the first of his many animal friends, a dolphin. I don't know how many times I heard him repeat the story and always with the same freshness and relish as if it had happened only the summer before. "As a boy," he would invariably begin, "I was a good swimmer—a regular fish, and at Bergeggi I was always in the water or with the fishermen in their boats. One day I'd gone out what might have seemed dangerously far, when I felt something nudging me. For a second I was scared. I thought: Sharks! Then I saw it was a dolphin and he was pushing me toward shore. After that he would often come and, jumping out of the water, catch the fish I held up for him." Varèse never failed to add, "The fishermen were *baba*—dumfounded." Evidently at the time neither the boy nor the fishermen had heard the many stories that have been told since antiquity of dolphins saving the lives of shipwrecked sailors by pushing them to the nearest shore or of their apparent affection for human beings.

Varèse was always convinced that his animals were in love with him as he was with them. *"Les bêtes m'aiment,"* he would say and *"Comme j'aime les bêtes!"* Like Colette, who said, "Not content with loving them, I wanted to shine in the eyes of these, my kin."

Other summers when he was older he would go mountain climbing with his paternal uncles in the Alps near Pignerol, his father's birthplace. Pignerol is in the Piedmont, a part of Italy that frequently changed nationality—sometimes French, sometimes Italian. His father, Henri Varèse, was Italian on his father's side, French on his mother's. His mother's name was Pauline Monet; one of her sisters married a Pasquet, and there were also Rivoires in the family. Varèse mentioned, as well, a great-great-grandmother who was Spanish. I remember a few odd bits of family history Varèse let fall at one time or another: The French ancestors came to Pignerol in the seventeenth century with Marechal Nicola Catinat, and a Monet, a great uncle of his grandmother, had been a doctor in Napoleon's army in the Russian campaign. Except for one of his father's uncles, Varèse detested the Italian side of his father's family and would get very angry if journalists mentioned the fact that he was partly Italian. He was deeply troubled by an ugly element in his nature ("my devil," he would call it), that he had inherited, he believed, from the Varèse "tribe." It was more than a violent temper. There were moments when, for apparently no reason, he would be seized by cold fury, a blind brutal hate. "Sometimes I could kill," he once told me. "I am afraid of myself." A dramatic exaggeration, I thought, until one evening: We had been having an intense, though as I thought, amicable discussion about something, I don't remember what, as impersonal as art, poetry, or philosophy, and I had just disagreed with him emphatically when suddenly he became furious and I was confronted by a stranger.

A complete change of personality occurred in an instant. What he said I hardly took in, but the brutality with which he spoke, the cruelty and coldness of his look horrified me as it astounded me. It was as if a leer should suddenly appear on the face of a child or a Buddha. All I could think of was: "This is what his father must have been like." Becoming cruel in my turn, I said aloud: "You are just like your father," before bursting into tears and rushing out of the room. Waking when it was already beginning to grow light, I was not surprised to find that Varèse had not come to bed. Then I noticed a large sheet of paper that had been slid under the door. Varèse had written: "Pardon, Pony [or Toto, I forget which of my names he was using then], je suis un C——," and in very large letters, "LE GRAND EMMERDEUR." This was the self-deprecatory name he had given himself for which I know no translation. I opened the door and looked over the banister. He was sitting at his table in his workroom, and when I went down to him he said, "You were right. I always said I should have killed that bastard." He told me that for days he had felt an oppression, a stifling, undefined hate, a desire to fight. Luigi Dallapiccola, the Italian composer, soon after he met Varèse, wrote in his diary on June 29, 1951, "In 1942 I happened to be present at an outbreak of Webern's anger and today of Varèse's; very different the one from the other, but equally interesting and instructive." One only wishes that Dallapiccola had enlarged upon this tantalizing observation. That Varèse in the end succeeded in controlling his "Varèse devil" was a triumph of will. Unfortunately the other dark side of this "man full of sun," as his former pupil Chou Wen-chung has called him, his crippling depressions, continued to handicap him.

I think it was the bitterness he nurtured against his known Varèse family that later led him to search for more acceptable forebears. He always said that they came originally from Corsica and he procured a book entitled *Armorial Corse* by Colonna de Cesari Rocca (in fact he had two copies, both in French) in which he found a Varèse family from the town of Bastia on a list of those families whose nobility was recognized by Louis XV in 1772 after Corsica had been annexed to France. More pertinent, he also discovered possible musical ancestors in a Fabius Varesus or Fabio Varese who composed sonatas and canzonets in the sixteenth century and a Giovanni Baptista Varese, composer of motets and masses around 1624. Curious, this mature interest in ancestors by someone who as a youth, to a tableful of people talking about theirs, had said, *"Moi, je suis l'ancêtre."*

Henri Varèse was an engineer, a graduate of the Polytechnique of Zurich. It followed in his pater familia mind that his eldest son should be an engineer and like him a graduate of the Polytechnique of Zurich. And so, directed to this end, from elementary school on, his son's studies were largely scientific and mathematical. It was also understood that his son should later on use his engineering knowledge (Henri Varèse had mining interests) to become a successful businessman which, because of his passion for litigation, his father was not. "He ruined not only himself, but also my grandfather with his damned law suits," Varèse told me with great bitterness, "so that Grandpère, in his old age, had to go on cultivating his few hectares of land when he was almost crippled with rheumatism."

When Varèse had shown an early and dangerously serious predilection for music, the piano was locked up. It was one thing for a father to play the violin accompanied by his wife at the piano ("playing sentimental trash," said Varèse), but quite another for an elder son to adopt music as a career. A precarious profession and scarcely respectable. So Varèse received no musical instruction until he was seventeen, when he met Giovanni Bolzoni, director of the Turin Conservatory, who took an interest in him and gave him private lessons.

Although lacking professional guidance, Varèse taught himself and composed in his own way—a way he continued to follow even after he had been taught all the textbook ways. This is how he described to me his first ambitious composition: "At the age of eleven I composed what I grandly called an opera. My company consisted of a few musically inclined schoolmates with choirboy voices, my orchestra, a mandolin my grandfather had given me. I monkeyed with the strings until I managed to get some sounds I liked, not a bit like the silly twiddle of the mandolin—and the frame was my first percussion instrument."

He wrote his own libretto, based on the heroic love story *Martin Pas* by Jules Verne. When I expressed surprise that he had not rather chosen one of Verne's prophetic science-fiction tales, which, as he told me, so excited his imagination, he explained: *"Martin Pas* seemed to me more dramatic and more romantic and therefore a better subject for an opera. After all, I lived in operatic Italy!" I think Varèse was a very romantic little boy and indeed a secret romantic all his life—like his music. Varèse himself once said: "What we need is a great romantic—I say romantic advisedly, for indeed in my estimation all great creators in science or art have been romantic. Genius is romantic. It is the work which is classic after it has withstood the test of time."

The first woman he fell in love with as a boy was Abbé Prévost's Manon Lescaut, and one of the first operas he heard was Massenet's *Manon* when he went with his grandfather to Paris for the exposition of 1890. But the Manon opera he really loved was Puccini's. Although he often said that opera today was an anachronism, beautiful voices gave him exquisite pleasure, and I noticed many times that whenever he sat listening to Manon on the radio there would come over his face a special Puccini expression of relaxed pleasure and he would say: "No one has ever equaled Puccini in writing for the voice." Of all the many beautiful voices he had heard in his long lifetime there were four that remained hauntingly in his memory: Nina Koshetz, who sang his own songs, *Offrandes;* Irène Joachim, the "only" Mélisande; La Niña de los Peines, the Flamenco singer; and Chaliapin, especially in *Boris Godunov.* In fact, Varèse wrote *Ecuatorial* with Chaliapin in mind. Soon after he began the score, one evening at a party, we were sitting with Chaliapin drinking champagne, his favorite drink (how many times the waiter refilled his glass I failed to count), when Varèse in his eager way began describing his work and dramatically recited part of the text, an invocation from the Maya's sacred book, the *Popol Voh,* in the Spanish translation.

"What nobility!" Varèse exclaimed. "But I simply must have a bass voice with a baritone—a lyric quality (an oratorio bass would kill it) and absolutely a singer who is an actor with imagination." Then he laughed and said to Chaliapin, "You see what I mean!"

At which Chaliapin, matching Varèse's enthusiasm with true Russian responsiveness cried: "I'll do it! I must be the first to sing your work. Waiter, champagne!" And we drank to the coming collaboration. Unfortunately the first performance of *Ecuatorial* took place without Chaliapin and with a bass without Chaliapin's qualities.

How many miles I shall now have to retrace my steps, my thoughts, how many years, to continue to pull out of my cluttered memory impressions entangled there, of Varèse's stories of his youth in Turin, in what he called the "prison" of his father's house. Twice as a small boy he ran away from it, once with two little school friends. When their provisions, including bread and a block of butter—a *"motte de beurre"*—appropriated by one of the boys from his family larder, gave out and after hunger and fatigue became stronger than their thirst for freedom, they had ignominiously returned and suffered the inevitable paternal beatings.

When he was fourteen his mother died at the age of thirty-one.

Varèse: A Looking-Glass Diary

Knowing that she was dying, she asked for her eldest son and when they were left alone she said to him: *"Veilles sur tes frères, ton père est un assassin* (Protect your brothers; your father is an assassin)." However bitter Varèse's hatred for his father had been before, I think it was at this moment that it became fanatical and murderous. Friends of Varèse have suggested that Henri Varèse could not have been the monster that throughout Varèse's life stalked his memory. Perhaps. But what can hardly be exaggerated is the harm he did his son. Varèse used to say, "I would probably have been a monster too, if it hadn't been for Grandpère."

At Turin Varèse attended the Institute Technique, which he said would correspond to an American science high school. Although Varèse liked to insist that he was a bad student, he could not have been too bad since he remembered so much of what he was taught. For example, he never forgot his Dante, and years later could recite long passages of the *Divina Commedia*. He explained this by saying that he liked his teacher, a Dante fanatic, whose name was Betrazzi and who must have been a very good teacher to so inspire his pupil with his own enthusiasm. For his professor of history Varèse wrote a paper, which won a competition, on the maritime republics of Italy: Genoa, Venice, Pisa. His little comic drawings and doodlings show that his hand never lost a skill due in part to the discipline acquired in his classes in mechanical drawing. Moreover, a passionate interest in science lasted throughout his life.

Naturally plagued as he was by a restless spirit and forced by his father to do the equivalent of five years of school in three, it is not surprising that he rebelled against so many hours of confinement and welcomed release in sports. When he was old, and a knee that had been injured in a ball game when he was sixteen became incurably arthritic and very painful, leaning heavily on my arm, he would say angrily (prefacing his remark with the *mot de Cambronne*—which I called *"le mot de Varèse"*): "And I once could outrun any boy at school!" He felt thwarted because his spirit now outdistanced his legs. "But what I really liked when I was a boy," he used to say, "was street fighting. If a brute of a boy, even much bigger than I was, teased me or in any way roused my awful temper, I would go for him with all my comparatively puny might and when I got home, bloody and with my clothes torn, I'd get another beating." I think each blow Varèse gave another boy was directed against his father and relieved his pent-up resentment. When his father once threatened him with reform school, Varèse retorted: "All right. But when I get out I will kill you." There must have been something in his son's spirit of independence and nonconformity that goaded the father. Not being able to tame him by brutality or threats, his father tried sarcasm. *"Naturellement,"* he would say, *"Monsieur n'est pas comme tout le monde."*

During his boyhood and youth in Turin, fully occupied as he was with studies, sports, brawls, and music, Varèse always had time for Maurice and Renaldo, his two younger brothers. He must have been quite an extraordinary brother. He not only helped his brothers with their schoolwork but encouraged their natural predilection for playing hooky by signing his father's name to notes of excuse—a really rash act of defiance.

When Varèse reminisced about his life in Turin I cannot remember his ever mentioning his sisters, Corinne and Yvonne, except to say that Yvonne was the youngest of the five children—in fact she must have been at least ten years younger than Varèse, for she was born in Italy—and that Corinne was next in age to himself.

During those years in Italy, Grandpère was Varèse's great consolation, his safety valve, to whom he could pour out all his fierce angers and unbearable frustrations. They also enjoyed some good times together. Grandpère took him to the opera, to concerts, and once they went to Paris together to the World's Fair of 1900. Varèse said that Grandpère had a naturally happy nature and a wonderful sense of humor. "When we got away from the damned house we were like two children playing hooky."

Of his first teacher, Giovanni Bolzoni, Varèse always spoke with great warmth, affection, and gratitude. He must have treasured his memory, for he kept the score Bolzoni had given him,

Sei Preludi for organ, in the same drawer with the inscribed scores of Debussy and Busoni. Bolzoni had inscribed it: *"All' Egrègio Allièvo,* Edgardo Varèse, Giovanni Bolzoni." It was to him that Varèse went when he felt that he could not endure his life at home any longer and had decided to leave. He begged Bolzoni to help him get to Paris so that he could go on with his music free from his father's harassment. Bolzoni kept the boy with him for a couple of days and finally with the kindly support of a friend, Monsignor Spandre, the Bishop of Turin, made him understand that he would not be able to cross the frontier and that his father could have him brought back. Varèse was still in his seventeenth year. Bolzoni sent word to Varèse's father and Henri Varèse stormed in angrily demanding his son. Varèse described the scene: "The three of us, Bolzoni, Monsignor Spandre, and myself, were standing at the top of the stairs looking down at my father in the hall below. Monsignor Spandre took command. With all the authority of the Church and the eloquence and dignity of a high churchman and an Italian, he impressed upon my father that his son had influential protectors, including Cardinal Riscelmi. I can't remember all he said. I was too angry and jubilant, but he succeeded in awing the bastard, who left me alone after that."

Henri Varèse had capitulated. As Varèse said, "Bullies are easily bullied." He scarcely demurred when Varèse refused to continue his studies and even gave his rebellious son a job in his office. It must have been at this time that Varèse was allowed to have a piano of his own.

After knowing Bolzoni, Varèse enjoyed a fuller musical life. He met many musicians, those who lived in Turin as well as the many visiting singers, instrumentalists, and conductors. Varèse mentioned many names, famous at that time. I remember one, a singer—"the Great Tamagno," as Varèse called him, and two opera conductors: Pasquale Gramegna and Rudolpho Ferrari. One of them was the conductor who, so fortunately for Varèse, became ill one day, thus giving him the chance to conduct a rehearsal of *Rigoletto*. Varèse used to relate the story with all the youthful excitement he had felt on that day. For

Early Years 1883–1915

the first time, when the *Concerts Colonne* came to Turin, Varèse heard the music of two composers who were later to become very important in his life, besides influencing his early works: Claude Debussy and Richard Strauss.

Henri Varèse, besides his mining interests, had other business affairs, one the manufacture of chestnut sapling fences, which Claude Cortot, his father-in-law, managed. Now that Varèse had refused to become an engineer, his father had another scheme for weaning him away from his foolish musical obsession—by making over this business to him. But Varèse soon settled the question of his future for himself. He went to Paris.

After the death of Varèse's mother, his father had married again. Varèse told me that his stepmother had always been good to him and to his brothers and sisters. One day Varèse saw his father raise his hand to strike his wife, and in a burst of rage Varèse attacked him. Turning the tables at last, he beat his father instead of being beaten by him. This time he left home for good. His father's concessions had not succeeded in tempering Varèse's hostility, and when later his father came to Paris, Varèse refused to see him.

Now began a period of exhilaration and extreme poverty. Varèse's pockets were empty but he was free. Sometimes he almost starved and sometimes he had no place to sleep. But he had music and he was young. He told me of nights when he slept under the arcades of the Louvre, grateful if the *flics* (cops) left him in peace, protected at least from the rain, if not from the cold. At other times he had a lodging but no money for food. And the hungrier he was, the more imperative his pride.

Varèse told me that one evening when he had not eaten for twenty-four hours he dropped into Picasso's studio—then in the Bateau Lavoire, that famous building of studios in Montmartre —and found him eating his dinner. When Picasso asked him if he had eaten and Varèse said no, Picasso rejoined: "You dine late." So Varèse swallowed his saliva without a word. But he had only to remember, as he said, the "comforts" in the house of *ce salaud de mon père* to find his present discomforts unimportant. And so he was spared that worst degradation, self-pity.

29

Varèse: A Looking-Glass Diary

In Paris Varèse sought out a friend who had been a classmate of his at Turin and who had come to Paris to study architecture at the Beaux Arts. For a little while Varèse shared his room in one of those very cheap, very drab little hotels which in Paris seem to have been a special institution for poor students. I have known pretty drab Paris hotels myself, where Varèse and I used to stay, and I still shudder when I think of the wallpapers, the one dim electric bulb hanging from the ceiling that went off when you turned on the lamp by your bed, and the limp, one-a-day towel! Varèse said that his student hotel was worse!

I don't know the address of Varèse's next lodging. It may have been the little attic room under the sloping mansard roof with a candle-end for light at night, so small that Varèse used to say: "To put on my shirt I had to open the skylight," and where one of the many amusing incidents of his student days occurred. This is the way Varèse used to tell it:

> One day two friends were there with me, sitting on the bed and my one chair (the rest of my furniture: one table). There was a knock at the door and an old gentleman with jet black hair and goatee (also much too black) asked to see Monsieur Varèse in private. I went downstairs with him to the café on the street, and over a *café-crème* he told me, lowering his voice like a conspirator, that he had composed a melody he would like to have "harmonized." It was written over some nauseating verses. "I must first ask you," he said, "to give me your word of honor that you will never disclose that you had any part in this work. It is for someone very dear to me." The old fool. He didn't know how easy it was for me to be honorable in this case! When I got back to my friends I said, "We'll eat tonight. This crap will take me an hour at the most." "Don't be a fool!" they said. "He'll think it was easy and won't pay you enough. Wait a day or two." So I did. When I took it to him he handed me an envelope saying, "I trust, monsieur, that this is adequate remuneration for your work." Adequate, my God! The smallest paper money at that time was fifty francs, and I had never hoped for that much. When I got out of the house I opened the envelope. One hundred francs! I know now what it is to be on a flying carpet. I don't remember my feet touching the ground be-

fore I came to earth at the café where I was to meet my friends.
That night we didn't have dinner; we had a feast.

Varèse soon entered the Schola Cantorum, introduced by his
cousin Alfred Cortot, the son of one of his grandfather's three
brothers, who later became a fashionable pianist. Cortot was
friendly with Vincent d'Indy, then the head of the Schola, and
obtained for Varèse the job of librarian so that he could pay
the tuition. There, with Albert Roussel he studied composition,
counterpoint, and fugue; with Charles Bordes, medieval and
Renaissance music; with d'Indy, conducting. He also attended
d'Indy's "pedantic" (Varèse's adjective) lectures.

With the exception of d'Indy, Varèse liked his professors at
the Schola. Albert Roussel became a good friend whom, twenty-
five years later when we were living in Paris, we used to see
quite often with his wife. He was intelligent and had a lovely
sense of humor. Varèse's other teacher, Charles Bordes, was the
founder of the Schola Cantorum together with Alexandre Guil-
mant—and not, in spite of the dictionaries, with d'Indy, who
only later became director. Bordes had devoted all his life to
early church music and it was with him that Varèse first studied
the old polyphonic masters, whom he came to love passionately
and whom he always gave the predominant place in the reper-
tories of his various choruses.

At the Schola one of his classmates who became a lifelong
friend was the Breton composer Paul Le Flem. He succeeded
Bordes as conductor of the famous *Chanteurs de Saint Gervais*
when Bordes, their founder, left Paris. Later he was for many
years music critic of the Paris newspaper *Comoedia*.

Among Varèse's papers I found a friendly little note from
d'Indy saying that he was enclosing a word for Durand, the
publishers, which Varèse had asked him for. Varèse hoped to
obtain work from them, and did, I believe, copying music, that
being one of the ways he earned money for his almost daily
bread. The friendly relations did not last long. Varèse soon
began to resent what he called d'Indy's bigotry, pedantry, and
arrogance. In his *Musiciens d'aujourd'hui,* Romain Rolland, al-

though an admirer of d'Indy, had to admit that his "intelligent eclecticism was perfectly suited to developing the critical faculty, rather less to forming original personalities" and described him as "a mixture of Christian humility and aristocratic pride"—the latter being what Varèse called his arrogance. How could Varèse, pagan and rebel, have anything in common with such a man, and one who said, "At the base of all art is this essential condition: teaching. . . . The aim of art is to teach, gradually to elevate the spirit of humanity." Varèse liked to tell how d'Indy, analyzing a score of Beethoven's, explained to his class: "Here Beethoven failed to modulate in time." Varèse used to say, "D'Indy wanted all of us to become little d'Indys and I thought one was enough."

So, after a year, Varèse left the Schola Cantorum, which Romain Rolland compared to "a window looking out, not on the open, but on a courtyard" and which Debussy called "a kind of musical high school." He took the Paris Conservatoire examinations and was admitted to Charles Widor's class in composition in January 1905.

Besides d'Indy, Varèse soon made another powerful enemy of a would-be patron. Before he left Turin, a sculptor, Leonardo Bistalfo, had given him an introduction to Rodin. When over a year later, Varèse finally went to Rodin's studio on the rue de l'Université, the great man opened the door himself. He told Varèse that he was engaged with his secretary for a moment and suggested that while Varèse waited he should look around the studio, which was full of sculpture, Rodin's own and that of others. When Rodin returned he said, "Tell me, young man, what did you like best?" Without hesitating, Varèse pointed to a little terra-cotta figurine. "Ah," said Rodin unruffled, "you have good taste. That charming little Tanagra is a gift which I received only this morning." Rodin must have found the young man who preferred a Tanagra figurine to a Rodin sculpture in Rodin's presence unusual. At least, Rodin was not offended and moreover found the impolitic boy sufficiently interesting to invite him to come to live with him at his home in Meudon, as a kind of secretary-companion. In addition, Rodin could not have been insensitive to Varèse's good looks, which were, I judge by hearsay, extraordinary. Romain Rolland a few years later, in a letter to a friend, described him as "a young Italian Beethoven painted by Giorgione." And in Berlin in 1922, reminiscing to me about the young man he had known fourteen years before, Ferruccio Busoni (composer, great pianist, pioneer musical theorist, and formidable personality) said: "He was so handsome— lean and pale in those days—that even men turned to look at him on the street, a compliment men usually pay only to women." Then Busoni added: "And the beauty of it was Varèse was totally unconscious of his looks—preoccupied with only one thing—his music." This was true of Varèse all his life. He failed to make use of this gift of the gods as a less dedicated and vainer man would have done. However, he fully enjoyed one result, attracting without trying *"les jeunes filles en fleurs,"* as well as matrons in full bloom.

In any case, on February 22, 1905, Varèse received a letter from Rodin's secretary giving him instructions to Meudon and including a sketch indicating the way to Rodin's house from the station. At Meudon he was lodged upstairs in a little garden pavilion where on the ground floor marble, tools, and odd pieces of sculpture were kept. His duties were not arduous, some clerical work, letters, and so on, and on the days Rodin spent in Paris he was expected to meet the six o'clock train which brought Rodin back to Meudon. He had plenty of time to work, although I suppose (though Varèse made no mention of it) he must have gone to Paris himself more than once during this brief stay at Rodin's, for in January he had been enrolled in Widor's class at the Conservatoire. Rodin, Varèse said, used to talk to him at length about his musical future, about the people he intended to interest in his career as a conductor, evidently considering Varèse his permanent protégé. Then with one angry word Varèse wrecked all these plans.

Very soon after moving to Meudon Varèse had begun to feel resentment at Rodin's rather magisterial ways. *"Rodin ressemble au Père Eternel,"* Apollinaire said; so it was almost inevitable that such a godlike figure who also acted the part would irritate a youth who had run away from a father who had been the jealous god of his childhood. One day his rancor, exacerbated by disagreement on the sacred subject of music, led to a fatal quarrel. Varèse could not remember the point of the musical dispute, only how Rodin had enraged him. "He didn't know a damned thing about music," Varèse said. *"Il disait des âneries comme s'il était le bon Dieu* (uttered asininities as if he were God Almighty)." Always rashly outspoken and at the moment unreasonably angered, Varèse called Rodin *"un con"* (no equivalent in English), a very insulting and indecent epithet which seemed to dart out of Varèse's mouth of its own accord whenever he was disgusted beyond words. A relief word. That he was addressing an older man, a famous man and his host, was at the moment an irrelevant abstraction. Nor was he deterred by the consideration that Rodin was prepared to be useful to a very ambitious and a very poor young composer and future conductor. (How many times on other occasions which hardly seemed to justify such an expenditure of emotion Varèse would charge blindly like a hurt bull as though stung by too many *banderillas.* Anger and impatience often made Varèse act foolishly from a practical point of view, but it cannot be said that he ever acted venally. Among his papers, I found a clipping in which he had underlined a quotation from Franz Kafka: "Impatience is the greatest sin." Recognizing in himself this sin or, rather, as he thought of it, this destructive element in his nature, all the more hated because he believed it to be an inheritance from his father, he struggled against it all his later life, with at least moderate success.)

That same afternoon Varèse left Meudon and never saw Rodin again.

Several months after returning to Paris, Varèse was invited by his friend the poet Leon Deubel to share his quarters on the rue de Fürstemberg at the offices of the *Rénovation Esthétique,* of which Deubel had been made an editor by its founder, the painter Emile Bernard. In a letter to Bernard, Deubel gives a picture of Varèse at that time. After saying that he was to be introduced to Sar Péladan by Varèse with the hope of getting his book of poems accepted by the *Mercure de France,* Deubel writes:

> I am warmly recommended to him by the young composer Edgar Varèse, who has been lodged for some time at the Rénovation. He is to do an opera on his *Fils des Etoiles.* Speaking of Varèse, Goutchkoff has asked him for articles on César Franck, and Mme la Comtesse de Chabannes de la Palisse, known as Armande de Polignac, composer and writer on music, has also promised us articles and has subscribed. She is a personal friend of Varèse and takes a great interest in him. I have never spoken to you of this young maestro. He is at the Conservatoire in the class of composition preparing his *Prix de Rome.* I like and admire him very much. He is in the true tradition. Evenings I enjoy listening to him play Wagner and Beethoven. His works are already remarkable and I am sure would please you. At the moment he is finishing a *Prélude* to my *Fin d'un Jour* for an orchestra of 120 musicians which is colossal.

The Armande de Polignac, or Mme Chabannes de la Palisse, mentioned by Deubel had been a classmate of Varèse's at the Schola. When I met her many years later in Paris she had the round blue eyes of a child, the calm of a Buddha (in fact she told me she was studying Chinese philosophers), and the merriest laugh I have ever heard. Even the very fine wrinkles of her very fine skin were lovely.

Deubel's letter continues:

> On November 25, at the Athenée Saint-Germain we are going to give our first soirée of the associations we have founded together, which we call Mansarde, which includes a poet, a musician, a sculptor, and an architect. Willy has agreed to be our godfather, and Armande de Polignac our godmother.

La Mansarde, of which I know nothing more than this mention by Deubel, must have been the first of the many societies Varèse founded in his lifetime, but unfortunately the only one including all the arts—still a good idea.

Varèse: A Looking-Glass Diary

One remark in this letter mystified me. Why did Deubel make a point of implying that Varèse was a traditionalist when he must have known he was a rebel? I found the answer in an old issue of *Les Nouvelles Littéraires* in an article on Leon Deubel. Louis Thomas, the author, writes that Deubel "has been made editor of the *Rénovation Esthétique,* a curious publication founded by the painter Emile Bernard *for the defense of tradition in contemporary art"* (my italics). Evidently Deubel did not want his boss to think he was harboring a nonconformist, as Mr. Thomas calls Varèse in the following sentence: "This was the year without worry for the poet, who lived on rue de Fürstemberg in the little locale which served as the offices of the review with another nonconformist like himself, Edgar Varèse."

After Deubel's suicide on June 12, 1913, at the age of thirty-four, Guillaume Apollinaire, who for many years had been writing a column captioned *La Vie Anecdotique* in the *Mercure de France,* asked Varèse to tell him his impression of the poet while they were living together. He took down Varèse's oral account and published it in his column for November 1, 1913, captioned, "Leon Deubel":

> Although the musician, Edgar Varèse is less known in France than in Germany, where he is considered one of the most original talents today, it will not be long before he conquers Paris as he has conquered Berlin. The *French musician,* as he is known over there, is for the moment in France and I heard him make some remarks on Leon Deubel, a comrade of his, which I think worth recording. I copy them here just as I took them down.
>
> "Leon Deubel," Edgar Varèse said, "was very misanthropic and a misogynist. To my knowledge he only loved one woman, Anna, a German and very ugly. The comrade for whom he had a really warm affection was Louis Pergaud, in whose literary future he had great faith. He also liked Emile Bernard, who had always been very good to him and had placed him at the *Rénovation Esthétique,* where he was very well lodged. For me he had at least esteem, since he invited me to share his quarters. During the time I lived with him he read me everything he wrote. We spent enjoyable evenings together drinking the white wine he was very fond of and that he went out to buy at the Co-opera-

tive, rue Cardinale. I set several of his things to music: a sonnet called *Souvenir,* two rhythmic prose pieces, written expressly for me and which I do not think have been published in any review. I also wrote a symphonic poem, *Le Prélude à la Fin d'un Jour,* to serve as a prologue to his *Fin d'un Jour,* one of the poems in *Lumière Natale.*

"I said that Deubel was a misogynist; he was above all extremely inept with women. Being full-blooded and also sensual, he suffered from the contempt he imagined women showed toward him. One evening at the *Rénovation Esthétique* several other comrades were with me. Deubel recited one of his most poignant poems on the subject of woman. When he had finished he literally fell onto his chair and burst out sobbing. He was hungry for fame and very much flattered when anyone wrote something about him. His ambition was to be published by the *Mercure de France.*"

Varèse kept a particular affection for that rue de Fürstemberg, where he had lived with Deubel. When we went to Paris for the first time together in 1924, he hardly gave me time to powder my nose at the Hotel Jacob before rushing off to see the *"plus jolie rue de Paris."* It is still the prettiest street in Paris and one of the shortest, beginning at the rue de L'Abbaye and ending in the rue Jacob. Only the rue Cardinale, which curves so pleasantly into it and where Deubel went for his white wine at the Cooperative (no longer there), is shorter. Varèse often spoke of the "Place" instead of the rue de Fürstemberg because almost immediately after leaving the rue de L'Abbaye it widens into a charming square with benches and trees before narrowing again after rue Cardinale. The windows of the *Rénovation* overlooked the trees. In the rue de Fürstemberg you will also find the Musée Delacroix. That summer I think Varèse took me to all the streets where he had lived as a young man, and as he changed domicile frequently I should never have remembered them all if he had not named them in a letter years later. I also had to visit the most important street of his boyhood, the rue de Lancry, where Grandpère's bistro was located at the corner of the boulevard de Magenta, and afterward, walk down rue de Lancry to canal Saint-

Martin so he could show me where he played as a little boy. When, in 1954, in Paris for the première of *Déserts,* Varèse took Odile Vivier and Al Copley on similar tours of his old haunts, his enthusiasm and evident delight was such that they were convinced that he adored his native city. Yet by that time Varèse had for years been insulting the most beautiful of cities and, together with a like-minded friend, would reiterate ad nauseum the same refrain like a needle stuck in the groove of a record, *"Paris me dégoûte."* A letter Varèse wrote me at the time explains away the paradox:

> Last Sunday morning, I went to relive my twenties in the 6e arrondissement: Place Furstemberg—Mazarine—Dauphine—Ancienne Comédie—St.-André des Arts—Séguier—St.-Augustin . . . de l'Echaudé, etc. etc.—and all the passages and courtyards. It was as if I had never left Paris. I went automatically from one courtyard to another—one passage to another. It is fantastic how my memory stowed everything away at the time and the element of novelty was definitely, automatically fixed.

It was his youth relived, which had endured intact, and the fidelity of his memory that had moved Varèse; Paris of the past, not Paris of the present. On a postcard dated December 22 of the same year, Varèse wrote me:

> This morning—gray sky, low-lying huge gray clouds—moving lazily—wet streets and pavements. I have the feeling that I am going to meet Rutbeuf and Villon at the next corner. It's funny Paris—I walk—and all at once—whether it is the Place de la République or Place de la Bastille, Blv. St.-Martin—de Strasbourg—the 6th arr.—the Panthéon—no matter where—in the most disparate places—a corner—a courtyard—an alleyway—and I lose the sense of the present. It is like a dream—one doesn't know where one is or under what circumstances. It is fantastic how one's childhood is engraved in the memory.

Another comrade of those early days was François Bernouard, also a poet, but the contrary of a misanthrope. He was gay, with the quick wit and repartee of a Paris *voyou* like that other François, poet and real *voyou.* Even years later when I met him, although he was a serious master typographer and responsible head of the *Belle Edition,* he had lost none of his urchin charm, with his little nose that crumpled like a bunny's when he laughed.

He was as fond of practical jokes as Varèse was. I know that practical jokers often go to a great deal of trouble, but in that respect one of the practical jokes Varèse used to describe has, I am sure, never had an equal. Varèse and a couple of other friends were visiting Grandpère in Le Villars. One evening they were strolling through the fields where on one side of the path beets were planted and on the other was a plowed field. All at once a hilarious idea occurred to them. They would transplant the beets from one side of the path to the empty field on the other, the jest being the thought—just the thought you understand—of the expression on the face of the farmer when he saw his beets on the wrong side of the path. It took them most of the night, for they spent much of it doubled up with laughter. "It was backbreaking labor," Varèse said, "which none of us would have done for any amount of money but, in our little 'union' we would always settle for laughter." I wonder how many bottles of wine from Grandpère's vineyard they had drunk that day!

In his ardent book on Varèse, Fernand Ouellette, the French-Canadian poet, has an astrological note in reference to Varèse that I find arresting:

> According to astrology, Varèse would have the sun in Capricorn and the ascendant in Gemini. The extraordinary mobility of Gemini, his comedian nature, would often protect him from his other. In this way his profoundly tragic Capricorn nature would escape superficial observation. One might say that Varèse was the center of a dialectic between play (homo ludens) and despair. The astrologer André Barbault elucidates the Capricorn-Gemini nature thus: "The one is disciplined, severe, serious, stable, restrained, the other all youth, mobility, adaptability and lightness."

Whether or not the stars had anything to do with it, certainly no psychoanalyst, knowing all the dreams Varèse ever dreamed, could have analyzed Varèse's ambivalent nature more accurately.

Varèse: A Looking-Glass Diary

François was as poor as Varèse and they shared their penury with the lighthearted ingenuity of Paris urchins. On the leanest days they would go to *les Halles* and, eyeing stray carrots or other vegetables fallen from the peasants' carts, would nonchalantly kick them along as though accidentally until they could pick them up and run.

Sometimes at *les Halles* Varèse earned enough pennies to buy his own carrots by holding their horses for the peasants, who liked to go off to a wine shop for a *coup de rouge,* quick glass of red wine, while the *forts des Halles,* those giants with enormous hats, on which they carried their burdens of provender, unloaded the wagons. One *fort des Halles,* coming up to unload, looked curiously at the handsome (my adjective) young man at the horse's head. "You're not a workingman," he said. Varèse, quickly resentful, always anticipating criticism (his father again), retorted: "What's that to you? I'm doing my job." But the man soon mollified him and when Varèse told him that he was a composer and was in the class of Widor at the Conservatoire, the man, a fanatic of music and an admirer of the great organist refused to believe him. *"Sans blague!"* he said. "I don't think you even know what it is to be a composer." When Varèse succeeded in convincing him, this *mélomane fort des Halles* took him to his bistro nearby and said to the proprietor: "Whenever this young man wants to come here and eat, it goes on my slate. *Monsieur Varèse est compositeur!"* After that he used to take Varèse to concerts with him and for the first time Varèse sat in the orchestra instead of among the "children of Paradise."

Varèse's means of livelihood while he was a student at the Conservatoire—in fact for most of his early life—was copying music, orchestrating other people's scores, and teaching. In November 1905, he had at least two pupils. In one of his letters Grandpère writes in his gently understanding way: "I received your good and charming letter and was happy to know that you are well and content with your composition and your pupils and I hope they will multiply with time."

Varèse had two good friends at the Conservatoire, Widor and Massenet. Massenet, who had been a professor of advanced composition since 1878 and was more than old enough to be Varèse's father, addressed him in one of his affectionate little notes as *Mon cher confrère.* He was evidently out of favor with Conservatoire officialdom when he wrote in another note:

> My dear Varése: I want to prove how much I am interested in you; find some other way for me to be of use to you—my relations with the "high administration" make it impossible for us *at this moment! Très à vous. M* Massenet [the first M is twice underlined. Why *M* when his name was *Jules??* A shared joke no doubt.]

Debussy has left a very sympathetic appreciation of Massenet in his *Monsieur Croche, Antidilettante:* "Massenet was the most truly loved of contemporary composers. . . . His confrères could not readily forgive his power of pleasing which, after all, is a gift." Varèse used to contrast the cold dogmatism of magisterial Saint-Saëns with Massenet's extraordinary charm and simplicity.

Through the good offices of Massenet and Widor, Varèse received the Bourse de la Ville de Paris en musique, a monetary award given every year by the municipality in music, architecture, painting, and sculpture. There was great excitement on the street (I think Varèse said it was the most plebeian part of the rue Monge) when a Garde Républicaine in all his impressive regalia arrived on horseback and sent the concierge to bring down Monsieur Edgard Varèse (a Garde Républicaine never leaves his horse). After Varèse appeared and had been duly presented with the Bourse, he invited the neighbors who had gathered around— his friends all of them—to celebrate with him at the nearby wine shop (*Vin et Charbon*). The next day, much to their surprise, he paid the butcher, the baker, and the *bougnat* all that he owed them.

Varèse admired Widor both as a great organist and as an understanding teacher. When Varèse once remarked to Stravinsky that professors were "ruled like music paper" he was speaking of professors in general and in particular of d'Indy only. He used to say that Widor was the opposite of d'Indy, human, unpretentious, open-minded, and that he had a sense of humor. Once when Widor, examining a score Varèse had brought to him for criticism, came to some rather unorthodox bars, he observed: "I can't say I'd advise that, Varèse, but perhaps the textbooks will have to be changed." Widor gave Varèse extra lessons in his own apartment and Varèse enjoyed telling this incident: One morning when he arrived for his lesson, after quite a long wait, Widor opened the door a crack, obviously without much on and "his two hairs *en bataille.*" "Pardon, Varèse," he said. *"Je ne peux vous recevoir, j'ai du monde* (Excuse me, Varèse, I can't receive you, I have company)." It was funny as Varèse told it, imitating Widor's lisp. Varèse was a devastating mimic.

About this time certain unorthodox conceptions about music began to germinate. These ideas—the "liberation of sound," "spatial music," and music as "organized sound"—were later on in America to run through most of Varèse's interviews and lectures until electronics did actually "liberate sound" and make all sounds available to composers for transformation into music. In more than one lecture Varèse has described the inception of these ideas during his student days. In one, specifically, he related:

> When I was a student at the Paris Conservatoire, I came across a definition of music that was the first to satisfy me completely, suggesting as it did a new and freer conception of music. Hoene Wroński, physicist, chemist, musicologist, and philosopher of the first part of the 19th century, defined music as "the corporealization of the intelligence that is in sounds." Looking back, it seems to me that it was this definition which started me thinking of music as organized sound instead of sanctified and regimented notes. I began to resent the arbitrary limitations of the tempered system, especially after reading at about the same time, Helmholtz's description of his experiments with sirens in his *Physiology of Sound.* Wanting to experiment myself, I went to the *Marché aux Puces,* where for next to nothing you could find just about anything, and picked up two small ones. With these I made my first experiments in what later I called spatial music. The beautiful parabolas and hyperbolas of sound the sirens gave me and the haunting quality of the tones made me aware for the first time of the wealth of music outside the narrow limits imposed by keyboard instruments.

Early Years 1883–1915

It was during Varèse's second year at the Conservatoire that he organized a mixed chorus of working-class men and women and gave concerts at the Château du Peuple, under the auspices of the Université Populaire du Faubourg Saint-Antoine. Founded in 1899, this was the first of the people's universities that sprang up in that period of the apotheosis of idealistic liberalism. An enthusiastic socialist-positivist, George Deherme, writing about them in the social-missionary tone of the day, describes the neighborhood where the first one was established:

> In the Faubourg Saint-Antoine, whose population is the most intoxicated by absinthe, where homicidal bars are everywhere overflowing with customers, the Université Populaire must have appeared as a lifesaving beacon.

The Château du Peuple was a free theater for working-class people, where singers, poets, actors, musicians, donating their talents, gave a variety of entertainments. Among them I remember Varèse mentioning his friends Apollinaire, de Max, famous actor of that time, and Louis Jouvet, who staged plays. Varèse kept a copy of a weekly review of Paris events, *La Chronique de Paris*, which describes one of these entertainments at which Varèse played two of his own compositions:

> The Château du Peuple, way off behind the Porte de Madrid, near the Drilling Grounds—Sundays workingmen come with their families; dinner costs 20 sous; and after dinner arrive the artists. Sunday it was Edgar Varèse, a composer whose name you would do well to remember. Before this audience of simple people, he played—and with what success—his *Colloque au Bord de la Fontaine* and his *Apothéose de l'Océan*, vast *poème symphonique*, exuberant and magnificently young.

This enthusiastic journalist in similar vein speaks of the singer Germaine Le Senne and of others who recited poems by Baudelaire and Barbey d'Aurevilly and of de Max, "simply marvelous in *Les Cloches* and *Les Départs* by Rodenbach."

Of his choristers, all much older than their young maestro, Varèse said: "They could all have been my father or mother."

The men had a protective attitude toward him and, in the beginning, after rehearsals in that absinthe-intoxicated environment, several of them would always act as his bodyguard to see him safely out of that unhealthy neighborhood because, as they told him, *"les mauvais garçons* (apaches) don't know you yet." What was it in Varèse that made them so confident that once these ugly customers knew him he would have nothing to fear from them? Was it his fearlessness, his humanity, his simplicity? Varèse could get along with gangsters, working people, and aristocrats, but never for long with rich smug bourgeois, and not always with musicians. Varèse used to tell a rather touching story about one of his apache acquaintances. A friend of his was an intern at one of the Paris hospitals and Varèse would sometimes drop in on the young doctor on night duty. One night an apache who had been knifed was brought in. He was bent almost double and as Varèse put it, "He was holding his hat over his belly to keeps his guts from spilling out." He was in great pain and Varèse lighted a cigarette and put it in his mouth. The man, because he believed that hospitals didn't give a damn whether his sort lived or died, was sullen and suspicious. Varèse set about reassuring him. "You'll see," Varèse said. "My friend is good and he's going to operate on you. He's young, but he's far better than most of the big shots. Don't worry. You're in good hands." Months later a stranger came to Varèse's door. "You don't know me," he said, "but I know you. You saved my life." Then Varèse saw that it was his wounded apache. He took him into his room. "Didn't I tell you my friend would pull you through?" he said. "It wasn't your friend," the man rejoined. "It was you and the cigarettes you gave me and the way you talked. I just came to say if you ever need a job done, *si quelqu'un t'emmerde,* I'm your man."

In the competition for the Prix de Rome in the spring of 1906, Varèse failed. Unlike Berlioz, who succeeded only after three trials, Varèse decided not to try again. He was beginning to feel that he had had enough of academic teaching, was already dissatisfied with the limitations imposed by Conservatoire tradition, and had lost his ambition for academic prizes. He was considering leaving the Conservatoire when his departure was decided for him. In his own words, as quoted by Gunther Shuler in an interview: "the immediate cause for leaving was a rather nasty exchange of unpleasantries with Fauré, who, as administrator of the Conservatoire, kicked me out." Debussy, whom Varèse met in 1907, must have applauded, for he once wrote: "One should leave the Conservatoire as soon as possible to look for and discover one's own personality." On the occasion of the Centenary of Debussy's birth, Varèse wrote of his first visit to Debussy at 80 avenue du Bois de Boulogne:

I had the privilege of knowing Debussy when I was still a student in Paris and from the many long talks I had with him I have kept the image of a man of great kindness, intelligence, fastidiousness, and wide culture. He was also something of a sybarite and loved beautiful things and all the pleasures of the senses. I remember a carved sandalwood fire screen he kept in front of his wood fire, and how he delighted in the warm fragrance of the precious wood that filled the room. He was in his middle forties when I first knew him, I in my early twenties, but he treated me simply as a colleague without the least condescension. He was too intelligent to be self-important.

Before I met Debussy I had heard on all sides that he was quite unapproachable, bearish and disagreeable. Later I told him I had felt very ill at ease the first time I came to see him because of this reputation. His response was charming. He put his hand on my shoulder and said: "And have I given you cause for complaint? (*Avez-vous à vous plaindre de moi?*)" Being a rebel himself, I think he liked my somewhat aggressive independence and my revolt against conformity. Although the tendencies in the scores I showed him were too foreign to his nature for him to really like them, he approved of them objectively. He would say: "You have a right to compose what you want to, the way you want to if the music comes out and is your own. Your music comes out and is yours. (*Votre musique sort et elle est de vous.*)" Everybody knows Debussy's aphorism: "Rules do not make a work of art."

Debussy was far from happy over the compliment of having his style imitated by enthusiastic followers. He once said to me:

"These so-called Debussyites will end by disgusting me with my music." He also suffered from his "interpreters." I once wrote to him from Berlin that I was practicing the piano, to which he replied: "You are quite right to take up the piano . . . one is so often betrayed by so-called pianists. I can vouch for this personally, for you have no idea how my piano music has been distorted, to the point that I scarcely recognize it. Excuse this personal burst of temper. But really I have plenty of excuse." He was also critical of journalistic criticism. When my score *Bourgogne* was performed in Berlin by the Blüther Orchestra in 1910, I wrote him that it had been very badly received by public and critics. Debussy replied: "You are quite right not to be disturbed by the hostility of the public. The day will come when you are the greatest friends in the world. But give up the idea right away that criticism is more clairvoyant here than in Germany, and don't forget that a critic rarely likes what he is called upon to discuss, and that often he even makes a point of misunderstanding. Criticism might be an art if it could be exercised under the necessary conditions for making independent judgments. And it should also be said that the so-called *artistes* have done much to bring about this state of affairs."

At that time I was very poor and Debussy tried to help me with introductions and recommendations. When I returned to Paris in 1928, the first time I saw Gaveau (head of the piano firm of that name) he told me that he had me to thank for the only Debussy autograph he possessed. This was Debussy's signature on a letter he had written Gaveau asking him to put a piano at my disposal.

Everybody agrees that Debussy was one of the greatest innovators of all time, but few people know that he was also one of the kindest of men.

A score of the 1905 edition of *La Mer* which Debussy gave Varèse in 1908 has several corrections in Debussy's handwriting, and before these were incorporated in later editions conductors used to ask Varèse's permission to see the score and to make these changes in their own copies. It was also precious to Varèse because it was inscribed: *"A Edgard Varèse en sympathie avec mes meilleurs souhaits de réussite—Claude Debussy."*

At the Conservatoire, which was at that time officially called Le Conservatoire de Musique et de Déclamation, Varèse met Suzanne Bing, a student in the department of Déclamation—that is, she was preparing for a stage career. Her ambition was fully and happily realized six years later when, after leaving Varèse, she became one of the first actresses of the Théâtre du Vieux Colombier, founded in 1913 by Jacques Copeau.

Suzanne and Varèse were married in November 1907, and soon went to live in Berlin.

That Varèse chose Germany is not strange. Except for Berlioz, Varèse preferred the German masters—it will be remembered that Deubel mentioned his playing Wagner and Beethoven—and though Debussy certainly played an important role in his development, his greatest admiration among contemporary composers at that moment was for Richard Strauss, the great orchestrator. Moreover, he had just read and been stirred by the prophetic little book *Entwurf einer neuen Ästhetik der Tonkunst* (Sketch for a New Esthetic of Music) by Ferruccio Busoni. It encouraged him in his own private musical rebellion, and Busoni lived in Berlin.

But why he left Paris is another matter. To Fernand Ouellette he once gave his reason: "I left Paris out of disgust for all the petty politics, to escape myself, to get away from bourgeois ideas —ideas that neutralize the efforts and the sensibility of the keenest and most intellectual people in the world and whose elite is the finest." In other words, Roussel, Widor, Massenet, and Debussy might represent an elite of France but the bourgeois majority in Paris were personified for him by d'Indy, Saint-Saëns, and Fauré, men responsible for that "constipated" Paris he deplored—the men who, according to Varèse, kept music static, stayed the imagination, and stopped the flow of life. Varèse always gave reasons for his sudden changes, but not the reason, unconscious of it as he was, that gave them the final impetus: his demon of unrest.

Berlin did not prove to be the haven and musical Eden that Varèse had envisioned. There was for some time the language difficulty and to the end of the German hegira his financial situation was precarious and his health suffered also from hopes constantly deferred. Of course, he soon found friends, for although he was shy in certain instances, as both Rolland and Hofmannsthal remarked, on the other hand he had the gift of picking up Gemini friends with the ease of a picaresque hero—enemies too—but the importance of Varèse's Berlin experience lies in his contact with men of great achievement who gave him the encouragement he needed and confidence in his own future. These were: Karl Muck, Richard Strauss, Hugo von Hofmannsthal, and in particular Busoni. One cannot overassess the importance of Busoni's influence on Varèse in his twenties. Varèse was not only stimulated as never before by Busoni's brilliant personality and caustic intelligence but in Busoni Varèse found the first musician whose ideas on the future of music were, as Varèse has said, like an echo of his own thoughts. So, in spite of poverty, illness, and moments of dark despair, depression such as he was to endure intermittently all his life, nevertheless, of those six years, in retrospect, only a golden glow remained. Even after two wars when Germany was the enemy of his country and of the world, no amount of hysteria and propaganda could shake his love of Germany and Germans. He even liked to say, "I am not French. I am Burgundian, therefore Germanic." Unlike Varèse, Suzanne never learned to like Berlin or German ways.

When I met her in New York at the time of Vieux Colombier's New York engagement, she confided to me how much she had hated Berlin, how miserable she had been there. She reminded me of what Debussy had written Varèse: "It seems to me that you have found Berlin very hospitable and I am glad and congratulate you. All the same it must have taken a great deal of courage to get used to a foreign country! So many things, customs must be disconcerting, not to say offensive. Wherever one goes one more or less drags one's own country along. . . ." Debussy and Suzanne were both too French to be happy anywhere but in France. Not Varèse, by nature a cosmopolite.

I don't know how long Varèse was in Berlin before he went to see Busoni. Probably not too long. Busoni's little book, *Sketch for a New Esthetic of Music,* seemed a sufficient introduction. Of the fruitful friendship that followed his first visit Varèse has given the following account:

In 1907, still in my early twenties, I went to Berlin, where I spent most of the next seven years, and had the good fortune of becoming (in spite of the disparity of age and importance) the friend of Ferruccio Busoni, then at the height of his fame. I had read his remarkable little book, *A New Esthetic of Music* (a milestone in my musical development), and when I came upon "Music is born free; and to win freedom is its destiny," it was like hearing the echo of my own thought.

From the beginning Busoni took an interest in my work and let me bring my scores for criticism. But one day—by then I had known him for three years or more—I brought him my latest score—whether *Les Cycles du Nord* for orchestra, or an opera based on Hugo von Hofmannsthal's *Oedipus und die Sphinx,* I cannot remember. In any case he seemed surprised and expressed pleasure at the way I had developed. He went over the score with special attentiveness and asked many questions. At certain places he suggested modifications which I found contrary to my conception. He asked me if I didn't agree with him, and I said emphatically, "No, Maestro," and gave him my reasons. "So," he said, "you will not make these changes." "No, Maestro," I repeated, somewhat belligerently. He looked at me for a moment and I thought he resented my rejection of his recommendations as youthful conceit. But then he smiled and, putting his hand on my shoulder, said, "From now on it is no longer *Maestro* but *Ferruccio* and *Tu.* We spoke either Italian or French when we were alone together.

Having become acquainted with Busoni through his extraordinarily prophetic musical theories in his *New Esthetic of Music,* I was surprised to find his musical tastes and his own music so orthodox. It was Busoni who coined the expression "Young Classicism," and classicism, young or old, was just what I was bent on escaping. He could never understand how *most* of the works of such a master as Mozart, his favorite composer, could bore me as they did and still do. But it was also Busoni who wrote: "The function of the creative artist consists in making laws, not in following those already made."

49

Varèse: A Looking-Glass Diary

Together we used to discuss what directions the music of the future would, or rather should take and could not take as long as the strait jacket of the tempered system ("the diplomatic two semitone system," as he called it) continued to keep it unmovable. He deplored that his own keyboard instrument had conditioned our ears to accept only an infinitesimal part of the infinite gradation of sounds in nature. However, when I said that I was through with tonality, his quick response was: *"Tu te prives d'une bien belle chose."* He was very much interested in the electrical instruments we began to hear about and I remember particularly one he had read of in an American magazine, called the Dynamophone, invented by a Dr. Thaddeus Cahill, which I later saw demonstrated in New York and was disappointed. All through his writings one finds over and over again predictions about the music of the future which have since come true. In fact, there is hardly a development that he did not foresee, as for instance this extraordinary prophecy: "I almost think that in the new great music, machines will be necessary and will be assigned a share in it. Perhaps industry, too, will bring forth her share in the artistic ascent." How right he was, for it is thanks to industry that composers today compose by means of electronic machines invented for industry's benefit but adopted by composers, with the assistance of engineers, for theirs. To musicians who have known Busoni only as a pianist, or through his scores, this ambivalence will come as a surprise. It was as though his heart, loyal to the past, refused to follow his adventurous mind into so strange a future. In any case I owe a most tremendous debt of gratitude to this extraordinary man—almost a figure out of the Renaissance—not only one of the greatest pianists of all time, but a man of wide culture, a scholar, thinker, writer, composer, conductor, teacher and *animateur*—a man who stimulated others to think and do things. Personally, I know that he crystallized my half-formed ideas, stimulated my imagination, and determined, I believe, the future development of my music. Treating me as he did, as a colleague and a friend, was as fructifying to me as the sun and rain and fertilizer to soil. He liked to have young people around him and has written: "I prefer to look forward rather than backward, and my preference for young people is connected with this fact." I was very lucky to have been young at that time.

Busoni gave generously of himself. I know that not one of the pupils of his whom I knew personally ever paid for their lessons with him. Connecting music and money he found distressing. He also had an almost exaggerated sense of what he owed pupils and colleagues. When a composition of mine, *Bourgogne,* was to be played by the Blüther Orchestra—the first orchestral work I had ever had performed—I was, of course, anxious for Busoni to hear it, and he had promised to be present. But when I phoned the day of the concert, Mrs. Busoni, who answered, told me it would be impossible as her husband was in bed with a fever and his doctor had forbidden him to go out. It was a terrible disappointment. To my great surprise that evening I saw Busoni enter the concert hall, supported on either side by Zadora and Petri, two of his pupils. In spite of my joy, I protested that he should not have come, to which he replied simply: *"C'est mon devoir."*

Busoni, who was half Italian and half German, was all Italian in a very conspicuous trait of his many-faceted personality, his sense of humor, which I used to call his Florentine sarcasm. He was not malicious but had an overpowering sense of the ridiculous and could not resist poking fun at anybody who struck him as ridiculous, pretentious, or affected. On occasion he liked to prick the inflated adulation of his admirers, and he was not above punning. I remember one evening at his house, when a singer by the name of Frau Pissling came up to him to say good night, he took both of her hands in his and, keeping a very serious face, said, "Dear Frau *Piss*ling, every night before I go to bed I think of you."

In 1922, after an absence of eight years I returned to Berlin for three months, principally to see Busoni, whom I had heard was ill. I also wanted my wife to meet the man who had meant so much to me. I found him still as brilliant, still as sarcastic, now drinking milk prescribed by the doctor but, in spite of the doctor, still drinking the white wine he loved, and still ready for new departures. He joined me in forming a branch of the International Composers' Guild, a society devoted entirely to modern music, which I had founded in New York the year before. A composition of his and one of mine were performed at the first concert. Busoni was too ill that night to be present and could no longer defy his wife and doctors as he had in 1910.

Berlin was a sad place that fall of 1922 with the terrible

mounting inflation that made us, with our American dollars, rich, but pauperized the Germans. Sadness also mingled with my happiness in being with Busoni, for I felt that when I said good-by it would be for the last time. Busoni died in 1924, less than two years after we left.

My most precious reminder of the days when I first knew Busoni in the wonderful Berlin before the First World War is the published score he gave me of his *Berceuse Elégiaque* with this dedication: "All'illustro Futuro, l'amico Varèse, affezionatamente, F. Busoni, 1910." A dedication that made the young composer very proud.

Although Varèse spent most of the seven years before the First World War in Berlin, he made yearly visits to Paris, where he, with two *copains,* François Bernouard and the painter Claude Chereau, formed a like-minded trio who enjoyed doing all the Gemini things together. I wrote to Chereau, the last of the trio, asking if he had any photographs of the three of them together. He replied that he was sure he had several taken at the *Belle Edition* and would make a search for them. Unfortunately, the search was unsuccessful. Instead of the photographs, to compensate me for my disappointment, he sent me this evocative picture in words:

I knew Edgard Varèse through François Bernouard about the time I became associated with the latter at his *La Belle Edition.* It was located in the same building where Rémy de Gourmont lived, 71 rue des Saints-Pères, at the back of the courtyard. *La Belle Edition* was already bringing out the magazine *Schéhérazade,* which published the works of all the young intellectuals of the Saint-Germain-des-Prés quarter, and soon added other reviews, among them, *La Vogue Française, Panurge,* etc. In short, our offices became the meeting place of young writers and artists who would congregate there to talk about all the problems of the times that concerned them. We would linger for hours, afterward continuing our discussions at the bistro Chez Ayral, at the corner of the rue des Saints-Pères and the Boulevard Saint-Germain. At the bar on arriving, we would play a game of ace poker with the proprietor. When one of us lost we would order only the cheapest drinks, but when it was the proprietor who lost, nothing was too expensive for us. This arrangement was not to the taste of the proprietor's wife. But, as it gave her husband so much pleasure, she did not interfere. After that, those who were going home for dinner left, and the rest of us sat around the table in a little room reserved for us at the back of the restaurant near the kitchen.

From the moment we met, Varèse and I became very good friends, and he was at once incorporated into our little band, which included Guillaume Apollinaire, André Salmon, André Billy, Francis Carco, Jean Cocteau, René Bertrand, Dunoyer de Segonzac, Maurice Rostand, etc.

Hardly a day passed that Varèse failed to appear, strolling along, his hands in his pockets, looking as completely nonchalant as a Parisian *flâneur* without a care in the world. I soon understood, however, that this young man I found so likable was perturbed and that something very serious was going on in his head. He had been living in Germany and had come to Paris only a short time before. He knew all the contemporary composers and saw them frequently. When we became more intimate he talked to me about his boyhood in Italy and of a little village in Burgundy, where I believe he was born, in any case where his grandfather lived. When I published my first book of nudes, with a preface by André Salmon, it was Varèse who took a copy to Claude Debussy. I was rewarded with a charming letter from the author of *l'Après-midi d'un Faune,* which I have always treasured.

It will not escape notice that among those whom Chereau names in the group that met at *La Belle Edition,* there were painters as well as writers but that Varèse was the only musician. Varèse himself, in one of his lectures years later, was to point out this phenomenon in his life. He said:

Although in my youth I had the extraordinary good fortune to be sponsored and aided by such musicians as Debussy, Strauss, Muck, Mahler—even Massenet—and, as I have already mentioned, Busoni, most of my life I have been rather more closely associated with painters, poets, architects, and scientists than musicians. Perhaps this is why my point of view has differed so

Varèse: A Looking-Glass Diary

radically from that of most musicians. Or vice versa, my musical views, having made me an untouchable, I sought and found sympathy and corroboration from the practitioners of other arts.

He then quotes Jean Roy, who, after the first performance of *Déserts*, wrote of Varèse that he was a composer "who set his watch at the same time as the poets and painters."

In passing I should add that Bernouard's *Belle Edition* not only brought out literary reviews, but was responsible later on for several special editions, typographically outstanding, of such writers as Barbey d'Aurevilly, Bloy, and Jules Renard. I don't remember whether or not Varèse ever met Jules Renard, but I know that he had a brotherly feeling for Renard's young *Poil de Carotte*, who said, "Everybody isn't lucky enough to be an orphan." Varèse loved to quote him.

To name all of Varèse's friends and acquaintances in Paris between 1904, when he left Turin, and December 1915, when he came to New York, would be to make a list of almost all the young artists, writers, and musicians who have since made their mark on the several arts—and many who haven't. One of the most picturesque and outrageous characters Varèse knew was the compatriot of Picasso, the sculptor Manolo, around whom so many stories have accumulated. Apollinaire speaks of him as "that singular Manolo, who began by sculpting in blocks of butter." Varèse told a lecture audience the following Manolesque anecdote, not as funny, perhaps, in cold print as in Varèse's perfect imitation of Manolo's terrible French accent:

Before the First World War, when cubism was still shocking, it was in 1912 or 1913, I was in Picasso's studio with the Spanish sculptor Manolo. Mediterranean by race and culture, Manolo's preoccupation had always been to keep his art within the purest classical tradition. You can imagine what happened when Manolo's impassioned purism clashed with Picasso's originality. After a heated discussion, Manolo, having exhausted all his arguments, pointing to one of Picasso's cubic women, said: "Anyway, in spite of all your cubism, Pablo, you can't keep me from being your contemporary."

An older man, and a good friend of Varèse's, was the sculptor Despiau. When Varèse went to see him, whether or not he and his wife had finished their frugal meal (for he too was poor at that time), Despiau, unlike Picasso, seemed to know when Varèse needed tactfully to be fed, if only those ubiquitous lentils, which, from Varèse's accounts, as soup or salad, they seemed always to be eating.

Varèse was particularly fond of Modigliani—so handsome, so gifted, so poor, so drugged, so drunken, and so tragic. They used to meet at the Closerie des Lilas when that café was for the moment the favorite of artists. For food they would go to Chez Rosalie, rue Campagne Première because, as Varèse said, "Rosalie had a soft heart—sometimes." That "sometimes" was echoed later by Kiki, inimitable model of Montparnasse, when in her book she speaks of this same Rosalie: "I'd be bawled out for having the nerve to spend only six *sous* for a plate of soup. At other times Rosalie fairly wept and fed me for nothing."

Varèse also used to go to Modigliani's studio in Montmartre not far from the Bateau Lavoire, where Picasso and the poet Max Jacob then lived.

In his associations as well as in his music Varèse was, as Boulez called him, *marginale* in the sense of belonging to no system, no coterie. He was a lone wolf, but a friendly one. He would give his support to any new movement which sprang from the will to free whatever arts were in question from the inertia of academism. In this marginal capacity he took an interest in that group of ardent apostles of the arts of writing and painting who in 1906 joined in a communal experiment, taking a house in Créteil, near Paris, which they called with a bow to Rabelais, *L'Abbaye de Créteil*. There they lived and worked together and printed their books on their own printing press. Henri Barzun, creator of what he has named "Orphic Poetry" and one of the charter members of L'Abbaye, has described it as "neither a Cloister nor a Tower of Gloom, our Abbaye was a youthful and enthusiastic Fraternity of French 'Brook Farmers,' 'Lakists,' and 'Pre-Raphaelites' all in one, whose aim was to adjust their lives to this Machine Age, whose ambition was to give the new Century a

Literature and Culture commensurate with its momentous desti-
nies." They lived in their Abbaye for two years, then brought
their movement back to Paris, where other adherents joined their
activities. Of the charter members one became an academician,
Georges Duhamel, and on his initiative a plaque was placed on
the wall of their former Abbaye by the municipality of Créteil.
Most of the founders were good friends of Varèse's: the cubist
painter Albert Gleizes, and the writers Henri Barzun, Alexander
Mercereau, Charles Vildrac, and René Arcos, who wrote a book
on Romain Rolland.*

In 1908, during Varèse's first visit to Paris after settling in
Berlin, he met Ravel. It was the year Ravel finished his *Gaspard
de la Nuit,* the charming piano piece that musically translates
three of Aloysius Bertrand's poems, *Ondine, Le Gibet,* and
Scarbo.

When I was translating the words for Emile Baume, who was
to play Ravel's work at his concert in January 1947, Varèse told
me of the first time he had heard it at Ravel's before the
première, played for a few friends by Ricardo Viñes, and I
remember his saying: "They're beautiful things, these poems of
Aloysius Bertrand. Ravel, like Debussy, loved poetry. They both
had exquisite literary taste, something that Schoenberg, for all
his genius, lacked, or he would never have chosen such a trashy
poem for his *Pierrot Lunaire.*" Varèse spoke with high praise of
Viñes, a Catalan francophile, who lived all his adult life in
Paris, and as Varèse said, "Viñes was the first pianist to under-

* Arcos was one of the friends of Deubel and Varèse who used to come to
the *Rénovation Esthétique* while Varèse was living there. In 1935, Arcos, receiving the first news of Varèse since the First World War, in a letter of
reply exclaims:

   Think of it! At this moment I have here with me in the country a
   Japanese sculptor who is the author of a monument to Leon Deubel
   which has just been inaugurated. Curious coincidence! What old memories!

I don't know what has happened to this monument. When I was in Paris
in 1967 I went looking for it in the modest little square named for the poet,
Place Leon Deubel, near the Porte de Saint-Cloud, but no monument was
there.

stand and perform Debussy and Ravel at a time when for the other pianists they were too 'avant garde' before they became 'geniuses' (Varèse always put the word *genius* in quotes)."

There were other friends at Ravel's that evening but I can only remember one that Varèse mentioned, the music critic of the *Mercure Musicale,* Jean Marnold, a devoted friend of Ravel's. In a letter to Marnold dated December 22, 1908, avenue Carnot, Ravel mentions Varèse:

> Mon cher Ami, If it hadn't been for Monsieur Varèse's visit this morning I was all set to come to you this evening. I was sure you had invited me for Sunday evening. . . . Mr. Varèse told me of your intention of getting us together another day. Any time you say.

Among Varèse's letters of that period is one from Marnold inviting him to another of these reunions:

> You will find Ravel, Viñes, and other friends you met the last time. I hope your *poème symphonique* is recopied. You promised to entrust me with it for a few days.

Usually, however, Ravel reserved Sunday evenings for the weekly gatherings at his great friends the Godebskis. As they received intellectual *"tout Paris,"* Varèse, sure of meeting some of his friends there, spent many of his Sunday evenings at their apartment on the rue d'Athènes when he came to Paris. He might find his former teacher Roussel, his old friend Paul Le Flem, or the composer Florent Schmitt; often Alfredo Casella, Satie, and Cocteau would be there, and Léon-Paul Fargue might drop in on the way to one of his countesses. Cyprien Godebski (or Cipa, as his entourage called him) had been a friend of Toulouse-Lautrec, who had painted a portrait of him. Our friend, Jeanne de Lanux, at that time a *jeune fille* and an intimate friend of the Godebskis' fifteen-year-old daughter, has told me of meeting Varèse there. "He intimidated me," she said. "He was *too* handsome."

Varèse: A Looking-Glass Diary

It was while Varèse was in Paris in 1909 that he went to see Romain Rolland. Although better known in America as a novelist because of his *Jean-Christophe,* which in 1916 was awarded the Nobel Prize and translated into English, Romain Rolland was an erudite music scholar and at that time president of the music section of the Ecole des Hautes Etudes. When Varèse knew him he had already written many articles on composers, among others on Richard Strauss and on Vincent d'Indy.

Romain Rolland received Varèse with such kindness, showed him such warm sympathy, gave him so generously of his time, that Varèse was disarmed, lost his wary reserve, and was his natural youthful, intense self, pouring out his likes and dislikes, his ambitions, frustrations, and despairs. First he took Rolland his score *Bourgogne,* and in reply to Varèse's request for his opinion, Rolland wrote to him still in Paris, staying with Mme Kauffmann, Suzanne's mother, at 12 rue Lesueur:

Tuesday, January 19, 1909

Cher Monsieur, I read your work several times with great pleasure. It is in spite of myself that I give you my impressions! I do not like to judge an orchestral work without first hearing it played; I believe an audition is absolutely necessary even for the most proficient readers. If, nevertheless, I write my opinion, it is because you insisted that I should, and I beg you to excuse me if I am wrong.

You seem to me to be remarkably gifted for the orchestra; and your orchestral matter seems light, supple, alive and full. The composition in general remains valid from beginning to end; and it is very limpid and clear. In spite of the influence of Strauss in the general movement (not to mention a few Debussy traits in the beginning), it seems to me very French in feeling and nearer to d'Indy than to Strauss. That is probably due to its calm and religious nature, but also to its clarity, with that figure of triplets, so characteristic, alternating with the *phrase carrée.* The development seems to me more in the orchestra, in the color, than in the conception or the spirit; and passion is always a little in the background, or to one side, as though exterior to the subject. It is true that your subject is really BOURGOGNE and not yourself. . . .

You are going to write a Gargantua. Don't describe, be Gargantua. . . . Don't be afraid of letting yourself go, like Strauss in the first page of his *Erdenleben*. You will never lose your French qualities of clarity and purity, of form and intelligence, which you have to a high degree.

But advice is always useless and almost always impertinent. One must be what one is. But one is always that. You seem to be master of your musical language. And there is in your work a youthful virility and the purity of a poetic sensibility that I like.

Varèse undoubtedly objected to Rolland's reference to d'Indy, for in a letter a few days later Rolland writes:

I regretted having mentioned a name in my letter that might have distressed you (knowing your feeling on the subject), the name, that is, of Vincent d'Indy. In fact, I said a little more than I intended; I only wanted to point out that there occurred in you a phenomenon a little like that which occurs in d'Indy when he is (or was) the most Wagnerian, that is, he always remains French in his sense of order, in clarity and in logic, perhaps to excess—not that I advise you against those qualities; but they must be instinctive and not flagrant. They must only be found where there is passion.

. . . . Excuse this long letter, written in a great hurry, and see in it only the proof of the sympathy I have for you and my confidence in your future.

This "long letter" included Rolland's expression of disapproval over Varèse's choice of Hofmannsthal's *Oedipus und die Sphinx* as libretto for an opera Varèse was planning to write.

I have many misgivings about *Oedipus und die Sphinx*. I know the work, I have seen it performed in Germany; and in spite of some very beautiful lyrical moments (or even psychological—like the first meeting of Jocasta and Oedipus), I find it very dreary and erudite.

He advises Varèse, if he is attracted by the "Hellenic Myths," to go back to the sources, Sophocles, Euripides, and so on, suggesting also several modern writers, both French and German. He writes:

> I can't believe that there is any future for works like *Œdipe et le Sphinx*. If so, the byzantism (overrefined) of the elite will have to get the better of the rising force of the peoples of the world that is being felt today throughout the universe; and I sincerely hope not.

Rolland was politically a devout liberal.

On the other hand, Rolland gave his entire approval to Varèse's choice of Gargantua as the subject for a work Varèse had begun.

> Your Gargantua, on the contrary, seems to me an ideal subject, alive and popular (in the sense of an entire people). But, above all, enjoy yourself writing it; if you don't exalt in writing it, it's not worth doing; get rid of all intellectual preoccupations; let yourself go.

No wonder Rolland approved of Gargantua as the subject for a musical composition, since he himself chose it for the score of his hero Jean-Christophe. As he explains it to his friend, Sofia Bertolini Guerrieri-Gonzaga, in a letter two days after the above letter to Varèse:

> Look, how strange, a second Jean-Christophe has just appeared. He is extremely handsome: tall, beautiful dark hair, blue eyes, an intelligent, energetic face, a kind of young Beethoven painted by Giorgione. He is only twenty-five; but has suffered hardly less than Dupin, though in an entirely different way . . . he is French with a mixture of German [*sic*] and Italian blood and his name is Edgard Varèse; he will soon conduct a concert in Prague. He has a passion for the orchestra. He showed me a symphony called *Bourgogne* (the country where he spent his childhood), which seemed to me interesting, and remarkably written, in particular from the point of view of orchestral color. He has a great admiration for Strauss; and though he lives in Berlin he has never dared to go to see him because he is afraid of being badly received and of losing his illusions about the man.

Though he is not shy, in this instance just because he adores Strauss, he is. I have thought that if he goes to see him it will be the scene between Christophe and Hassler. He has confided to me all of his troubles, people's cruelty, that of colleagues and other artists. He has almost worked himself to death. He is now out of the woods. It makes me happy to feel that young independent artists come to me, and they are right to come; for I can in fact be useful to them—intellectually, and even in a practical way. Jean-Christophe attracts his brothers who are struggling in the world.

But I haven't told you the most amusing part of my meeting with this Varèse; he is writing a Gargantua (symphonic poem). Well, at this very moment, Jean-Christophe is writing one too! After that don't tell me that my book is fiction. He is everywhere around us. My book is not fiction. Jean-Christophe really exists. I am only telling what exists. I invent nothing.

One is certainly ready to agree with Rolland after reading the following paragraph from *Jean-Christophe,* which so prophetically prefigures Varèse:

The difficulty began when he tried to cast his idea in the ordinary musical forms: he made the discovery that none of the ancient molds were suited to them; if he wished to fix this vision with fidelity he had to begin by forgetting all the music he had heard, all that he had written, to make a clean slate of the formalism he had learned, of traditional technique, to throw away those crutches of impotency, that bed all prepared for the laziness of those who, fleeing the fatigue of thinking for themselves, lie down in other men's thoughts.

On November 29 Varèse must have written a very unhappy letter to Romain Rolland, who at once sent him this touchingly sympathetic reply:

My poor boy, I pity you with all my heart. Don't be discouraged. Life isn't always very amusing, and there are some bad moments. I know something about that myself, I assure you. Go back courageously to work. Only work can console and avenge.

Say to yourself, not "I will conquer," but "I will be." To be,
even if nobody else understands you at first. The rest will follow later. But one must be a severer judge of oneself than anyone else. Courage. I have only a moment tonight; but I was so
distressed by your letter that I wanted to answer it right away.
Thank you for having confided your troubles to me.

Was it disappointment over the cancellation of the concert in
Prague that had depressed Varèse? Or was it perhaps about this
time that Stransky was making difficulties about conducting
Varèse's score *Bourgogne,* which Strauss had urged him to perform. After further pressure from Strauss, Stransky did play it in
the following year.

Soon after meeting Varèse, Romain Rolland had written to
Strauss:

> I talked a great deal about you this morning . . . with a
> young French composer, settled in Berlin for the last two years,
> who admires you so much that he doesn't dare go to see you; his
> name is Edgar Varèse, and he has talent, he is particularly gifted
> for the orchestra. I think he should interest you. He has what I
> believe you prize (like me) more than anything else and what
> is so rare: life (*de la vie*).

Later the same year Varèse met Strauss and Strauss did indeed
take an interest in him.

But before taking Varèse back to Berlin, I must speak of a
part of his life that concerned another place and another person,
for even when he was in Paris or in Berlin they were never far
from his inner life. The place: the village where he had grown
up as a child; the person, Claude Cortot, his grandfather, who
had returned to Le Villars from Turin about a year after his
grandson's stormy departure in 1903.

I have before me a packet of letters from Grandpère to his
cher petit fils, which Varèse had kept all these years and which
are so endearing that I should like to include them all. Until
1905 they are from Turin; after the spring of 1905, from Le

Villars until the end of 1910 when he died. They make one understand Varèse's enduring devotion to the memory of this gentle, loving, simple, understanding, humorous man, abounding in so much "intelligence of the heart."

From those written in Turin it is evident that he was disgusted with his life there and longing to get back to France. They also reveal a distressing financial situation, the exact nature of which can only be guessed at. In one of them at the end of 1904 he writes: "I would not like to leave your father until his affairs have been settled." Did this refer to one of those disastrous law suits Varèse spoke of with such bitterness? It was a time when Varèse was almost destitute in Paris and it caused Grandpère the greatest distress that he could not help him. "I should like to buy you things, *mon cheri*, but you see how impossible it is for me. If I were only at home, I would find some way of coming to your aid. In this country, in this business there is nothing to hope for but to die of hunger." He still owned land in Le Villars, and he promises: "When Uncle Joseph receives my rents I shall ask him to send you a little money." He also writes that he is exhausted: "Plenty of fatigue but no work," and speaks of the cold with a touch of wry humor so much like Varèse: "I am sitting beside my stove and my pen escapes from my fingers—O beautiful sky of Italy—or rather, Siberia." He speaks of Varèse's brothers, most often of "Nate," as he calls Renaldo, the younger of the two: "All the family is well. Every day they ask me if I have heard from you, especially Nate. A little card would give the poor child such pleasure, he loves you so much." The only time he shows a moment of ill humor is in speaking of Henri Varèse's second wife, who is going to have a baby. "I'm afraid of having to stand godfather, that's one reason I'd like to get away. But I don't believe she wastes any more love on me than I do on her. I don't like to talk about anything so disagreeable, but I owe you the truth. Write to me but don't allude to what I have said. Let me know what your situation is, for I think of you all the time."

Considering Varèse's extreme hostility toward his father, Claude Cortot's references to him are of peculiar interest. From them it appears that Henri Varèse wrote to his son, whenever he knew his address, sent him a little money, and in November 1904, Grandpère tells Varèse: "Your Papa is having your winter coat repaired and is waiting until he has news of you to send it and other things. I know it isn't with what he sends that you will be happy." So, Henri Varèse, in spite of that terrible beating which took place with the family looking on, was trying to become reconciled with his rebel son. Was it thwarted possessiveness, sentimentality (a common trait in bullies), or a kind of cantankerous pride *à rebours* that made him refuse to let his son escape him? Claude Cortot, in another letter, reveals the father in a particularly revolting light: *"Mon cher petit fils,* I received your good letter—at second hand—your father having gone to the concierge's saw and opened it. . . . I need say no more." Like Grandpère I feel no comment is necessary.

One last word on the disagreeable subject of Varèse's father: When Grandpère is back in Le Villars, and Varèse with him, in a letter addressed to both, a brother-in-law of Claude Cortot writes:

> I wonder how you managed to get away from Italy—it must have been something rather serious. . . . Well I hope Edgard will be kinder to you than his father ever was.

Yet Grandpère bore no malice. Over and over again in his letters he urges Varèse to write to his father, who complains of his son's silence. I think Grandpère was tolerant almost to a fault, with one exception: toward his son-in-law's second wife he shows a bitter and uncharacteristic resentment.

From the letters written after he left Italy, when he was living once more in his native village, I shall quote at length, for, even in translation, though something of his personality is lost, they still give a vivid picture of the man Varèse cherished, of his village, and of his *cher petit fils.* I regret that I never read them with Varèse, who would have explained references that must now remain obscure. The first time I knew of them, perhaps twenty-five or thirty years ago, was one day—one of many—when we were searching for a straying something (our house has always had its mischievous poltergeist who hides things), Varèse picked up a packet of letters, saying: "These are Grandpère's." I wanted to look at them right away but Varèse said, "Not now, we haven't time." Why did we always have so many current things to do, to think about, to worry about? Although there were moments when Varèse felt impelled to talk about his past, it was against his principle: live in the present and face the future. Reading Grandpère's letters with me would have been too deliberate an indulgence.

When Claude Cortot returned to Le Villars he became a peasant again and, though already an old man, began bravely to dig his livelihood out of the soil. He had left Italy in March 1905, when Varèse was already at the Conservatoire studying with Widor. That was after Varèse had left Meudon and before he went to share Deubel's quarters at the *Rénovation*.

The second letter Grandpère writes to Varèse after his return to Le Villars is dated February 3 and is addressed to 22 rue Monsieur le Prince. One sees him facing bravely, but with some misgivings, his new life and senses that he is very tired.

> I received your two missives but delayed answering the first one, being worn out by work. I am cultivating my grapes, which have been neglected while I was away. There is plenty of work on all sides. Today I was to spade Mme Vernay's garden but it is raining so I am taking this opportunity to rest and to write to my little Gogo. I am badly lodged but Mr. Janot has promised me something in the Prieuré with the view you love so much.

Le PRIEURÉ! The word alone is enough to evoke Varèse for me when, overflowing with nostalgic memories, and forgetting his principles when the mood was on him, he would talk to me about Burgundy, "the country of stone and wine," as his stone-cutting sculptor friend Mathivet called it. This twelfth-century Prieuré that once housed Benedictine nuns, together with the Romanesque church adjoining it, and the magnificent abbey church of Saint-Philibert in Tournus only a few kilometers away, these were for Varèse his particular patrimony, the heritage from his Burgundian grandfather. They were the "manure," as Varèse once said, that fertilized his imagination.

The Prieuré is a long stone building that stands on a high bluff overlooking the Saône. Below it the river is so still it seems to have forgotten that it is on its way to the sea, and on the other shore lie the equally quiet meadows of Bresse, while on both sides cows add their reposeful personalities to a view that says softly, *"Pax vobiscum."* No wonder Varèse loved it. For a moment at least it must have given his unquiet spirit rest. The little house in the Prieuré into which Grandpère moved not long after writing the above letter was, with two other small houses, in recent times built into the old building, changing part of the façade that opens onto the square. In the original façade is an old doorway faced with the pale pink stone from the nearby quarry of Prêty, the same stone that gives the rosy glow to the nave of Saint-Philibert. A lovely little twelfth-century church stands next to the Prieuré and not far off Oncle Joseph's house and forge. Varèse, then *le petit Gogo,* used to play in the grounds around the Prieuré and in the graveyard where Anatole France buried his inimitable Abbé Jérôme Coignard, hero of *La Rôtisserie de la Reine Pédauque,* that adorable classic temporarily out of fashion. The church (now *Monument historique*) is famous for the architectural oddity of having twin naves, one formerly reserved for the Benedictine nuns of the Prieuré. Today only one is in use where, twice a month (or is it once?), the curé from Saint-Philibert comes to celebrate mass for the women of Le Villars. The men, true *Bourgignons,* prefer a bottle of wine at the café across the road and a game of *boules* afterward on the square. When a little older, but still a very small boy, Varèse would take the road along the Saône to Tournus where his friend Mathivet lived, and together they would play in the cloisters of Saint-Philibert, explore the crypt, whose slender columns make one think of Greece, climb up the spiral stairs to the Chapelle Saint-Michel, with its elephantine pillars and Romanesque stone carvings, built over the narthex, and which through arched openings overlooks the nave. Varèse told me that even as a little boy it excited him to look down from the chapel into the nave, which seemed to him mysterious so far below—not the dark mystery of Gothic cathedrals but with a mystery of light and lightness. The nave of Saint-Philibert! Even Varèse, in spite of his enthusiasm, never did complete justice to it in words, any more than the photographs he showed me. It was in 1927 that I first visited it with Varèse and with Mathivet, the latter reciting dates and architectural terms which I don't remember. I saw it again in 1967, when I spent two days in Tournus, and I remembered what Proust says somewhere in *Sodome et Gomorrhe,* that to know the full pleasure that *"les belles choses"* can give, one must be alone. It was only then that I fully understood Varèse's passion for Saint-Philibert. Remembering the nave of Saint-Philibert I become tongue-tied. Books describe it, photographs reproduce it, but all photographs make the stones look too smooth, like the photographs of a woman with all the marks of life removed from her face to make her look younger. And the architectural descriptions give no idea of its strong delicacy. You have yourself to touch with eyes and fingers the misty pink roughness of the great pillars (they too are built of the pale rose stone of Prêty). You must stand yourself in their midst. In spite of the soaring height and the huge circumference of the pillars, one has the sense of extraordinary grace as well as of great strength. Varèse once said to me: "If there is any strength or beauty in my music, I owe it to Saint-Philibert." Burgundy is rich in Romanesque abbey churches, many that are not very far from Tournus Varèse knew: Brancion, Uchizy, Cluny. He knew and loved them not as an archaeologist, a scholar, a connoisseur. He had grown up with them. They were his happiness. He knew the rose-pink columns of the nave of Saint-Philibert, the huge gray pillars of the narthex and the Chapelle Saint-Michel, not as examples of great architectural art, but as part of his daily life. He loved them as he loved his grandfather's vineyards, his great-uncle's forge, the quiet Saône below the Prieuré. I have much to be grateful to Varèse for, and one of the most precious possessions

I owe to him is Romanesque architecture—*his* architecture—
which, if it had not been for his passion, I might never have come
to know.

Not only Burgundy but all France is rich in eleventh- and
twelfth-century abbey churches. Rémy de Gourmont in his *La
Petite Ville,* which is Coutances in Normandy, describing one of
them, speaks of "the proud sobriety of Romanesque architecture."
It is not surprising that Varèse had no use for the eighteenth
century or for rococo art.

The spirit of Saint-Philibert must have hovered over the creation of at least two of Varèse's early works for, although only the
titles, *Rapsodie Romane and Bourgogne,* remain, the words of
two very different commentators of those days bear witness to the
"proud sobriety" of the music. They were Romain Rolland and a
young journalist from Bayonne. The latter, who visited Varèse at
the *Rénovation,* mentions it in an article about Varèse in the
Courrier de Bayonne of September 21, 1905:

> In the studio-bedroom of a young composer, Edgard Varèse, I
> —the only Bayonnais left in Paris during the vacation—with a
> few intimate friends, had the great pleasure of hearing four of
> his compositions: *Dans le Parc, Colloque au Bord d'une Fon-
> taine, Poème des Brumes, Rapsodie Romane.* We were deeply
> moved by the medieval spirit of the works of this young artist.
> Among others, *Rapsodie Romane* written for large orchestra.

There follows what I might call a short rhapsody on Varèse's
Rapsodie, which had evoked for the writer: "Solemn convent
bells, shimmering autumnal twilights, ascetic souls in prayer,"
and so on. The article ends:

> Edgard Varèse, vibrant passionate soul, has a brilliant future
> ahead. With all my heart I wish him the Prix de Rome for which
> he is working at present.

Three years later Romain Rolland, writing to Varèse of
Bourgogne, speaks of its "calm religious character." The quiet
flowing Saône and the rose nave of Saint-Philibert had got writ-

ten into it. They perhaps seem strange words to describe a composition that was to shock music critics the following year when it was performed in Berlin. One critic said it was even worse than Schoenberg, whose *Pelleas und Melisande* had been performed not long before. Yet not so strange when one stops to remember that if there is anything unacademic or technically unfamiliar in a new work it makes most critics deaf to its musical content. Also, it might seem strange in a pagan like Varèse that both Romain Rolland and the Bayonnais journalist should have felt a religious spirit in his music, until you recall Varèse's passionate admiration for the great Catholic polyphonic composers he had studied with Charles Bordes and conducted under Vincent d'Indy at the Schola Cantorum and whom he called *"mes copains et mes contemporains* (my pals and my contemporaries)."

On June 10, Grandpère, not yet installed in the little house in the Prieuré, writes:

> Mon cher petit fils, I have received sad news of your health from your Papa. He tells me that you are coming here to me. I am not very well lodged at the moment but will soon be moving where we'll be very comfortable and where I'll do my best to take good care of you. I am worried about your health. Don't keep me on tenderhooks any longer.

What this illness was I don't know. When in later years Varèse suffered periodically from nervous depressions and respiratory difficulties, aggravated, if not caused by claustrophobia, he said that these handicaps dated from boyhood. As a little boy in Paris he could not walk under the arcades of the rue de Rivoli without suffering a sensation of suffocation, and it was always torture for him to ride in an enclosed elevator. As a young man, for his depressions, he consulted a pupil of Charcot, the great nerve specialist. Varèse quoted this doctor as saying, *"Vous êtes un grand nerveux,"* which, though not a doctor, I discovered myself even before we were married.

By the time Varèse arrived in Le Villars, Grandpère had moved into the little house in the Prieuré. Two touching letters follow his visit, the first dated August 8, 1905.

Varèse: A Looking-Glass Diary

My dear grandson, I received your good letters and the *reviews Music*. I see with pleasure that you are happy about your composition and most of all that your health is good. It is the same with me, although tired, I am well. Since you left I haven't stopped cultivating my alfalfa. I'll be finished this evening. Too bad you left so soon. The peaches and the grapes are ripe. A strong wind for two days—the peaches are all under the trees. Tomorrow I'll put up some preserves. If I didn't answer sooner it is because you know all my little doings by heart and it's always the same. Evenings after the day is over and after dinner I sit at my window and admire the beautiful sunset you loved so much, thinking of you and wondering what you are doing at that moment. I seem to see you hurrying along, preoccupied and anxious, through that beehive. . . . Oncle and Tante send their love and all your numerous friends send their good wishes.

Enclosed in this letter is one from Varèse's cousin Marthe Cortot—little Gogo's big sister. Marthe became a teacher and later the Directress of Schools in Mâcon. The few letters of hers I have read show her as an intelligent, sensitive, and very frustrated woman. They are rather literary but show a gift of expression, the style tainted, Varèse said, by her normal-school education. Like Grandpère, she had a nice sense of humor. On that August day she wrote:

> Your grandfather and Mama are jellifying (*confiturant*). It is pouring and like Sister Anne I don't see anything coming. I went for a few days to stay with some old friends and made the acquaintance of some fresh and blooming babies, and nothing could have made me regret more my old maid existence. I received yesterday a card from my old friend (*ami*), who is vacationing at Coppet, with this simple phrase by de Staal: "Since they are reduced to seeking fame, those who might have been satisfied with affection, well let them attain it." It's rather pathetic, but he is right. This same phrase is expressed differently by I don't remember whom: "At the bottom of all feminine talent there is hidden sorrow." Those who obstinately search for oblivion in work are accused of pride and ambition, when they are only unhappy. One must say Lord, *fiat voluntas tua*, and take life as it comes, bravely and without bitterness.

I embrace you most affectionately and beg you to tell us in your next if the amelioration persists as to your health; avoid humidity in these autumn days, and then . . . abstinence, if you please, sir, in all things.

Your grouchy old cousin,
Bema

Your grandfather has a rare pointillistic talent; a genius in which he excels; I have never seen him write a letter without spots.*

Over two weeks later Grandpère still writes nostalgically of his grandson's visit:

I received your good card and the magazine, thank you. You can't believe how I miss you and what an emptiness your departure has left. I keep thinking I hear your voice calling *Pépé*. How short and how agreeable those days we spent together. But I must make the best of it since I know the separation is necessary for your future and I wish a good and happy one for you, *mon cheri*. I hope you will triumph and overcome all the difficulties you will have to overcome, but with the help of the eminent connections which will not be lacking, your task will be less difficult. Friends and relatives all send their best wishes and pray for your happiness and ask for news of you.

Tomorrow I am having Farquet take back the piano. I spent all day Sunday thinking of the pleasure it was to have you for a little while—much too short, but I must resign myself, hoping for the future.

On the first of November Grandpère is in the hospital of Tournus. After thanking Varèse for a postal order of twenty francs he continues:

I don't know how but I caught a sudden chill and as I couldn't take care of myself, I got Mme Vernay's carriage to bring me

* To appreciate this postscript you would have to try deciphering Grandpère's undecipherable handwriting. This feat was accomplished by my friend Jeanne de Lanux, who wrote out all the letters for me in her own beautiful hand.

here to the hospital. I am doing very well, I have no fever and am having a good rest after the heavy fatigue of last spring—too depressing to think about. But I am going to be as good as new, so don't worry, *mon cheri*, I shall leave here healthy and as merry as a cricket!

Poor Grandpère, no wonder he caught a chill, out in all weathers at his age, for he was past his mid-sixties, engaged in the hardest of physical labors, making things grow. Burgundy, where winters are very cold, summers very hot, is a good country for grapes but not for old men who are farmers. Over and over again Grandpère excuses his handwriting because of the stiffness of his fingers:

> Can you decipher my writing? I've been cutting wood and there's an icy drizzle falling and I have no feeling in my fingers. [And again:] You mustn't mind my scribbles, my hands are so numb from handling the pickax I can hardly hold a pen. [Later it is his legs:] I work with a will, and if it weren't for my legs the work doesn't tire me. And I can't go to Tournus anymore because my feet don't want to follow me.

Peasants and farmers seem to age sooner than most people. If you want to keep young into old age the profession you should choose is conducting, never farming. The agelessness of conductors is astonishing, especially when you consider the atmosphere they breathe at morning rehearsals (judging by those I used to attend), not to mention the air in concert halls (exception: Philharmonic Hall). Varèse was right perhaps when he said that "the virtue of fresh air is very much exaggerated." He thought the American habit of sleeping with windows open was unhealthy and an indication of physiological ignorance. "Look at the birds," he would say. "They put their heads under their wings at night. When you're asleep you don't need much oxygen —lungs and heart want a rest." The case of farmers as compared with conductors would seem to support his theory.

Varèse, not satisfied that Grandpère was telling him the whole truth about his condition, wrote to a friend in Tournus, Mme

Chapuis, asking her to let him know. In a letter dated January 1, 1905, Grandpère reassures him:

> Yesterday I had a visit from Mme Perrin and Mme Chapuis, who is charming. She said that she had received a letter from you asking whether I was not worse than I said. Don't worry, *mon cheri*, I'm as fit as a fiddle. I would be home already except that work is not pressing and the weather not favorable, so I am in no hurry.

I like Grandpère's, "Mme Chapuis, who is charming." As Varèse used to say, "Grandpère liked the attentions of attractive women and they loved him even in his old age." Like grandfather like grandson. In another letter feminine beauty again gets an approving mention:

> Sunday Marthe was in my garden with Mlle Bagout and we talked at length about you. It seems she had a crush on you, she kissed me for you. She is more beautiful than ever.

Grandpère enjoyed his convalescence in the hospital, sitting around an "enormous stove" with other patients "more or less ailing." He is in a gay mood when, referring to a photograph Varèse has sent him of a group taken sometime before in Le Villars, he writes:

> Tell your photographer friend that it took quite a while to sort out the group. You are not too bad, but I look as if I'd been dragged out of the Saône after a sojourn of several days under a boat.

Early in 1906 Varèse succeeded in getting exempted from military service through the intervention of Clemenceau. How Varèse obtained an interview with Clemenceau I don't remember, but how it ended Varèse often enjoyed telling:

When Clemenceau, bringing the interview to a close, had said, "Yes, yes, my boy, I promise you," Varèse with youthful impertinence—his special kind which did not always offend, as in this case—rejoined: "I know what politician's promises are worth." Whereupon Clemenceau burst out laughing and said: *"Sacré gosse!"* which might be translated, "What a boy!" Varèse got his exemption.

Grandpère, congratulating him in a letter dated the second of February, says: "Now that you are free and have nothing to worry about, you can give yourself up entirely to your work." I detect in this remark of Grandpère's a secret worry of his own in the knowledge that his little Gogo, freed of one worry, would soon find another to disturb his work.

In the same letter is this arresting mention of Alfred Cortot:

> Marthe showed me the newspaper that speaks of Alfred in very flattering terms. . . . Do you think that he is capable of putting obstructions in your path, trying to harm you?

I knew that Varèse disliked his cousin intensely; this letter indicates that he also had reason to distrust him. Cortot was certainly capable of trying to harm Varèse in official musical milieus and, now that he was beginning to be successful in his career, probably succeeded in that too. Varèse had the gift of wit, quicker than thought it tickled laughter and so pat that winged repetition was inevitable. In short, a boomerang.

Unprejudiced persons, among whom I am not, may question whether it was wit or resentment that started this cousinly feud. I think it was incompatibility; a question of character. Of Cortot's I was given a shocking revelation by Mme Romain Rolland, whose husband's first wife had married the famous, or as it seems to me, infamous pianist. He treated her very badly, Mme Rolland said, and when, during the occupation, she at first refused to give him a divorce, threatened to tell the Germans (with whom it is said he was on excellent terms) that she was a Jewess.

The following remarks, I once heard Varèse make:

> Alfred resented me and soon began avoiding me and lying about me. He was a filthy snob and wanted to forget his peasant origins and to conceal them from the people on the social hill he

was bent on climbing. I talked too much about my peasant grandfather whose name was also Cortot and who was his uncle. He disgusted me and he thought I was a menace to him. He licked boots to get ahead, or I should say slippers, for he had been boosted to popularity by women more easily flattered than men by a man.

I think I should say here that in all the years I lived with Varèse I never knew him to try consciously to hurt anyone. In fact he wasted a good deal of time trying to help people. I admit, his wit could occasionally be cruel.

Cortot's father was Grandpère's brother, Denis; his mother, I believe, was Swiss, and he was born in Switzerland. As far as I know, he had never set foot in Le Villars, at least not after he reached pianohood.

When I went to Le Villars in May of 1967, I was vaguely considering how Varèse's name could be permanently attached to the village he loved so much, perhaps a plaque somewhere near the church where there is already one in memory of Anatole France's fictitious hero; or I might buy Grandpère's little house, which had belonged to Mathivet and was now, since his recent death, for sale.

Please try to imagine—after considering what I have said about Cortot contrasted with what I said about Varèse in relation to Le Villars—my horror, my utter consternation, I cannot think of a word strong enough, when on a wall abutting the church I saw a memorial plaque to Alfred Cortot and learned that he had been buried with honors in the little country churchyard nearby! What if I were instrumental in having a plaque with Varèse's name placed next to his ignoble cousin's, wouldn't Varèse leap out of his grave (if he had one) and haunt me for the rest of my life?

After leaving Deubel and the apartment in the *Rénovation* sometime in April (a falling-out of two difficult and contrary temperaments at too close quarters), Varèse moved to 86 rue Saint-Honoré, moved again in September to 41 rue Monge. He was now giving concerts with his chorus at the Château du

Peuple and was in consequence stimulated and filled with an ever-vanishing and ever-recurring euphoria. In this state of elation he longed for his grandfather and wrote to him that he was taking an apartment where the two of them could live together in Paris. But Grandpère, wiser than his impulsive *petit Gogo,* replied cautiously in a letter dated September 25, 1906:

> You say you have taken a little apartment for the two of us, but do you think, *mon cheri,* that our resources will suffice to meet such an expense? I know that with my economic experience we could live very well with very little. But we have to look ahead. I know we would be happy to be reunited, both of us, but first we must be sure of certain resources and know what we are doing. Give me more details so as not to act lightly.

In his next letter Grandpère writes:

> So, it is decided for the present, but patience, later on we'll be reunited, so I hope. Next year I'll have a good harvest to sell, potatoes and the wheat I have just sowed. If things turn out well, in January I'll receive a certain old-age subsidy, which will help liquidate the loan I contracted last year. See if you couldn't take one room, less expensive than an apartment. . . . As soon as you are installed I'll send you some provisions and a few sheets.

This loan, referred to several times in Grandpère's letters, seems to have been a constant worry to him; he also knew the precariousness of Varèse's situation and the uncertainty of his periods of extreme euphoria, considerations that outweighed his longing to be with his grandson.

Varèse's next move was in November, to 27 rue Descartes. From the description Varèse used to give of this place it could hardly have been the "little apartment" he and Grandpère were to have lived in together, but rather the one room which Grandpère in his hard-earned wisdom had advised. It had no stove and only three solid walls, the other being formed of burlap that moved like an arras with every draft. Often in winter Grandpère complained of the cold, but the cold of Burgundy is nothing compared to the damp chill of an unheated room in Paris. It used to seem to me, when I lived there many winters ago, that the cold was not in the streets but came out of the houses when those great outer doors opened.

Grandpère's hope that he and his grandson would be "re-united later on" was never realized. That winter Varèse lived alone in his refrigerator of a room, and it was Suzanne, and not Grandpère, who, the following spring, came to share it with him. In a letter dated June 24 Grandpère inquires:

> I see that my newspaper was addressed by an unknown hand, the hand of a friend of yours, so of mine too. Whether masculine or feminine (*ami ou amie*), I send my greetings to the person to whom the hand belongs.

This letter shows—and not for the first time or the last—Grandpère's touching eagerness to become friends with all of Varèse's friends, an almost obsessive longing to share his grand-son's life. The unknown hand was that of Suzanne Bing, who before the end of the year would become Varèse's wife. Soon after this Varèse took Suzanne to Le Villars to meet Grandpère. He immediately opened his generous warm heart to her and she soon became "*ma petite Suzanne cherie.*"

I have already mentioned that Varèse often took friends with him to his grandfather's village. Afterward Grandpère always referred to them in his letters as "my friends," and it was not long before they understood Varèse's devotion to him, for they came to love him too.

When Edouard Gazanion, a poet, perhaps not one of the best, but one of Grandpère's most devoted young friends, was visiting Le Villars with Varèse in August 1907, he wrote a poem dedi-cated "to Monsieur Claude Cortot," which was inspired by the "view" so often mentioned in Grandpère's letters. He entitled it *Fenêtre*—that is, *Window*—the window where Grandpère used to sit watching the sunset, dreaming of his *petit Gogo* and long-ing for his next visit. It describes the quiet Saône, the barges slipping silently toward the north, the pastures, the sheep, and the hills beyond. It ends (in translation):

> And the river so slow near the fertile fields
> That it seems, in the hollow of its peaceful shores,
> Just a meadow more limpid that sleeps and rocks
> Without eddies or islands or dipping oars.

With Gazanion that summer was Julio Gonzales, the Catalan sculptor who later became famous for his forged and welded iron sculpture, a technique which he may have invented, though I believe there are other claimants. More important, his iron sculpture is beautiful. While Gazanion was picturing Varèse's beloved Saône in words, Gonzales drew sketches. He also made a fine drawing of Grandpère, which Varèse mentions in his tribute to his grandfather.

Other frequent visitors were a certain Jama often mentioned in Grandpère's letters but whose family name I don't know, as I can't remember Varèse ever mentioning him, and of course Varèse's childhood friend from Tournus, Desiré Mathivet, who was then living in Paris. He was also a sculptor and later made several regional monuments in honor of Burgundy's grapes and war heroes.

The following letters from Jama and Gonzales to Varèse, who had failed to keep a rendezvous in Le Villars, give an idea of the gay reunions in Grandpère's village. Gonzales wrote:

> Greetings, my dear Edgard! Here I am in Le Villars as I promised Grandpère. He is certainly looking very well. Mathivet was waiting for me in Tournus, we stopped to say hello to his grandmother, then took the path along the Saône and there on the terrace were the charming Grandpère, a little, but very little sheep,* and old Jama.

* The "little, very little sheep (*le petit, tout petit mouton*)" was, of course, Suzanne. The nickname puzzled me until Jeanne de Lanux, who knew Suzanne in Paris after she and Varèse had separated—when Suzanne with other members of the Vieux Colombier were taking lessons in rhythmics at the Dalcroze School, where Jeanne was an instructor—explained that Suzanne's hair was cut very, very short and was very, very curly like a *"petit mouton."* He calls her "little, but very little" because she was.

We drank a bit of Spanish wine left over from my trip, afterward some *gnolle* [brandy] to your health, to that of Grandpère, to that of all of us.

We went for a little walk, as far as the *Mar aux Grenouilles*, tried some of the grapes around there, came home for dinner, and I, dead tired, fell asleep in my chair. I got up today feeling fine and your *mouton* wants to make me eat everything in the house, wants to cut off my mustache with great big scissors, in short is very naughty, tells me all about what you are doing in Berlin, etc.

Finally, I must say, old man, I regret not seeing you in Le Villars for, without you, Le Villars isn't the same and as I am leaving right away I won't have that joy.

All the best from my mother and sisters. We talked about you, awaiting the day when you will conduct an orchestra in Barcelona.

Tout à toi, je te dis au revoir, et je t'embrasse, mon Edgard.

Jama begins his letter without preliminaries:

Just one absentee, old man, you, when, as first inhabitant, you should have been waiting for us and have prepared our downies! It's deplorable, and I insist that as soon as you receive this letter, after distributing all the requisite kicks in the various Berliners' backsides, you pack your bags and demand a ticket *nach* Le Villars *ohne* return ticket.

Last night at Richy & Co. we slept like princes, both in the bed and on the floor. The fleas, scared by this invasion of the barbarians, kept quiet, and it was a good thing for them they did, for Mathivet has a special talent for cannonading that's enough to make the walls tremble. Gonzales woke up this morning fresh and fit and, like the rest of us, awaits your coming, O Messiah! We have been making diverse plans for a future house in the Prieuré for the four of us together. A house built with our own hands, old man! We call for your ideas on the subject, and for your mug, and your hair and your entire person.

Tout à toi, je t'embrasse, mon cher, avec pleine amitié.

J. Arand [or Araud]

The idea of a house in the Prieuré was still echoing in Varèse's memory when, in 1927, we stopped in Le Villars on our way to

Varèse: A Looking-Glass Diary

Paris from Antibes, where we had spent the summer. Mathivet was living in Grandpère's little house, which he had bought, and for a brief moment Varèse and I played with the idea of buying, if cheap enough, and renovating a bit of the old building next to him. Luckily nothing came of this emotional impulse. A legend should never be reduced to a reality.

In 1908 Varèse was asked to organize a mixed chorus in Berlin and to be its musical director. He accepted with enthusiasm, not that it would do very much toward solving his financial problems (his salary was seventy-five marks a month), but conducting a chorus was an activity he enjoyed perhaps above all others.] He began rehearsals with his new chorus, The Symphonischer Chor, the following January. Anyone who has ever heard Varèse talk about the masters of the Middle Ages, the Renaissance, and early Baroque—Perotin, Josquin Deprès (of whom Luther wrote: "He is the supreme master of notes, which must express whatever he wants them to. Other composers only do what the notes want."), Victoria, Heinrich Schütz, Monteverdi, to name only a few of the dozen or more he liked best—or seen him conduct them with such concentrated fervor will not have to be told that they constituted the principal fare of his chorus. His chorus also took part in two of Max Reinhardt's productions: *A Midsummer Night's Dream* and Goethe's *Faust.* Reinhardt was at that time director of the Deutches Theater in Berlin and in 1908 produced Hugo von Hofmannsthal's *Oedipus und die Sphinx.* When Varèse saw it he decided it would be just the opera libretto he had been looking for, and after he met Hofmannsthal in the winter of 1909 he obtained his permission to adapt the drama and his promise of collaboration. Hofmannsthal's long collaboration with Richard Strauss had already begun with *Elektra,* which was first performed by the Dresden Court Opera that January. I seem to remember Varèse telling me that he and Hofmannsthal met at the Fritz Andreaes' in Berlin, where Varèse was often a guest. Andreae was a banker and his wife an accomplished hostess who gathered in her drawing room a great variety of civilized people from many countries with French as the lingua franca. Being

German and Jewish, she loved music and musicians and was particularly kind to at least one young composer. She was the sister of Walter Rathenau, who later became foreign minister in the Weimar Republic and was assassinated by the Pan-German-ists in 1922. That spring Hofmannsthal invited Varèse to visit him in his home at Rodaun near Vienna. Before Varèse left, Hofmannsthal gave him a copy of *Oedipus,* inscribing it: *"A Edgar Varèse en souvenir de Rodaun*—Hofmannsthal—May 1909," and in a letter the following June he wrote: *"Je garde de votre visite le souvenir le plus charmant."*

When Varèse was planning to give the Berlioz oratorio *L'Enfance du Christ* with his chorus, he wrote asking Hofmanns-thal to translate the words into German. Hofmannsthal replied:

> The words of the symphony *Enfance* are impossible in Ger-man. I have done my utmost but the translation sounds stilted and silly. There is a chasm between the two languages. But since everybody here understands French, why not leave it in French?

Of the remarkable men who sponsored Varèse during those early years Hofmannsthal was the one most concerned with his day-by-day welfare. Indeed, he seems to have worried about him not a little and to have taken it upon himself to see that he and Suzanne did not starve. Although it is true that it was Richard Strauss who was instrumental in getting Varèse's *Bourgogne* performed in Berlin in 1910 by forcing the mediocre and unwill-ing conductor Josef Stransky to play it, Hofmannsthal, as Varèse used to say, was the *"eminence grise."* It must have been soon after he met Varèse that Hofmannsthal began trying to interest Strauss in Varèse and in his music. On February 2, 1909, he wrote to Varèse:

> When I left, Strauss had only had time to glance through your score; he said that already he was willing to vouch for your fu-ture. I shall try in a little while to get his opinion in writing.

In spite of Romain Rolland's disapproval of *Oedipus,* Varèse had continued his collaboration with Hofmannsthal. In May he went to Rodaun and the letter Hofmannsthal wrote following that visit shows his active concern for his young collaborator. After the first few lines about *Enfance* (which I have already quoted) the letter continues:

> I am enclosing a letter for Mr. Bie, a very advanced critic and a charming fellow. Go to see him. I have written directly to Mr. Fischer, whose office is at Bülowstrasse 91 (the same as Bie's) and his home Grunewald, Erdenstrasse. I shall shortly write to Madame Guillette Mendelssohn and to my friend Frankenstein. I had a letter sent to Mr. Hans Heye, a young painter whose young wife is looking for a professor of harmony—*Harmonie-lehre*. . . .
>
> On the fifth or sixth of June send the symphony, registered parcel post, addressed: A. M. Richard Strauss for Herr Hofmannsthal, Villa Strauss, Garmisch, Oberbayern.
>
> I wrote to the manager of S. Fischer, my publisher, that I owe you 300 marks and that he should be prepared to pay them to you on request, either in part or the entire amount. I beg you, my dear Sir, to make use of this money without waiting until you are in real need—someday you will pay it back.

Memory is often unconsciously selective and, as I have said, Varèse, looking back on his life in Berlin, recalled only what had enriched him. He forgot or failed to mention the dark Berlin of illness and poverty, dwelling only lightly on a nervous disorder and mentioning that principally because of the devotion of his doctor, Dr. Flies, disciple of the "great neurologist Jean Martin Charcot," and his pecuniary difficulties only because he liked to recall how he was helped by those remarkable men who had befriended him. Not till I read Hofmannsthal's letters to Varèse and to friends on his behalf, as well as Varèse's letters to him, did I learn that Berlin was not all exhilarating moments with Busoni, meetings with Strauss, with Muck, and the friendship of Hofmannsthal. On July 26, 1909, Varèse wrote:

> Cher Monsieur,
>
> Thank you for your good card and for having written to Madame Mendelssohn. The latter (whom my wife saw) was ador-

able. As I am very ill nervously and can hardly keep going, she sent me 2000 marks so that I can go to our rich Burgundy to rest. So I am leaving in a couple of days and shall let you have news of me as soon as I arrive. Thank you again for all you are doing for me which I shall *never forget.*

He adds a postscript:

I can't wait to get back to work. I think of nothing but getting well quickly.

He spent July and August in Le Villars and was back in Paris that autumn. On September 12, Hofmannsthal wrote to him:

Cher Monsieur,

You have given yourself very little rest. At least if you begin to work again it must be calmly and without fever (apart from that of inspiration). You must give yourself inner repose, for if, by a sustained effort of your will you do not get back peace and joy within yourself your work will suffer. For the moment and for the immediate future you are not without sufficient means; afterward you will receive aid and with no difficulty at all, with no more than a word from you. As for Strauss I will introduce you; also viva voce I'll succeed in getting a more detailed judgment of your symphony, which it has been impossible to drag out of him by letter. I have written to my friend Frankenstein, Ansbacherstrasse 53, Berlin, to get in touch with you. The Fischers have told me that they will be very happy to see you again and to meet Madame Varèse. Madame Mendelssohn has written me the most charming things about you, which have really moved me. As for your work, I suppose *Gargantua* comes first. In regard to *Oedipus,* forgive me. I find myself at a critical moment in my work. It absorbs all my strength, which is not enormous. I cannot do what I promised you for another eight or ten weeks. And frankly I believe that it would be better if you were to do the whole thing yourself. I think you should so penetrate the work that you will finally know what use to make (or not to make) of Kreon, better than I would myself—and understand the *Motiv* and *Gegenmotiv.* The work I think should tell you everything, I nothing. Am I wrong?

The first part of this letter indicates clearly that Varèse was going through one of those periods which kept recurring all his life, when he would be incapable of getting down on paper ideas that never ceased to swarm through his head. Yet he could never stop trying, as he was unable at this time to take the wise advice so kindly proffered by Hofmannsthal. Disappointment over a concert he was to have conducted in Prague, which for some reason was cancelled, may well have had something to do with it. In April Grandpère had written: "I see in the *Lion* of the troubles in Prague." In April a friend, René Morax, inquired: "Will you be going to Prague soon for your concert?" And Romain Rolland's letter of March 23 ends: "I see that you are in Prague. I hope everything will be settled satisfactorily." But nothing was settled at that time and it was not until 1914 that Varèse conducted the long-postponed concert in Prague.

Varèse continued to work on the libretto by himself. On an undated postcard, Hofmannsthal writes:

> I went over *Oedipus*. . . . Very good. It is excellent, especially your suppressing everything from page 170. I am *very pleased* with the way you have penetrated the drama.

Among Varèse's books are the two small copies of the play, published by Fischer in 1906, which Hofmannsthal had sent him in 1909. In one, changes and omissions for the libretto are indicated through the first act in Hofmannsthal's handwriting. Throughout the other (Varèse's working copy) the marks are all by Varèse in colored crayons, with the exception of one or two penciled suggestions by Hofmannsthal.

Hofmannsthal did not, after all, introduce Varèse to Strauss. As it happened, meeting Strauss one day on Kurfürstendamm, and not being as timid as Romain Rolland supposed, Varèse introduced himself, and having seen his score, Strauss was extremely cordial and soon joined Varèse's other distinguished protectors in trying to help him. On October 30 Varèse wrote an ecstatic letter to Hofmannsthal:

> Just a word to say that I have made the acquaintance of Richard Strauss, who is interested in me—without saying a word to

me he has arranged with Mr. Stransky of Hamburg to have *Bour-gogne* played here this winter—and he will try to get me work to do. He has even told me I could use his name as reference anywhere it would be useful—and he offered to use his influence with all the personalities of the music world whom I might like to know so as to facilitate my career. He proposed all this himself, spontaneously. Wasn't it good of him?

The following postcards Strauss sent to Varèse show that he did, indeed, try to help him in getting work. The first is dated the twenty-ninth of October:

Cher Monsieur,
    Monsieur W. Klatte, professor of counterpoint at the Stern Conservatorium and critic of the Fr. Lokalanzeiger, has promised me that he will help you in getting lessons. Please go to see him tomorrow, Saturday afternoon, between 4 and 5, Nettlestrasse 24. Do you speak German?

Yours,
D. Richard Strauss

The second was written the following month:

Monsieur,
    I have spoken to my publisher W. Krenenstrasse 16/1. I hope he will be able to give you work. He expects you tomorrow at his office.

D. Richard Strauss.

Strauss also wrote a very warm letter of recommendation to Paul Kupfer, president of the Association of the Workers' Chorale of Germany:

Dear Sir,
    I take the liberty of recommending very warmly Mr. Varèse as conductor for your association. If the fact that he speaks very little German is not a hindrance, you will have acquired in him an excellent musician and an admirable conductor (he is also a talented composer). I am sure in choosing him you will bring credit to your organization.

Varèse: A Looking-Glass Diary

By the time I met Varèse many years later, and after I came to know his musical predilections and aversions, his enthusiasm for Strauss's music had abated. Not that he admired less the virtuosity of Strauss's orchestration, but he found the themes, the motifs, really too "cheap." *Elektra* he still enjoyed, while the *Rosenkavalier* was, in his own simple words, *"de la merde."*

In Paris about 1929 or 1930 I had just discovered Proust and was gorging on him, when I came across this passage on Strauss in *Le Côté de Guermantes:*

> people who have an instinctive taste for bad music . . . when, dazzled—and rightly so—by Richard Strauss' brilliant orchestral colorings, discover this musician adopting vulgar motifs worthy of Auber, they are delighted to find in so high an authority a justification for what they really like, and listening to *Salome,* they let themselves be enchanted without scruple and with twofold gratitude by what they were forbidden to admire in *Les Diamants de la Couronne.*

I was overjoyed to find this tidbit and could hardly wait to read it to Varèse, hoping to convince him that I was not an idiot for admiring a writer whom he (without the prejudice of having read him) dismissed with a pun: "I can't read him, he gives me a proustatite." Varèse responded to the quotation with surprised approval: *"Tiens, il n'est pas bête (he's not stupid)."* However, he still avoided the volumes of Proust I left lying about, his pun absolving him from the necessity of reading him.

It was probably in 1908 or 1909 that Varèse met Karl Muck, who had been appointed general music director of the Berlin Royal Opera in 1908. Of all the conductors whom Varèse had occasion to compare during his long life of concert-going, Muck for him was incomparable. "He never gesticulated," Varèse used to say, "a look was enough." Muck also wrote letters on Varèse's behalf. In the same month of April 1909, both he and Busoni wrote to the president of the Paul Kusynski Foundation recommending Varèse for a grant. This is Muck's recommendation:

> M. Edgard Varèse is a gifted musician and possesses a remarkable culture. I know a symphonic poem which shows a rich

and personal inventiveness, a vivid imagination and a complete mastery of his technical means. The information I have received from my Parisian friends is very favorable to M. Varèse: warmth, energy, tenacity of will, an upright and correct attitude in the face of the difficulties of daily life. It is approximately in such terms that the judgments from three different sources are expressed.

Eight days before Muck's letter, Busoni had written to the same foundation:

In the interest of my dear young friend Mr. Varèse, I take the liberty of calling your attention to the intelligence and the talent of this youthful artist. These, among other pronounced qualities, are deserving of consideration and support.

Varèse received the grant. He liked to tell how he happened to have in his possession the letter Busoni had sent to the president of the foundation:

When I went to the foundation to receive the grant, the president, after he had given me the money, handed me a letter and said: "Do whatever you please with the money, young man, but I advise you to keep this letter from the person who wrote it."

It was Busoni's letter of recommendation.

It was through Hofmannsthal that Varèse had met Mahler in May 1909, after his visit to Rodaun. Still in Vienna on the twenty-fifth, he wrote Hofmannsthal: "I met Mahler, who was very cordial and asked me to send you his regards." Varèse considered Mahler a great conductor and I remember his saying: "It is scandalous that after a Mahler the Philharmonic and the New York musical public should have put up for so long with a Stransky!" As a composer, Mahler was not at least one of Varèse's intimates.

The following November, Varèse wrote that in a few days he would send Hofmannsthal the text of *Oedipus* with the alterations he had made for the libretto. He also told him that through

Professor Klatte, to whom he had been recommended by Strauss, he had a pupil, a young Swede who would study with him until Christmas, when he was returning to Sweden. He said too that he was working on *Gargantua* but added: "I am not yet very strong and often my head doesn't work (*ma tête me manque*)."

The year 1910 was an eventful one for Varèse, a joyful and a tragic year: his daughter was born, his symphonic poem *Bourgogne* was performed, but his beloved grandfather died.

At the beginning of the year Varèse had two pupils, one, his Swede who paid, the other, Ernst Schoen, whom he taught gratis. Schoen was a friend of Busoni's son, Benvenuto. He wanted to study music and Busoni recommended Varèse as a teacher. When I met Schoen many years later in Berlin he told me: "I was Varèse's first and worst pupil. When I asked him his fee, he said it was ten marks or nothing. So it was nothing"—a fee of ten marks at that time being preposterous. Varèse knew that Frau Schoen, who was a widow, had very little money—though he himself had even less. Busoni also, Varèse told me, later advised two of his rich American piano students to study with him.

In any case that winter of 1910 Varèse was relieved of his desperate money worries thanks to Hofmannsthal, who on January 3 wrote:

> My dear Varèse,
>
> Beginning this month the publishing house of Fischer on the 15th of each month will send you 250 marks till the end of 1910. Mr. Fischer has nothing to do with it personally, I use him as my banker. Don't write me any more about this. I receive too many letters and I am working like a madman.

He adds that Mme Mendelssohn has nothing to do with this "economic arrangement" either. Varèse was unpredictable about accepting money—without a qualm from some sources and not from others. In this case evidently he had been pestering Hofmannsthal to know to whom he would be obligated and Hofmannsthal does not conceal his exasperation. Varèse had also his salary from the Symphonischer Chor. It may have been that year that Reinhardt engaged the chorus to take part in his production of *Faust*. In this winter of comparative affluence Varèse's deepest satisfaction came from his ability to send money regularly each month to Grandpère, who was then over seventy and was finally admitting, "I cannot work as I used to in the past." In one letter he says that it is not so much stooping that he finds difficult but "straightening up again." Each month now he thanks his grandson for a money order of twenty-five or thirty francs.

By the end of October 1910, however, Hofmannsthal had again begun to worry about his young protégé's situation and health. On the twenty-fifth he wrote to Mrs. Hedwig Fischer, the wife of his publisher:

> The time has come for me to remember our conversation when you were so kind as to offer your help for the musician Varèse. . . . Varèse has again reached the point where help is needed, in order to prevent a hopeless ruin of a delicate and certainly valuable organism. Since he is too proud to mention his distress in any of his occasional letters, I have asked a young musician, a friend of mine who lives in Berlin, to look him up. He found him looking very exhausted again. He is under medical care, is getting injections. He is struggling like a drowning person, running from one publisher, one agent to another. . . . In addition to all this he has to support his wife and his grandfather in France. He told my friend that he has only 300 marks left from Mrs. Mendelssohn's gift. This may last for three or four weeks, then what? . . . In a few months I shall again be able to do something for him and after that will find someone else, and finally hopefully he will obtain lessons and support himself.

And a month later:

> you know how concerned I am about this man. For the past year I have barely kept him afloat. . . . But now another year is coming, shall help suddenly stop? . . . In September these people had a child. Perhaps you didn't know this yet. . . . I had several letters from him never complaining but mentioning that he needs treatment for his nerves, etc. I am afraid the bad past years have exhausted his nervous strength.

Often it must have seemed to those who at that time extended a helping hand to Varèse that they were grasping quicksilver. Like his double, Jean-Christophe: "One day wiped out another and he was a very different person from what he had been a month before." Varèse had moments of unaccountable stubborn pride when he wanted to owe nothing to anybody; at other times he would accept help quite ingenuously. Of all the eminent sponsors and friends of this mercurial young man, Hofmannsthal, the most sensitive and the least egotistical, was also the most understanding and patient.

There was a repetition of the question of accepting Hofmannsthal's aid in 1911 and again in 1912, each time Varèse raising objections, each time Hofmannsthal, with tact, insisting:

> I have written Fischer to send you 100 marks during the year 1911 on the 15th of the month. I beg you not to refuse this. It is addressed not to you but to the child.

And again in 1912:

> I had instructed Fischer's to continue to send you the same monthly amount for the year 1912. I thought this little aid would be useful to Madame Varèse for the little girl's needs. You have written Fischer asking him to stop sending it. I understand that you felt that there were others whose needs were more urgent than yours. But I beg you to reconsider your decision, which I am not willing to regard as final.

Until *Oedipus* was finished, Varèse's pride rebelled against accepting any more help from Hofmannsthal, to whose generosity he already owed so much.

It was in September 1910, that Varèse's daughter, "the child" referred to in Hofmannsthal's letters, was born and, of course, was named Claude in honor of his beloved grandfather, Claude Cortot. Surprisingly Varèse adored his baby. I say surprisingly because Varèse had a horror of babies and children in general. He who loved all animals (except horses) considered all children pests. Perversely children were drawn to him just as animals were. Yet in his own baby girl he took great delight and pride during the three years she was with him in Berlin. I remember later in New York during our very first conversation he found an excuse for taking a photograph of Claude at three years old out of his wallet to show me.

It was with deep feeling that Debussy wrote to congratulate Varèse on the birth of his daughter, for, as Varèse told me, Debussy adored his own little girl, "Chouchou."

> First of all, let me wish you all happiness in the birth of your little daughter. You will see how much more beautiful this is than a symphony and that the caress of a child of one's own is better than glory.

Grandpère was, of course, overjoyed. "Embrace my little Claude for her grandfather until I can do it myself." This great joy he was never to know. Varèse and Suzanne had planned to take the baby to Le Villars in the spring, but Grandpère died in December. Expressing his sympathy, Hofmannsthal, always so sensitive to Varèse's moods, in a few simple words shows his comprehension of the precise effect of this loss on his young collaborator.

> My dear Varèse, I understand so well your sorrow, and know that at this moment nothing counts, neither success, nor even your work. I think of you very affectionately.

Happily, Varèse had no premonition of this, the greatest sorrow he would ever know, and could during the preceding months enjoy fully his baby and the anticipatory excitement of the coming concert when an orchestral score of his would be performed for the first time and he would hear the actual sounds which so far had withstood only the test of his inner ear.

It would seem a very cruel trick of fate that the ardently awaited performance of *Bourgogne* should have been scheduled just eight days after the death of Grandpère. Yet wasn't it, on the contrary, the most fortunate thing that could have happened to him at that moment? He was forced to attend rehearsals, and rehearsals and concert forced his attention away from his sorrow. Now the performance of *Bourgogne,* dedicated to "Mon Grand-père, Claude Cortot," inspired by his grandfather's Burgundy, became a memorial to Claude Cortot, *Bourguignon.*

Among Varèse's papers is a typewritten excerpt from a letter in German from Stransky without date or address which, translated, reads:

> Since your work has been warmly recommended by Dr. Richard Strauss, I herewith announce that, without having seen it, I am ready to conduct it on March 16 at the fifth Symphonic Music Evening. You may consider this decision definitive and make whatever use of it you choose for publicity and in the press.
>
> Yours faithfully and in haste,
> Josef Stransky

Why was the performance of *Bourgogne* in Berlin postponed from March to December? I don't know. I only know that Varèse said there were moments when he thought Stransky was going to refuse to play the work, that he raised objections, concocted excuses. Was it, perhaps, after he had seen the score? At any rate, he was finally brought to heel by Strauss and the work was rescheduled for December. At a rehearsal when Strauss was present, Stransky's attitude seemed so disparaging, his rehearsing so negligent that Strauss called out to him in front of the orchestra: "Careful, Stransky, you had better be nice to my friend Varèse or you will have me to reckon with."

Bourgogne was performed December 15 and was received with hostility by both public and critics. This reaction must have come as something of a shock and a disappointment to Varèse, for he had left France for Germany expecting rather too much of that "music-loving people," and, as Romain Rolland at that very moment was writing about his Jean-Christophe: "It had not occurred to him that even in Germany there are not many more real musicians and that people who matter in art are not the thousands who understand nothing about it but the few who love and serve it. . . ." *Bourgogne* was performed before the con-

ventional music-gorged Berlin audience, which was like audiences
of the great symphony orchestras the world over who listen to
music with their memories. Difficult as it may be, one should
(substituting in George Moore's recommendation *ears* for *eyes*)
listen to music with innocent ears. But few people could have
been less innocent than the ones in that Berlin audience listening
to Varèse's work. One critic, his ears stuffed with bias and
Brahms, called it "infernal noises, the music of cats." In the
twenties with a total lack of individuality, it was barnyards and
zoos that Varèse's music evoked for the New York critics. Of the
two notable exceptions I shall speak later.

In the Berlin of 1910, the exception was a literary, not a music,
critic. Alfred Kerr, critic of the great daily paper the *Berliner
Zeitung,* wrote to Varèse on January 3, 1911:

> Monsieur,
>   I have still to thank you for *Bourgogne.* I found it full of
> thrillingly beautiful things. Would you like to say something of
> your way of envisaging art; your habits and your loves in music?
> I can put at your disposal the review *Pan,* where I have a certain
> influence. I was told that one day you said to Saint-Saëns: "I
> have no desire to be an old fossil (*vieille perruque*), like you."
> So it is evident that you have a talent for expressing yourself
> valiantly in other mediums besides music. It is what (before
> Wagner) Berlioz and Schumann did. So send me your article. I
> will translate it and have it published.

Unlike most gossip, what Varèse said to Saint-Saëns had become toned down in the telling. With retrospective naughty-boy
relish, Varèse informed me that the word he used was not *vieille
perruque,* but the same word that had banished him from
Meudon and which used to slip out with economical ubiquity
when the *mot juste* came too slowly for his impatience. I think
I should pause here in case those who never knew Varèse should
get a wrong impression. Varèse was never vulgar. He could say
the most appalling things, use all the taboo words, tell "dirty"
stories, without shocking prigs, prudes, or puritans. He was too

impersonal to be offensive, too charming and too funny. Nobody who knew him will ever forget his Olive and Marius stories, the meridional accent, and the laughter. After meeting Varèse, Dallapiccola, struck by the Varèsian vocabulary, wrote in his diary:

> The display of unrepeatable—not to mention unprintable—adjectives on the part of Varèse, their variety, their richness, is a kind of Rabelaisian *divertimento*.

Rodin and Saint-Saëns were not shocked; they were incensed at the affront to their dignity and the lack of respect due to their greatness.

Hofmannsthal summarily dismissed the critics in a letter of January 5, 1911: "The critics were just what I expected. The only thing to do is to forget them (which isn't difficult)."

Varèse must have expressed comparable unconcern for critics and public (how he felt is another matter) in a letter to Debussy, who, in his reply (quoted in Varèse's monograph on Debussy), applauded Varèse's attitude, adding his own criticism of criticism and predicting a friendlier relationship in the future between Varèse and the public.

Later Debussy's prophecy came true. I have been present at many concerts when the public wildly demonstrated that they were "the best friends in the world." When the audience happened to be a mixture of those who listen with innocent ears and those who listen with their memories—then there was pandemonium.

In 1911 Varèse had resigned as music director of the Symphonisher Chor. When later he used to talk so enthusiastically about his chorus and the music he gave them to sing, he never mentioned his resignation and the reason for it. Was it his health—the nervous condition mentioned by Hofmannsthal in his letter to his publisher's wife? When one knows what Varèse kept silent about, one understands much that appears as contradictory in his character. It seems paradoxical that anyone as ordinarily frank and eagerly outspoken as Varèse should have guarded certain secrets so jealously. They were, like most people's, usually connected with his pride—his pride of life, his passion for life, intensified by his horror of the dark, the "negative" side, as he called it, of his nature; and his obsessive hatred of illness, old age, and of death, which all his life stalked his dreams.

Early in his life Varèse discovered and embraced Nietzsche— in fact, there was a time when he liked to think of the great poet-philosopher as his alter ego; ignoring his own protean and —in spite of his repudiation—Italian nature, he failed to see that the bond was intellectual and spiritual affinity, not consanguinity. Nietzschean he was in his moral judgments. I have spoken of his aversion to pity. He believed with Nietzsche that "pity stands opposed to the tonic emotions which heighten vitality"; so, as Varèse allowed himself none for his own weaknesses, sufferings, depressions—only repugnance—he had succeeded in blacking them out of his memory of Berlin where only tonic emotions survived.

After his resignation, Varèse received the following letter from the Board of the Symphonischer Chor:

Symphonischer Chor   March, 1911
Berlin

Mr. Edgard Varèse
Wilmeredorf
Nassauischestrasse No. 61

Under separate cover we are sending you your fee for February in the sum of 75 marks, and may we ask you to be so good as to acknowledge receipt of this sum on enclosed statement.

We take this opportunity to express our warm appreciation for your activity with our chorus. We have had the opportunity during your eighteen months with us of learning unfamiliar works which have been of great interest to most of us. We keenly regret that it is no longer possible for you to remain at the head of our chorus, but rest assured that you will be remembered with high esteem.

> Respectfully yours,
> The Board of the
> Symphonischer Chor.
> I.A.
>
> Carl Gutner

Hofmannsthal's kindness to Varèse and his family and his understanding sympathy seem to have been inexhaustible. He had, of course, met Suzanne and "the child," had visited them in their apartment on Nassauischestrasse. With those sensitive antennae of his he would not have failed to perceive Suzanne's discontent. So he thought of a plan that might perhaps reconcile her to Germany by procuring for her a charming friend. Here is Hofmannsthal's proposal in a letter of May 28, 1911.

> Mon cher Varèse,
>
> In April when I stopped at Neubeuern, we eagerly discussed the project of having Madame Varèse and the little girl spend at least a few weeks there. My mind is really set on this because something tells me that ties of reciprocal sympathy will be formed between the Countess de Degenfeld, a young widow, alone in the world with a little daughter, and Madame Varèse. The Countess D. is the sister-in-law of Madame de Wedelstadt. But naturally we had in mind July and August. . . . And now you talk of two trips. . . . After all Munich is on the road to Paris (it goes without saying that I would ask your permission to offer this trip to Madame Varèse). . . . What dates would you like me to propose to Madame de Wedelstadt?

In a sceond letter dated June 5, Hofmannsthal writes:

> It is no longer possible to arrange for the months of June and July. . . . But I am authorized by Madame de Degenfeld to invite Madame Varèse to visit her at Hinterbor, a charming lodge a half hour from Neubeuern and perhaps even more agree-

able than the castle and to spend the last days of August and the
first days of September.

And finally on June 13:

> Here is the address: Gräfin Ottonie de Degenfeld, Schloss Neu-
> beuern am Inn. Oberbayern. Bon voyage!

I remember Varèse, when telling me about Hofmannsthal's
great kindness, mentioning this invitation but not whether
Suzanne with Claude actually visited Mme de Degenfeld. By this
time Suzanne was perhaps not in the mood to meet any more
Germans, no matter how delightful; perhaps she was already
considering a move which took place only a little over a year
later: a return to Paris and the beginning of her stage career.

I should, perhaps, before going on with Varèse's career, correct
an impression these notes may have given, that his whole life
in Berlin, through his illustrious older friends, was given up
entirely to furthering it. His youth and, above all, his nature had
other needs. He had young companions his own age with whom
he would forget ambition, poverty, and ill health, become
"homo ludens" (a psychosomatic necessity) and his Gemini self.
One of his most intimate friends was a young Hungarian painter,
József Bato (Jóska to his friends), a companion such as Gonzales,
Bernouard, Chereau were in France. Like all young artists everywhere, they spent a great deal of time in long discussions on art
and all imaginable subjects and long nights in drinking and
laughter—that laughter Varèse used to recall when he said: *"On
ne rit plus,"* and which Auden has defined as "the spirit of Carni-
val, where we laugh *with* and *at."* In 1922 in Berlin listening to
Bato and Varèse reminiscing with relish about their life at that
time, *"noctambular but auroral,"* I caught glimpses of gay, and
some very startling escapades. In 1911 a friend of Bato's—a
musician, Egon Kenton (he was later viola player in the first
Hungarian string quartet)—came to Berlin from Budapest. In

Varèse: A Looking-Glass Diary

New York, not long ago, he talked to me about the Varèse he had known then. I was amused when he told me that Varèse insisted on always going to a little Italian restaurant in Berlin, Bertoli's, to eat spaghetti and drink Chianti, for it had become a joke among our friends that Varèse could never feel at home anywhere until he had found a *"bon petit restaurant italien."* When we were in Brussels for the opening of the Corbusier Pavilion and *Poème Electronique,* even in that city celebrated for fine cuisine, Varèse was not content until he had discovered Italian Gino's, where we dined whenever we were free and drank Valpolicella, and where our friends Diane and Touma Bouchard, and Frederick Kiesler, arriving for the exposition, had to eat, too. The first time Varèse took me out to dinner in New York after I met him toward the end of 1917, it was to a *"bon petit restaurant italien,"* of which there were several very good ones then—family affairs with real Italian home cooking, where the father was chef and the mother and children waited on table and where the abundant course dinner including California red wine, condescendingly called "red ink," cost one dollar!

From Egon Kenton I learned something else, more interesting to musicologists, if not to me. When Varèse told Ouellette, as he told me, that he had heard the first performance of Schoenberg's *Pierrot Lunaire* in Berlin in October 1912, we both jumped to the conclusion that Varèse had attended the première. Now I learn from Kenton that what he was undoubtedly referring to was a private performance given before the première at Busoni's, for a few friends, with the same *Sprechsinger,* actress Albertine Zehme, the same instrumentalists, and with Busoni's pupil Edward Steuermann, at the piano.

This is Kenton's account of the occasion:

> Varèse had been invited to Busoni's to hear a private perform-
> ance of Schoenberg's new work, *Pierrot Lunaire,* and he took
> me along. When we arrived the salon was crowded. Varèse made
> his way to the end of the room where Schoenberg was standing
> near the players. He introduced me and we stood there, Varèse,
> Schoenberg, and the violinist Arrigo Serato, during the perform-
> ance. Afterward, when the applause had subsided, Schoenberg,

timid and a little awkward, started toward the players, but Busoni, handsome and imposing, was already there, congratulating them. Then Schoenberg, screwing up his clever monkey face in a wry smile, turned to Varèse and said: "And now he's distributing the decorations."

Varèse's sorrow over the loss of Grandpère had aggravated his nervous condition. For over a year he was treated by Dr. Flies for what used to be called a "nervous breakdown." Nobody has them any more. Now we suffer from something Freudian or post-Freudian. The Bible called it being "possessed by the devil," which I like better, for being poetic it is more meaningful. Jesus used to exorcise these devils and that is what psychiatrists today believe they can do. Unfortunately, an artist's devil has a Siamese twin, his angel, and you can't get rid of one without the other. In any case Varèse was never cured, but his devil would often get tired of torturing him and let him alone for long, medium, or short periods of creativeness, liveliness, extreme optimism, and often, ecstasy. When he seemed to show some improvement, Dr. Flies recommended a change of environment. So Varèse returned to France for three months. He was in Paris on June 17, 1912, for on that date Debussy sent him this *petit bleu:* "Here are two seats for tonight with my affectionate cordiality." Perhaps Debussy, a remarkable pianist, was playing his own works that night, or were the tickets for a performance of *Pelléas et Mélisande?* I know that Varèse saw Debussy's opera in Paris before World War I with Mary Garden as Mélisande, for he used to say, "Mary Garden was good then, for she was under the tutelage of Messager. Later she was just an ordinary prima donna without imagination." For Varèse the *only* Mélisande was Irène Joachim. She too was fortunate in having for conductor and coach the exceptionally sensitive musician Roger Desormière. There was mystery in her Mélisande and in her lovely voice, and great delicacy. Of course, Irène Joachim was very intelligent in her own right. When Varèse took me to hear my first performance of the work by the Chicago Opera Company in New York, he could not sit through it and stalked out angrily, disgusted particularly with Mary Garden. I, too ignorant, of course, to be critical, continued to sit spellbound by the music. When I joined Varèse afterward in the lobby, he said: "I envy you your ignorance." Today after many decades of listening to music with Varèse, I understand what he meant, for I too have become critical and rather than listen to and watch prima donnas victimizing Debussy and his Mélisande, I prefer to put on the record Varèse bought for me, conducted by Desormière with Irène Joachim giving me the illusion of listening to Mélisande herself, *ce petit être mystérieux.*

After Varèse returned to Berlin in the autumn of 1912, he wrote to Hofmannsthal:

> thanks to the affectionate care of Dr. Flies and even more to my three long months in France, everything is fine. My health being excellent, now I can get to work in earnest—something I have not been able to do for over two years. I am now finishing a symphonic poem that promises well, and then I return with love to our *Oedipus.* I am more and more keen about it. I know it almost by heart and now with my present understanding of German I can appreciate all its subtlety.

Varèse usually gave titles to his works after they were finished. One wonders what title he gave this *poème symphonique*—which of his early works it was. They have all been destroyed or lost and only this list of titles which Varèse gave me remains, all for orchestra: *Souvenirs, Chansons avec Orchestre, Prélude à la Fin d'un Jour, Trois Pièces pour Orchestre, Rapsodie Romane, La Chanson des Jeunes Hommes, Bourgogne, Gargantua* (unfinished), *Mehr Licht, Les Cycles du Nord, Oedipus und die Sphinx.* My own idea is that this *poème symphonique,* mentioned by Varèse in his letter to Hofmannsthal, must be either *Mehr Licht* or *Les Cycles du Nord.* This is not wholly a gratuitous speculation but is based on Varèse's description of the source— the "impetus," as he would say, of one of his works. He told me that once watching a display of the aurora borealis he felt an "unbelievable exaltation—an indescribable sensation" and that

as he watched those "pulsating incandescent streamers of light"
he "not only saw but *heard* them." As soon as he returned home
he wrote down the sounds that had accompanied the movements
of the light. The title that suggests either light or the north must
be that of the score in which Varèse incorporated the sounds of
the aurora borealis.

In a letter written on February 25, 1913, two months after first
mentioning his new work, he asked Hofmannsthal's permission
to dedicate it to him.

This is perhaps as good a time as any to explain what happened to those early scores.

Suzanne and Varèse, having amicably agreed to separate, early
in 1913 Suzanne left Berlin for good and went to Paris where,
soon after, she joined Jacques Copeau's new theatrical organization, the Vieux Colombier. After Suzanne left, Varèse kept his
little girl with him for a month or more, entrusting her finally
to the care of an old friend of his student days, a poet, Anne
Osmont, who was returning to Paris.* Among Varèse's books is
a copy of Villier de Lisle Adam's *Axel* with a dedication to Anne
Osmont by the poet's wife. When Anne Osmont gave the book to
Varèse, she added another dedication: *"A Edgard Varèse, seul
musicien digne d'*Axel, *ce livre en souvenir des mauvais jours
en commun."* It is dated October 15, 1907. (I wonder if anyone
still reads that fantastically romantic work of the symbolist
school, once so modern and so famous.) In that summer of 1913
Varèse gave up his apartment at Albrechtstrasse 2, Halensee,
and as he was going to Paris and then to Prague to conduct that
long-postponed concert and would not return to Berlin until
the autumn, he put whatever household belongings he had in a

* Suzanne's mother, Madame Kauffmann, then took complete charge of her
little granddaughter. Soon after, she moved to the Midi, first to Nice, finally
settling in Monte Carlo in Monaco. The arrangement was made with Varèse's
entire approval, for he and his mother-in-law were great friends. Varèse told
me: "She liked me better than her own daughter and always sided with me
in any dispute." He called her, but affectionately, *"la sorcière."* She had the
reputation for eccentricity and was certainly a personality. She adored Claude
and brought her up in the cult of her father.

storage house, as well as most of his scores. As things turned out, he did not return to Berlin until 1922 when he learned that during the Spartacist revolution the storage house had been destroyed by fire. He had kept out two scores and part of the last act of *Oedipus,* which he was revising. A day or two before war was declared he sent one of the scores—I think Varèse said it was *Les Cycles du Nord*—to Béla Bartók, who never received it, and before leaving for America he sent the fragment of *Oedipus* to a Berlin friend, Dr. Merton, then in Switzerland. As for *Bourgogne,* Varèse brought it with him to New York and later himself destroyed it. Such a renunciation of a work that had meant so much to him would seem inconceivable. Varèse explained that with *Amériques,* his first score written in New York, he had begun working in a new idiom toward which his earlier scores had only been groping. It will be recalled that, to the imputation that he was simply an experimenter and his works experiments, Varèse once replied: "I have always been an experimenter but my experiments go into the wastebasket." Nevertheless, as this infanticide occurred on a sleepless night during one of his prolonged depressions, I cannot help wondering if, at more objective moments, he did not have regrets—like the rest of us.

Unlike too many musicians, Varèse's interests were as catholic and eclectic as those of his friend across the ages, Leonardo. Consequently, as I have said, he felt at home in many different milieus and belonged to none. One of the circles he frequented in Paris was that of the Russian exiles, where, either in 1909 or 1910, he met Lenin. Later he also met Trotsky. Varèse, a rebel and an idealist, was not only in sympathy with their revolutionary ideals, but was attracted to them for the simple reason that they were Russian. For, Red or White, Varèse loved Russians and Russians loved him. Temperamentally he understood them and felt closer to them than to the people of any other country, including most of his cerebral countrymen, or the Germans, for whom, nevertheless, he professed so great a liking. About Americans, Varèse used to say, "I like Americans; they are natural like the Russians; they don't have the 'slavic charm' and are not mad, but more reliable." Of course he said other things at other times about them—not always flattering!

I think it was when the Russian Ballet was in Berlin that Varèse met Karsavina, or he may have known her before in Paris. She was not only Russian, but also beautiful. By a rose I judge that the attraction was mutual. Varèse's friend Bato told me this story in which he acted as messenger. Karsavina had invited Varèse to a performance of the Russian Ballet in which she danced *Le Spectre de la Rose* with Nijinsky, but as Varèse was ill that evening and could not go, he sent his friend to make excuses. Karsavina, with her arms full of roses, was surrounded by admirers, but as soon as she heard Varèse's name she turned her back on them and gave her entire attention to Varèse's messenger. She seemed, Bato said, very disappointed. Then she tore off a rose from the bunch she was carrying and handed it to him. "Give this to Varèse from me; tell him that I am sad that he is ill and tell him that he has been missed." That is what Bato told me. And Varèse: One day he was getting some papers out of a drawer when I heard him exclaim: *"Tiens!"* and he handed me a folded piece of paper about two inches square. In red ink he had written on it: "Karsavina, Berlin." Inside was a faded rose.

One of the most interesting among those who used to meet at the *Belle Edition* and go together to the little restaurant on the boulevard Saint-Germain was Guillaume Apollinaire. André Billy, one of the same group, and for many years a regular writer on the *Figaro Littéraire,* has written about sixty years later that he seems to recall (though he may, he says, be mistaken—as he was) that it was he who introduced Varèse to Apollinaire, and *"toute la bande"* at Mme Louise Faure-Favier's. The house of that "charming" young woman on the île Saint-Louis was another of their meeting places, as a note to the Deubel-Varèse *Anecdotique* also indicates: "Varèse and Apollinaire used often to meet at Louise Faure-Favier's, quai de Bourbon, in the charming Maison du Centaure, where she received her friends." I only wish that the note had also said something about "the House of the Centaur," for with a name like that, it must have a history, and Varèse, who was more apt to talk about people than the houses they lived in, never mentioned it.

Varèse called Apollinaire *"un animateur de génie."* Unfortunately our English word *animator,* appropriated by the cinema as a technical word, cannot be used, I am afraid, in the French sense to mean a man who stimulates, energizes, quickens all those around him, which was Apollinaire's role in the arts. He was the high priest of modernism, coined the word *surrealist* before the *ism* existed, discovered the Douanier Rousseau, was the first spokesman for the cubists and wrote a book explaining them. He had a rare gift for enthusiasm, exuberant vitality, and a fund of odds and ends of out-of-the-way knowledge. His *Anecdotiques* and other works are full of tidbits of fact and fancy, but the prose seems to me less pungent than I expected from Varèse's account of the man, lacking I suppose, the spice of his personality. I speak of the prose works only, not his lovely Villonesque-Verlainian-Apollinarian verse. Some of his chattings are startling, as when in *Le Flâneur des Deux Rives,* he quotes someone describing the New York Public Library ("Bibliothèque Carnegie") as "an immense building made of white marble which . . . is washed every day with brown soap." He invented designed verse, printed some of his poems in the form of the objects described (a fountain, a palm tree, rain, etc.), others were simply placed irregularly on the page, a device that became popular with poets for a time. The last one to favor it was, I think, e e cummings in his own syntactic way. Even Varèse wrote such a typographically set poem (*"en rigolant,"* he said) for the surrealist, Dadaist magazine *391,* founded and edited by Francis Picabia, the cubist painter who for a time in 1917 was Varèse's Gemini companion in New York.

Varèse and Apollinaire also often met at the Delaunays', Robert and Sonia, both painters as well as, in lighter vein, sartorial revolutionists, or, as Apollinaire calls them, "dress reformers." From the description of the clothes they invented, I think the hippies would have approved. But art in revolt was their passionate preoccupation as it was that of Apollinaire and Varèse too. There were enough *isms* in those days to keep café conversations very lively: waning impressionism, rising cubism, over-lapping fauvism, vociferous futurism, simultaneism, and others that died instantaneously. There was also Orphism, the origin of which became a matter of hot dispute, as a note in *Anecdotique* comments: "He, Apollinaire, made himself the exegete of *Cubisme orphique,* which he defined the year before in *Méditations Esthétiques;* and in his conversations with Delaunay he formulated the doctrine of simultaneism. It was not long before he came in conflict with H. H. Barzun, who claimed the paternity of the word *Orphism.*" Varèse, being a friend of both claimants, did not take sides. Besides, Orphism did not concern him. *Simultaneism* did. While poets were juggling words on a page and painters were producing curious juxtapositions of noses, ears, eyes, and breasts in the name of simultaneism, Varèse was beginning to wonder how it might be obtained musically. He believed that, given the means, simultaneism was literally possible in music. It was one of the objectives of his lifelong quest for what he called "the liberation of sound." René Bertrand, whom Varèse met in 1913, was already working on a new instrument that developed into the electronic dynaphone, conceived on the same principles as the Theramin and the Martinot. Years later Varèse was to say in a lecture:

One of the greatest assets that electronics has added to musical composition is that of metrical simultaneity. My music being based on movements of unrelated sound masses, I have long felt the need and anticipated the effect of having them move simultaneously at different speeds.

As for futurism, because in the early days Varèse had known their founder and "pope," Marinetti, and Russolo, the inventor of the *bruiteurs* (noisemakers that made so little noise), he used to be referred to as "the futurist composer," a label he resented and rejected. Since he had been thinking along the same lines as the futurists ever since he left the Conservatoire, indeed such ideas, encouraged undoubtedly by Debussy, had probably been responsible for his departure from that venerable institution, as well as, perhaps, his association with the painters in revolt at that time, he was in enthusiastic accord with many of the tenets proclaimed by Marinetti in his *Le Futurisme,* such as:

> Imitation has killed art. It is for us to resuscitate it. We can only succeed by getting rid of all worn-out formulas, by turning our eyes away from the already-seen, the already-done in order to observe the spectacle of modern life.

However, later on Varèse accused Marinetti's followers of committing the very offense their spokesman deplored, and in 1917 he protested in the Number 5 issue of Picabia's *391:*

> Why is it, Italian Futurists, that you slavishly imitate only what is superficial and most boring in the trepidation of our daily lives!

He shared Marinetti's enthusiasm for the mechanical modern world but not his desire to reproduce it. "The futurists," he used to say, "imitate, an artist transmutes."

I have been rereading lately Varèse's old copy of Marinetti's *Le Futurisme*—a frustrating feat, with most of the pages unsewn, with edges eaten away beyond the print and a downpour of "dandruff," as Varèse called the paper disease of French books. Before being completely buried under the paper sandstorm, I did glean passages that are of the essence of Varèse's own insurrection against musical academism such as these: "They want to imprison us in the cult of one ideal only, that of repetition." And: "The appellation *madman* with which they try to gag the innovator should be considered an honorific title." There is one chapter headed: "The Voluptuousness of Being Hissed"—a voluptuousness Varèse was to enjoy all his life until the very last years, when he knew a compensatory satisfaction in the plaudits, unspiced by boos and hisses, of the enthusiastic audiences that attended the special concerts of his music given to honor him. Though he has lost the honorific title of madman, that of innovator can hardly be taken from him.

Varèse certainly endorsed the Futurists: "Let us kill moon-light," and not only philosophically as standing for "romantic sentimentalism," but also astrologically, for he detested moon-light and always insisted on tightly closed blinds when the moon was full. In the Musicians Manifesto, their "must" especially came close to one of his own fundamental preoccupations: "We must free ourselves from the obsessions of dance rhythm, con-sidering it only one detail of free rhythm," for Varèse himself endlessly insisted: "Rhythm is too often confused with metrics. . . . Rhythm is the element of stability in a work—the generator of form."

Varèse did not agree with Marinetti that "an automobile is more beautiful than the *Victoire de Samothrace,*" standing, I suppose, for the consecrated sculpture of the past. Indeed, Varèse thought automobiles hideous though at times convenient. He did, however, subscribe to Marinetti's hyperbolic dictum that "nothing is more beautiful than the scaffolding of a building under construction," at least in one instance: the scaffolding around the unfinished Lincoln Center Opera House. Looking out from the upper glass promenades of Symphony Hall at the magnificent construction, Varèse and I with one accord ex-claimed, "Peranesi!" Certainly that particular scaffolding of that particular building under construction was more beautiful than the finished opera house.

However, in Varèse's manifestoes for the International Com-posers' Guild, which he founded in 1921, there does seem to be an echo of that very articulate period of revolt in the arts when hortatory manifestoes were popular—a world that was swept away in 1914 by the First World War.

Now let me try to recall other artists of that period whom Varèse knew—painters, writers, composers, and so on, who gave the pitch to a whole epoch in the arts:

Erik Satie, who has been called a composer *"en marge de son époque"* (Would that have the same sense as the *marginale* of Boulez on Varèse, although they were so differently *"en marge"*?), who, when he lived in Arcueil and was very poor, used to go on foot to Paris and back, carried a hammer in his pocket against apaches, and, as he told Varèse, when he saw anyone approaching would play drunk and tumble into the ditch—whose visits to friends, so legend had it, would last until the cognac bottle was empty—who wrote, among other better known works, the *Messe des Pauvres,* which Varèse found very moving, and the *Gymnopédies,* two of which Debussy orchestrated and conducted and which Varèse was the first to conduct in this country—who finally became the godfather and mascot of *les Six.*

Fernand Léger, one of the cubist painters, who was gassed early in the war and whom Varèse, through influential friends, got transferred out of the trenches, who quarreled with Varèse, accusing him of sleeping with his wife (his first wife), which Varèse denied but said: "Anyway, why only pick on me?"—who later in New York buried the hatchet, became friends with Varèse again, and gave him a painting.

André Derain, one of the *Fauves,* who illustrated Apollinaire's first published work, *L'Enchanteur,* in 1909—whose apposite dicta "Painting is made of light," Varèse used to quote as a pendant to his own, "Music is made of sound."

André Salmon, the poet who in a copy of his *Les Féeries,* which he had given Varèse in 1907, wrote: *"A mon ami Edgard Varèse, le grand cœur."*

Emile Verhaeren, the Belgian poet, classified a *symboliste,* but who, before much younger poets, expressed an affection for the cacophony of modern industrial cities in his *Villes Tentaculaires* and who Varèse said was *"si gentil."*

Firmin Gémier, actor and producer, at that time director of the Théâtre Antoine, later of the Odéon, who believed in sumptuous productions and despised the beggarly simplicity of the little new Vieux Colombier while envying its (to him) unaccountable popularity, who wrote to Varèse in 1920: "Copeau continues to bore people and by means of his productions spreads the notion that Shakespeare is a tedious writer"—to whom the *Times* drama critic Alexander Woollcott, of Algonquin fame, brought a letter of introduction from Varèse, then in New York.

Raoul Dufy, painter of the life of sunny sails on the Mediter-

ranean, whom much later I saw with Varèse in New York in a
wheelchair on his way to Boston to be treated for his crippling
arthritis with cortisone, the new "wonder drug," and who on
his return, about to sail for France, joyfully held out his hands
to Varèse. "Look," he said, "now I can shake your hand—mine
are alive again (*de nouveau vivantes*)."

Max Jacob, melodious, satiric word-juggler, who Varèse said
was *"malicieux comme un singe* (mischievous as a monkey)" and
loved to tease his friends—who became a Catholic convert and
then was martyrized as a Jew by the Nazis.

Paul Fort, elected *Prince des Poètes* in 1909; André Lhote,
painter and writer on painters, who went with Varèse to Bordeaux when Varèse left for America.

The famous actor de Max, who used to give grandiose parties
for *tout Paris* and whom Varèse used to parody reciting with
Comédie Française grandiloquence: "Voici des fruits: des fleurs
et des branches. Puis voici mon cœur qui ne bat que pour
vous. . . ."

Charles Cros, interesting because of his father who was the
poet-inventor Charles Cros, a friend of Rimbaud, and who wrote
verses as lovely and light as his monologues are ponderous, and
happily forgotten.

Francis Carco, who was associated for a time with Bernouard
at the *Belle Edition,* from whose book, *Nostalgie de Paris,* published in 1942, Varèse used to read me passages saying, "Listen,
you remember my telling you . . ." and others that brought to
his mind stories he had not told me before, such as that of the
melomanic *fort des Halles* who discovered a young composer
holding a peasant's horse:

"*Les Halles* teeming with strawberries and cabbages, with
porters (*fort des Halles*) and stout women in shawls, pleated
skirts, and sabots, with great quarters of beef, with poor penniless
devils, and *whinnying horses,*" the last two words Varèse had
underlined. In fact, Varèse has marked most of the passages he
read me which had reminded him of his exuberant youth in Paris
such as:

"Tuesdays at the Closerie des Lilas Paul Fort welcomed the

aesthetes from the two banks. . . . Moréas had just died but the 'Prince of Poets' upheld the tradition. We imbibed to saturation alcohol, theories, paradoxes, and tall stories. Boxers used to mix with artists. What wild elation! What an uproar around the tables, discussions ending in fist fights. . . ." Varèse also marked Carco's reference to Verlaine's *"gîte de la rue Descartes,"* for that was the street where Varèse had lived in 1907 in the room with the burlap wall. And two street cries of the peddlers of birds and old clothes which reminded him of the Paris of his boyhood when Grandpère had a bistro on the rue de Lancry. Then Varèse would chant them for me in the singsong of the street criers: *"Mouron pour les petits oiseaux"* and *"Habits et chiffons."*

I can also still hear Varèse's voice, with its warm, low timbre and with that power of evocation that was his, telling me about those days when music, poetry, and painting were all woven into a pattern of gaiety, and poverty was the muted accompaniment of intense living. I think it was Blaise Cendrars (Varèse knew him too) who wrote: "Poetry is in the streets and goes arm-in-arm with laughter."

And there was Léon-Paul Fargue, noctambulous poet and "pedestrian of the streets of Paris," who gave Varèse one of his books entitled *Poèmes*—which is in prose—inscribed *"A Edgard Varèse, mon ami, Léon-Paul Fargue, le 27 mai 1915."* He comes into an anecdote told me in 1927 by Juliette Gleizes in Paris. Varèse had known Juliette before she married Gleizes, when she was Juliette Roche and lived on boulevard Lannes, in the same apartment where she was once more living in 1967. "It was my bachelor-girl apartment," she said. "Varèse used to come here often with Léon-Paul Fargue. Sometimes they would spend the night."

Then in her high-pitched piccolo voice, peculiar to so many French women, and with the economy of all good storytellers, ending with an appreciative liquid chuckle that belied her eighty years, she told me the milk anecdote. First, I should explain that Varèse loved milk. When late at night, in cafés in Paris, or café-espresso-confectioners in our Italian neighborhood in New York, the rest of us would be drinking wine, whiskey, beer, coffee, or sodas, Varèse's nightcap, which he sipped with gourmet relish, would be a glass of hot milk. This is Juliette's story, in her own words as I remember them:

> One Sunday morning, having been informed rather pointedly by me that there was no milk for breakfast, since he had finished it before going to bed, Varèse disappeared. When the bell rang and I opened the door, there stood Varèse with his arms full of milk bottles. I was rather aghast when, putting down one bottle after the other, he explained, "I got this one at the door of the people on the first floor, you don't know them so it doesn't matter; I got this one on the next floor, you don't know them, so it doesn't matter," and so on until, putting down the last bottle, he said, "This one was on the floor below. You know those people, so it doesn't matter."

Varèse left Berlin sometime in December 1913 for Prague, where finally on January 4 he conducted that long-postponed concert with the Prague Philharmonic Orchestra. He chose for his program contemporary French works, all of them new to Prague and all considered very modern at that time: *Le Chant de la Destinée* by Gabriel Dupont; *Ariane et Barbe-bleu* by Paul Dukas; *Évocations: Les Dieux dans L'Ombre des Cavernes* by his old teacher Albert Roussel; and Debussy's *Le Martyre de Saint Sébastien,* performed for the first time in concert form.

To judge by the critics and a joyous letter Varèse wrote to his mother-in-law, the concert was a great success. The critic of the Prague *Tageblatt* wrote:

> The program alone should captivate all those who are interested in the originality and skill of modern French music. It was entirely composed of works that have never been heard here before and which, with the exception of Paris, have not yet been performed in Europe. But a joy as great as the program itself was making the acquaintance of Edgard Varèse. His splendid enthusiasm for the works of these masters was able to surmount all difficulties. After only three rehearsals with a strange orchestra he managed to disclose for us the soul of the works confided to him. The great love of art that exists in this tall, slender young

man, the noble fire, and the precise, clear manner of his conducting (which shows that Varèse knows what he wants) held the
orchestra under the spell of his charm and at once captured his
audience. The Varèse concert was a musical event, and it is to
be hoped that we shall soon again be able to hear this apostle
of the new school, both as conductor and composer.

Varèse wrote to Mme Kauffmann the same night:

Hôtel du Cheval Noir
Prague

Maman chérie,
Two words in haste—immense triumph—ovations—by the audience—and the orchestra twice stood up to applaud me—Every
important musician in Prague was there—The celebrated Bohemian string quartet came to congratulate me—as well as all
the other musicians—calling me *"maître"*—They are men in
their fifties—and with world-wide reputations. I am very proud
and you can be too—I am dead tired, having worked like a dog
—but it was a great joy to me to be so well seconded by this
splendid orchestra, who adore me. Kisses for my Claude, who
will bear a great name. . . .

                                                    Varèse

After the Roussel an immense wreath of laurel and palms—two
meters tall—was presented to me on stage. The audience went
wild.

Varèse must have written, either from Berlin or from Prague,
to ask Debussy to recommend him for the position of conductor of the Bordeaux Opera, since Varèse could hardly have been
in Paris on January 6, when Debussy wrote the following letter
to the mayor of Bordeaux:

Monsieur,
Allow me to recommend very particularly a young musician, Edgard Varèse, who is applying for the position of musical director
of the Bordeaux Opera. There is no doubt that he possesses the
necessary qualities to fill that function, and I should be person-

ally grateful if you would use your influence to assure him the possibility of making his career in France.

One hears in that last sentence an echo of Debussy's commiseration for anyone who would be so unfortunate as to be obliged to pursue his career outside of France.

Nothing came of Debussy's good offices and nothing turned up for Varèse that winter in Paris. For the following season, Gabriel Astruc, who was the manager of the Russian Ballet in Paris, had promised to arrange engagements for Varèse as guest conductor of the principal orchestras of Eastern Europe and a return engagement to Prague. But war broke out in August and war is no respecter of careers. It also prevented Varèse from going to Hungary, as he had planned, with a member of the Hungarian string quartet to spend a month at some lake resort and meet Béla Bartók, who was to join them there. Varèse stayed in Paris waiting to be drafted. On December 15, 1914, he wrote to Mme Kauffmann, who was then living in Nice with Claude:

> Life here gets more and more sinister. Since I may be drafted any day at the good pleasure of the military authorities, I can't attempt anything, undertake anything serious—I've been running around like mad without result—for nobody wants to take the risk with someone who may suddenly have to drop everything. It's ridiculous and agonizing—and this uncertainty about the future is nerve-racking. My only consolation—pretty meager, alas, is knowing that you and my beautiful darling Claude are more or less secure. I have several projects in mind but impossible to realize until after the war—When? . . . I am alone here, everybody has left and I await my convocation almost as a deliverance—for this forced sterile inaction is unendurable—all question of chauvinism apart.

Since he spoke German, in September he had applied as interpreter. In spite of official recommendations, there being a prodigality of German interpreters, his request was refused. Drafted at last in March, he was assigned to the Ecole de Guerre and became, as he said, "a heroic bicyclist," carrying messages back and forth from the rear to the front—he never got as far as the trenches. His military career was brief and he hated every minute of it, principally because he was bored—so bored, in fact, that he applied for active duty. However, after a physical examination, he was sent not to the front but to the hospital with double pneumonia.

In spite of Varèse's lack of enthusiasm for soldiering, thanks to *System D,** he received a citation. One day as he was lolling in the courtyard of the Ecole de Guerre, a truckful of codfish arrived and an officer came up to Varèse and ordered him to unload it. Varèse's eyes happening to light on a scale near the truck, quick as a flash he saw how he could avoid doing so nasty and smelly a job. He saluted with great show of alacrity and asked if he might get a detail of men to help him. His request being granted, he assembled his men, seated himself by the scale, and told them that after filling their baskets with fish they should come to the scale and weigh them, while he jotted down the figures. When the officer came by to see how the work was progressing he was impressed by such enterprise. The next day at roll call Varèse was cited for *preuve d'initiative*. He was very proud, not of the citation, but of his wily stratagem.

It was not long before Varèse was invalided out of the service. On June 18, after telling Mme Kauffmann that he has had a return of his "old lung trouble" he writes:

> My friends the Roches are very kind, as well as Cocteau and the Irishes, and have had me consult the best specialist in Paris, Professor Letulle. . . . So it has been decided that I leave for a month's treatment in the best Swiss sanatorium (Dr. Rollier). It is Gemier who is taking charge of that. I have only accepted on condition that my friends, even in a modest way (the case of my 50 francs a month), provide for a part of your and Claude's needs. . . . My relapse and attack of fever are the result of the privations of the winter . . . but everything is going to be all right. Astruc, a wonderful comrade, will take charge of my affairs. But he said again last Monday, "I shall get work for you only after your cure and with the permission of Dr. Letulle." For

* The equivalent of inspired goldbricking.

the moment I would not be able to conduct because I can't breathe.

("I can't breathe." How often in later years I was to hear that dreaded refrain!)

The father of Juliette Roche, whom Varèse refers to in his letter, was a senator and a man of some eminence who had more than once used his influence on behalf of Varèse. Who the Irishes were I don't know.

Varèse did not go to the sanatorium in Switzerland after all. Instead, he spent two weeks recuperating in the country. On July 7 he writes from Brignantcourt-sur-Marines: "Here I am since about a week at the Reskys'. A delicious welcome, pampered and spoiled. I follow scrupulously the prescribed regimen of recalcification and make myself keep fixed hours of chaise longue in the fresh air out of the wind. I dawdle a bit at my work and as soon as my strength returns I'll get down to it in earnest."

When he returned to Paris he wrote Mme Kauffmann that he had rented an apartment—*une garçonnière étonnante.* Although a bed and a piano were its only furniture, his new place, "full of sun," seemed heaven after barracks life. *"L'essentiel,"* he wrote, "is that I have my four walls where I can shut myself up with my work and create in calm and joy, without degrading promiscuity."

After his return from Prague, besides his fruitless preoccupation with trying to find a job and revising scenes from his *Oedipus,* Varèse was involved in a fascinating project with several of his friends. It will be remembered that the chorus Varèse directed from 1908 to 1911 had taken part in Max Reinhardt's production of *A Midsummer Night's Dream* in Berlin. Now news came that Reinhardt was planning to revive it, and this was evidently discussed by Varèse and his friends with Varèse describing and condemning it (as I judge by his comment on Reinhardt as we came away after seeing *The Miracle* in New York: "Pretentiously commonplace—Reinhardt's really 'Hollywood.' "). In any case the discussion must have triggered their combined wits to conceive a really original and altogether French presentation. Quite in keeping with the extraordinary popularity of the circus among artists at that time—as so many of Picasso's paintings bear witness—the delightful idea occurred to them of staging Shakespeare's comedy at the Medrano Circus in Montmartre—their favorite—with real clowns playing the roles of Bottom and his fellow journeymen. In a letter of June 1915, Cocteau wrote to Albert Gleizes, who was doing some scenic painting for him: "*Le Songe* can and must be a marvel—Medrano Orchestra, a potpourri of what we love conducted by Varèse"; and Varèse, when he gave a talk at Columbia University in New York many years later, jotted down the following memo: "1914: *Midsummer Night's Dream* project: Satie, Cocteau, Gémier, Astruc, myself. Satie's *Cinq Grimaces*. 4 interpolations by Florent Schmitt, Ravel, Stravinsky, myself and conducted by me. Project interrupted by war." Cocteau's "potpourri" was evidently the same as Varèse's "interpolations." Besides being the most active organizer, Cocteau had also translated the play—"literally," as he says, and with many cuts, *des grandes coupures.*

As I remember, Varèse once mentioned that Picasso was to have joined the group. He must have been replaced by Gleizes (whom Varèse failed to mention) and who must have been called upon very tardily, for Cocteau says in his letter: ". . . everybody has left—Picasso very ill—you save my life." He begs Gleizes to hurry as rehearsals are about to begin. This was in June 1915, and in June Varèse was taken ill and then went to recuperate in the country.

In the spring of 1915 the project was mentioned twice in *Le Mot,* a wartime weekly. Its managing editor was Paul Iribe, who also designed its covers, and Cocteau provided some prose and poems. It was diligently bellicose. All the cartoons, jokes, news items, articles either ridiculed or castigated the Germans. In a March number appeared the following item, captioned "ALLY":

> In Berlin they are putting on Shakespeare. The poster announces: "He has deserted to us from an unworthy country." For this Max Reinhardt makes very bad use of an enormous budget and the amorphous respect of a regimented audience. In Paris, in the midst of war, a group is planning to answer Rein-

hardt and all those who confuse your youthful effort with the vulgar stupidities of Munich. They promise us a sensationally new staging and French music for the *Midsummer Night's Dream* of our ally Shakespeare.

It was again referred to in June:

> Maître Saint-Saëns, always anxious to displease everybody and never failing to put his foot in it, now finds it clever to reply to Gémier, who plans to put on *Midsummer Night's Dream* with new music: "One does not give *Le Songe d'une Nuit d'Été* without the music of Mendelssohn."

However, the group scattered. Gleizes, who married Juliette Roche in September, left with her soon after for Barcelona, Varèse for New York in December, and, I suppose, the others were claimed by war. All that remains of this amusing plan by a prodigiously gifted group of artists is Satie's *Cinq Grimaces,* which, by the way, Varèse helped orchestrate, Satie not having yet mastered the art and science of orchestration and, as Paul Rosenfeld later suggested, Varèse having probably been "born with the orchestra in his veins." So *A Midsummer Night's Dream* was never played at the famous Medrano Circus with the collaboration of real clowns. What a pity!

It was at Cocteau's request that Varèse introduced him to Picasso. Whether Varèse took Picasso to Cocteau's, as Varèse related, or Cocteau to Picasso's, as Cocteau stated in the film *Portrait Souvenir* by R. Stephane, hardly matters. It only goes to show how tricky memory is and how risky it is for a biographer to be too categorical even when the facts are direct from the horse's mouth—that is if there is another horse, for as Durrell says somewhere, "Fact is unstable by nature." An example is cited by Apollinaire in connection with a performance of Alfred Jarry's *Ubu Roi* in the private theater of the sultan of Turkey. It having been described to him by two different friends, Apollinaire comments: "One of them told me that the play was performed by living actors; according to the other it was performed by marionettes!" At any rate, this meeting of Cocteau and Picasso that Varèse brought about resulted in a fruitful collaboration beginning with *Parade,* which was presented by the Russian Ballet in 1917 with Cocteau providing the scenario, Picasso the setting and costumes, and Satie, once more, the music. It was in the program of *Parade* that Apollinaire used the word *surrealism* for the first time.

In October Varèse had not given up all hope of obtaining a conducting engagement when he wrote to Mme Kauffmann: "Caillaux, as always, is very good to me and with his support I shall look into the possibilities of London." I don't know through whom Varèse met Caillaux, who in 1911 had become Président du Conseil. Varèse admired him and had been in complete sympathy with Caillaux's unpopular policy in the matter of closer relations between France and Germany. Like many French politicians (and too few in our country), Caillaux took a very personal and knowledgeable interest in music and the arts and, to judge by Caillaux's cordial note to Varèse, in that young composer. During 1914–15 Varèse had received a couple of small government grants and now Caillaux tried to get him a regular pension. He did not succeed and another two hundred francs from the Département des Beaux Arts in October did not solve Varèse's financial problems. He could not continue to depend on his very kind friends who had come to his aid during his illness. In the same letter he writes: "An American lady, a friend of mine, is looking into the question of an impresario." Does this mean a manager in New York? Varèse had Astruc in Paris (or had the war absorbed him too?) and besides Caillaux he writes of a Marquis de Breteil "who will launch me in London"; mentioning as well the Norwegian ambassador for the Scandinavian countries. Was Varèse really as optimistic as he evidently would like his mother-in-law to believe? It is true that Varèse was sometimes too quick to believe in conversational promises and to mistake good will for performance. At any rate, nothing came of all these hopes. It must have been *la dame américaine*—whose name, if Varèse mentioned it, I have forgotten—who put the idea of America in his head and a hope of engagements there. In any case he did decide to try his fortune across the Atlantic in that legendary America of his boyhood with its leatherstocking heroes, Indians, high skies, endless horizons and space! His passage was assured by a cousin of his old friend Armande de Polignac, the Comtesse de Boisrouvray.

Varèse boarded the S.S. *Rochambeau* on December 18, 1915, with eighty dollars in his pocket and a packet of letters of introduction in his trunk. At that time Varèse had not yet abandoned the piano and took part in the traditional shipboard concert, this time for the benefit of sailors wounded in the war. He played two pieces by Debussy arranged for piano, *La Cour des Lys* and *Le Laurier Blessé*.

PART II

New York
Varèse, Conductor

Berlioz's *Requiem Mass*

BESIDES an inadequate supply of money and an ample supply of introductions, Varèse brought to America two *idées fixes:* he would make his mark as a conductor and at the same time lots of money for his Claude *adorée;* second, he would create the new instruments he needed for the music he was going to compose.

During the first months in New York, his letters to Mme Kauffmann are like a barometer going from fair to foul, hope and discouragement alternating. On the ninth of February he writes that he has dined with Otto H. Kahn and that "Kahn and Vanderbilt" are taking an interest in him:

I believe they are arranging for me to conduct a concert next month here at Carnegie Hall (which is the largest concert hall) with the New York Symphony Orchestra. If this is successful, it will be the foundation of my future. Things move slowly here—everyone is suspicious but once you're in the saddle the rest is generally clear sailing. I am full of courage, energy, determination—I have something they don't have—so it is bound to go and *will go*. It only needs patience.

Ten days later, forgetting his advice to himself, he answers a question in one of Mme Kauffmann's letters with this disparaging account of New York:

New York: banal city and dirty and the inhabitants handsome sportsman type—not more. I see only Europeans with whom contact is possible. With the natives all conversation impossible no matter what the subject except the question of the "Dollar," which is the only one that is of any interest or importance to them. . . . I have 2 or 3 things in view but I don't count on them. People here are in an even greater funk than with us.

He had evidently heard no more about that concert he was to conduct and in his disappointment and *impatience* blames the whole city and its inhabitants. But by the end of March the wind has veered to fair and his letter on March 26 is all optimism once more:

In a little while you will have good news. My concerts have been postponed, the orchestra having previous engagements. . . . Things are going to be all right. I've got hold of what I need and next winter my music will be played—it's awaited with impatience and curiosity. I'm looking into the question of getting new electrical instruments made of my own invention. It's going to be marvelous. I am beginning to speak English—like the French, Americans have no predilection for languages.

Reading this confident letter, I think sadly that Varèse's life in America is, for the most part, going to be endless frustration in an endless search, with the exception of the six productive, satisfying years, 1921–1927.

In one of his first interviews to the Press Varèse tried to explain his ideas in his inexpert English, and this is the report of the young journalist from the *New York Telegraph* of what Varèse said:

> Our musical alphabet must be enriched. We also need new instruments very badly. In this respect Futurists (Marinetti and his *bruiteurs*) have made a serious mistake. New instruments must be able to lend varied combinations and must not simply remind us of things heard time and time again. Instruments, after all, must only be temporary means of expression. Musicians should take up this question in deep earnest with the help of machinery specialists. In my own work I have always felt the need of new mediums of expression. I refuse to limit myself to sounds that have already been heard. What I am looking for is new mechanical mediums which will lend themselves to every expression of thought and keep up with thought.

This was Varèse's credo in 1916 and no heretical doubts were ever to disturb his militant faith, which became, if possible, more indomitable, almost fanatical, over the years.

In May Varèse went to the Adirondacks to visit some of his wealthy American acquaintances, whom he calls "charming friends." It took Varèse some time before he learned not to mistake society cordiality and hospitality in America for friendship, or interest in his handsome, magnetic person for interest in his ideas. Varèse was always telling me after he had made new acquaintances that he, she, they "liked my ideas." Society was hardly the place for Varèse's profound seriousness nor for his Rabelaisian moods either. To have to emasculate his vocabulary (if he did) must have been a strain. Varèse could be a very entertaining guest, but his wit was apt to wither in unsympathetic company or when he was bored. Besides, too often seeing people through the deforming lenses of his protean moods—eager enthusiasm that embarrassed the conventional, dejection or boredom that repelled. He was not a good judge of the Americans he met—at least not of the American businessmen or the society women of those days, the very people who, for a conductor to succeed, had to be conciliated. Varèse in the end proved to be a failure at conciliation and compromise.

Varèse goes on to say that he "will succeed" but that it is difficult because "one lives among predators," adding, "but I'll be as tough as they are," which was a delusion.

In July Varèse is confident. He sees his future as assured. On the twenty-fourth he writes to Mme Kauffmann:

> All is well, especially my work. I hope to make lots of money. I think it is better just to let Claude rest [referring to an indisposition Mme Kauffmann has reported]. There is plenty of time for her to get herself stupefied later on—and if things continue in the same way, as seems probable, she will have enough to live as she chooses.

What promises had Varèse received that made him confident of so prosperous a future that he already had a vision of his Claude like a Cinderella in a golden coach?

Meantime he was meeting more congenial people connected with the arts. One of the most congenial and interesting, not only to Varèse but to all the French artists who had exiled themselves in New York from the war in Europe, was Alfred Stieglitz, photographer with an imaginative eye and prophet, in this country, of modern painting. They found a friendly meeting place in his little gallery, Photo-Secession at 291 Fifth Avenue. Its address had given the title *291* to Stieglitz's magazine, formerly *Camera Work*.

In the group of artists Varèse joined in New York were Marcel Duchamp, also recently arrived and famous in America since 1913 when his painting *Un Nu Descendant un Escalier* was exhibited at the Armory Show and caused a great deal of facetiousness; Marius de Zayas, the Mexican caricaturist at that time with *Life* magazine (not the same as today's *Life*); and Varèse's old friend Juliette Roche, now married to his old friend, the cubist

painter Albert Gleizes. Still homesick for Berlin, Varèse saw
many Germans, having been introduced to the German colony
by Karl Muck, at that time conductor of the Boston Symphony
Orchestra. Through Muck he also met the "charming, cultivated"
German ambassador, Count von Bernstorf. Among the Germans
he saw frequently was Fritz Kreisler. They often lunched at a
little Italian restaurant on Forty-seventh Street whose name I
have forgotten though later I often went there with Varèse. It
was frequented by many of the Metropolitan Opera people,
singers and conductors. One would often see the chef-proprietor's
wife and daughter emerge from the kitchen all dressed up for
an evening of Verdi, having received tickets from their operatic
clientele. As Varèse knew the Met's manager, Gatti-Casazza, as
well as many of the conductors and singers, he would often go to
rehearsals as he used to when, as a very young man in Turin,
he escaped from the inhibitive environment of his father's house
to enter the warm musical atmosphere created by Italian opera
people. He didn't have to like the Italian music to enjoy that
familiar ambiance in New York. Caruso, Varèse told me, explained to him the origin of that famous sob, so unfortunately
copied by tenors ever since. It was, Caruso said, an involuntary
trick of his larynx that he had never been able to control.

Through Marcel Duchamp Varèse met Marcel's friend and
patron, Walter Arensberg, poet, fanatical Baconian, and collector
of modern art whose spacious and hospitable apartment was another gathering place for artists, writers, poets, chess players, and
many of the rest of us. His collection of modern painting was
already overflowing up the stairs and into the bathrooms. It kept
on growing over the years and is now housed in the Philadelphia
Museum of Art. Another of Marcel's friends, Man Ray, photographer and painter, mentions Varèse in his book as "handsome
and popular with the ladies." When, at a party not so many years
ago, I met one of the ladies Varèse had enjoyed being popular
with, the beautiful Stella Adler, actress-daughter of the famous
Yiddish actor, she said: "Do you know that I was once madly in
love with this husband of yours?" Another of Varèse's American
feminine acquaintances who had found him attractive was Djuna

Barnes, famous later for her tortured little book, *Nightwood,* prefaced and praised by T. S. Eliot. I had first met Djuna as artist rather than writer when she came to show Allen Norton (a poet and journalist and my husband) her drawings for our frolicky little five-cent magazine, *Rogue.* Djuna was and is forthright and uninhibited. One day as Varèse and I were passing the Hotel Brevoort, Djuna, standing on the stoop, shouted to me for all to hear: "So, you've fallen for Edgard too!"

In quite a different category of acquaintances was Elsa Maxwell, of party fame. Varèse told me of driving down to Long Beach with Elsa and her friend Dicky Gordon and the Belgian violinist Eugène Ysaÿe, to visit Isadora Duncan, who was living with her girls in a house she had rented. It being one of her barren periods, friends who came to see her always brought food and drink. Varèse remembered particularly the quantities of wine they bought on the way and the very tipsy night that ensued with much running in and out of the bedrooms. Years later when Varèse happened to meet Elsa Maxwell at a cocktail party at Virgil Thomson's in the Hotel Chelsea, she fell on Varèse's neck and exclaimed: "He is one of my oldest friends," converting him next day into grist for her columnar mill. Any one familiar with Varèse's style will find very strange Elsa Maxwell's version of what Varèse said that day of another visit to Isadora Duncan. She quotes him as having said:

> "I went to call on Isadora Duncan at Long Beach and Elsa was there. Isadora was sitting cross-legged, illustrating by incredible movements some of the exquisite [hardly a Varèse word] things she found on Greek friezes from which she drew her inspiration [a word Varèse abhorred] for dancing. Also there were the late Eugène Ysaÿe, the great violinist, Isadora's special friend, and— SARAH BERNHARDT! [caps and exclamation] . . . It was the year before Bernhardt died." Varèse sighed.

The facts are: Varèse had an unqualified dislike of the "Divine Sarah" and Isadora's dancing bored him. Elsa was indulging in columnists' license.

When Varèse moved to the Hotel Brevoort on the corner of

Fifth Avenue and Eighth Street sometime in the spring of 1916, he found himself in a congenial and completely French atmosphere. I always want to say sentimentally, "the *famous* old Brevoort" for, to my generation, it is, and beloved and mourned, especially the café, which was on the ground level and you entered under the stairs of the high stoop that led up to the hotel. The Brevoort was Paris in New York. During the war it swarmed with French officers in attractive sky blue uniforms and American girls ready to be picked up by them; also French writers and painters who had a predilection for peace, as well as, of course, the usual American artist habitués, that is, all the drinking intelligentsia of New York, and their Bohemian camp followers, most of them from the far corners of the United States and almost as far from their native pastures as their French colleagues. Even before the war, without the French, and after in the "preposterous" twenties, the Brevoort was Paris in New York. The owner was French, the manager was French, as well as the *valets de chambre* who blacked the boots of the hotel clients and wore the same black and red striped waistcoats as their prototypes overseas; and the waiters were so Parisian that they never bothered you but clustered together out of earshot to talk politics after they had put the bottle of whisky or absinthe, with its ritual accessories, on the table, leaving you to *pour your own drinks!* and to uninterrupted conversation.

At the Brevoort Varèse's room had a social communicating door to the room of another new American friend, the sculptor Jo Davidson, who was a pet in the same wealthy milieu Varèse was frequenting at that time. He was a great favorite at society dinner parties due to his jovial vitality, his bold black eyes and virile beard, as well as his gift as a raconteur of amusing stories and bon mots, which he assiduously collected from his friends, Varèse included. He became the popular portrait sculptor of famous people, among others the President of the United States, Franklin D. Roosevelt, and the wife of the President of Formosa, Mrs. Chiang Kai-shek. Jo Davidson, who exercised more tact in society than Varèse and never let himself be bored as Varèse did, used to lecture his friend for showing so little zeal in catering to the tastes and prejudices of the people who could be useful to him and for failing to use his great assets of good looks and charm.

However, although Varèse later may not have come up to Jo's ideal of social diplomacy, at that time he nevertheless succeeded in impressing the "right people" sufficiently to achieve the first goal he had set himself. On April 1, 1917, he was to make his debut in New York as a conductor.

Sometime the previous winter Varèse had met with an accident. A wild automobile mounted the sidewalk where he was waiting for a Fifth Avenue bus and knocked him down. He was taken to the nearby St. Vincent's Hospital with a broken foot. In spite of his restless temperament and his dislike of staying in bed, his enforced confinement was made endurable not only by his many friends, who helped the days pass as well as his anxiety over the imminent loom of hospital bills by promised loans, but particularly by joyful anticipation. The concert was to be a grandiose and solemn affair, a memorial in honor of all the soldiers who had been killed in the war. It had been Varèse's idea to pay tribute to *all* the dead soldiers, not only to those of the Allies, but equally to those of the enemy who were just as dead. The program was to consist of one great work, the *Requiem Mass* of Hector Berlioz. By the time Varèse had to go to Scranton to rehearse the chorus of the Scranton Choral Society, though he still limped, he was able to abandon his crutches for a cane.

The concert took place at the old Hippodrome on Sixth Avenue between Forty-third and Forty-fourth Streets, whose huge auditorium was capable of seating up to 6000 persons and in which there lingered, as the music critic Irving Kolodin commented, "the pungent aroma from the annual invasion of the elephants and horses of the Dillingham Circus."

On the second of April at two o'clock in the morning Varèse wrote to Mme Kauffmann:

My first concert finished at 10:30 in the midst of frenetic ovations. It has been a marvelous debut—I am working on great things for the next season. . . . the public adores me. Everyone predicts that I'll be one of their idols. A big reception has just been given in my honor—I am full of champagne and happy.

Varèse must also have been pleased with the unanimously favorable reviews. The *Sun's* article gives a good account of the event:

> In the evening at the New York Hippodrome, the *Requiem Mass* of Hector Berlioz was performed as a Palm Sunday Memorial to the dead soldiers of all nations who have fallen in the European war. The work, which is seldom heard here, was given under the direction of Edgard Varèse, French composer, who planned the memorial and came to this country for this performance.
>
> The forces engaged in the production under Mr. Varèse's direction consisted of the Scranton Choral Society of three hundred members brought from Pennsylvania for the occasion, an orchestra of a hundred and fifty men recruited from the Philharmonic and the other New York Orchestra, and Lambert Murphy soloist.
>
> The performance was very impressive. Mr. Varèse proved himself efficient as a conductor. The singing of the chorus was commendable for good tone, attack and phrasing. The balance of the great ensemble, save for a few instances where the brass choirs over-powered in volume the voices of the singers, was generally good. All in all the rendering of the work was one of devotional spirit combined with much splendor of effect in musical achievement. The audience was very large. Much approval was shown Mr. Varèse.

Of Varèse, the *Evening Mail* wrote:

> Mr. Varèse, who made his American debut as a conductor, seemed to possess the inspiration of genius.

The *New York Herald:*

> the conductor, who is new to New York, put the proper fire into the musicians.

Varèse: A Looking-Glass Diary

In the *Globe*, Pitts Sanborn ended his review:

> In so far as the size and acoustics of the Hippodrome would permit, the performance was admirably effective. The *Tuba Mirum* recalled the fate of Jericho in quite the approved manner, and the *Lacrimosa* stirred the large audience to even more vigorous applause. The Scranton Oratorio Society and Mr. Varèse nobly earned their welcome.

Varèse once said of Berlioz: "One must not be put off by his superficial romanticism, for he has the proportion and luminosity of the Egyptians and the Greeks," which makes the following commentary by Paul Rosenfeld in the *Seven Arts Chronicle* particularly interesting:

> It is said that Mr. Varèse was sent by his government to this country to discover Berlioz to us. If that is so he has been most faithful, for Berlioz did manifest himself that night at the Hippodrome in a veritable blaze of power. He manifested himself in a manner that revolutionized all our conceptions. It is not as the romanticist, it is not as the literary musician, or the bizarre technical innovator. It was as perhaps the most classic artist who ever composed.

As for the reiterated rumor that Varèse had been sent to America by his government to be the propagandist of French music, let me quote from the rebuff Varèse received when in Paris he had offered himself in that role to a M. Humbert of *Le Journal* for whom a secretary replied: "He [M. Humbert] considers that at this moment there are more important things to worry about than the propaganda of our Art abroad." No, Berlioz was entirely Varèse's idea. France's mind, exclusively on war, had sent all those sky blue missions over most urgently to bespeak our aid. The Palm Sunday was, in fact, the day before the United States declared war on Germany, an event which abruptly ended Varèse's well-founded expectations. Dejectedly, he wrote to Mme Kauffmann:

New York Varèse, Conductor

> In spite of the great success of the *Requiem* I have little chance of looking forward to anything serious. For artists the situation is becoming as painful as in Europe—those who hold official positions cling to them for dear life—it's understandable—as for creating new organizations (my project accepted—a large part of the necessary funds already found) all that will have to be abandoned. America, which must get organized, is faced with a tremendous financial effort. I am working for myself and will try to manage somehow from the material point of view. It's tough.

Once more Varèse had fallen a victim of war; the same war had followed him across the Atlantic and defrauded him of the prize his second success as a conductor had won for him. However, as it turned out, this was only a setback. Less than two years later comes the story of the orchestra that he willed into being and its fated and fateful end. Of that more after several other happenings.

In the spring of 1917, a friend of Marcel Duchamp, the cubist painter and poet Francis Picabia arrived in New York from Barcelona, where he had started his Dadaist-surrealist magazine, *391*, abstracting the title from Stieglitz's *291* by adding a unit to the first digit. Soon after Varèse met Picabia, they became convivial companions and spent the summer in what, from Varèse's stories, must have been a very Gemini month of drinking, laughing, and girl-chasing. Picabia had charm, a subtle, seething mind, gaiety, and ruthless egotism, a combination of qualities that fascinated many people including Varèse. He was wealthy and loved speed; his legend has it that he bought 127 automobiles. At that time I was separated from my husband and living in a house that belonged to my mother in which I rented out two floors. The Gleizeses had taken the one above mine, and when I told them I was going West for the summer they suggested my renting my apartment to the Picabias. After Gaby Picabia left to visit her children in Switzerland, Varèse moved in with Picabia. With my apartment the Picabias had taken over Mrs. Kiernan, my housekeeper, so-called because of her extreme respectability, dignity, and gray hairs, though she did all the work. When I returned in the fall Mrs. Kiernan gave me an outraged account of the behavior of the two young men. "Mrs. Norton," she said, in a dramatically shocked tone, "I am an old woman but I have seen such carryings-on as I never dreamed of." It had been a hot summer (as usual) and Varèse and Picabia would lie around and stalk around the apartment within a few inches, if that, of stark nakedness, thus informally receiving their feminine guests. Among them was Isadora Duncan, who, as creator of barefoot dancing in diaphanous veils, thought nothing of nudity either.

During the five or six months Picabia stayed in New York he brought out three numbers of *391* to which Varèse contributed a poem and two epigrams. One of the epigrams contained his often reiterated creed and its title his lifelong battle cry: *Que la Musique Sonne.*

> Our alphabet is poor and illogical. Music, which should be alive and vibrating, needs new means of expression and science alone can infuse it with youthful sap. Why, Italian Futurists, do you reproduce only what is most superficial and boring in our daily lives? I dream of instruments obedient to thought—and which, supported by a flowering of undreamed-of timbres, will lend themselves to any combination I choose to impose and will submit to the exigencies of my inner rhythm.

Varèse was, however, very much annoyed when writers called his music "Dadaist." Varèse did not subscribe to Duchamp's antiart philosophy. Art, whether music, painting, sculpture, architecture, or poetry, was serious, was important—the only thing that kept life from being absurd: and music was the nucleus of his own life. He would never have said with Picabia: *"J'ai horreur de la peinture de Cézanne, elle m'embête."* However, he believed in fun and making-fun-of—especially of hypocrisy, mediocrity, and tradition, which he called "a bad habit." In his young days he had liked practical jokes, and always enjoyed *contre-pèteries,* limericks, and the Marius-Olive stories he told so well with the irresistible Marseillais accent. He liked the acrobatic wit and meaningful nonsense of *391* and felt a close camaraderie with Picabia and the other contributors for whom

Dadaism was, at least for the moment, their *dada*. Besides, through all the caperings of *391* thoughtful insights betray in poems and prose the well-stocked and brilliant minds of these clever clownings. Some of their names were: Walter Arensberg, Marius de Zayas, Erik Satie, Jean Cocteau, Louis Aragon, Tristan Tzara, Philippe Soupault, Ribemont-Dessaigne, Albert Gleizes, Ezra Pound, Max Jacob, Marcel Duchamp (who also signed Rose Selavy), Charchoune, Robert Desnos, Jean Crotti, as well as Varèse and Picabia (or as Picabia also signed, Pharamousse and Funny-Guy).

Examples of Picabia's Dadaistic humor:

> Morality is out of place in a pair of pants.

> The first phallus was Adam's rib.

> In America they have abolished alcohol and kept Protestantism, why?

> Men gain diplomas and lose their instinct.

And one of Satie's: "If you want to live a long time, live to be old."

Another happening that year—Varèse met me.

The Cincinnati Symphony Orchestra

It was sometime in that winter of 1917 that I first heard of Edgard Varèse. Marcel Duchamp, with whom I had been lunching at the Hotel Lafayette (French twin of the Hotel Brevoort a block away), asked me to go with him to St. Vincent's Hospital to visit a French composer who had had an automobile accident. *"Un garçon charmant,"* Marcel said. For some reason I could not go with him that afternoon, and it was not until the following autumn that I met Varèse.

Meantime I came to dislike a limping dark man in a green beaver hat whom I saw constantly at the Brevoort peering through the arches of the passage that led behind the café rooms to the bar on Eighth Street. He stared with a frankness that upset my very circumscribed ideas of good manners, for in spite of my antibourgeois rebellion, I remained ritualistically conventional. When one day, annoyed at his persistent staring, I asked the friend I was with if he knew who that glowering individual was, he said he had heard he was a French musician who had been wounded in the war. In those days it was taken for granted that a Frenchman who limped was a war casualty and a hero. Much later I learned that the man in the green hat was only an automobile casualty and Marcel's composer friend. Although that spring I met him once casually when, with Albert and Juliette Gleizes, we ran into him in a restaurant and they introduced us *en passant,* it was not until I returned from the West, where I had spent the summer, that I met, not the man in the green hat, but Edgard Varèse. He joined a party I was with at the Café Brevoort and sat down beside me.

As we talked the man in the green hat vanished forever though one of his bad habits did not—Varèse too was a starer and I had to become tolerant. It was not, however, as Ouellette says in his book on Varèse, "love at first sight" for either of us. That evening my antipathy gave way to liking and gradually, though I had no premonition of such an eventuality, to lifelong devotion. As for Varèse, a casual attraction turned into a need.

Varèse had to an extraordinary degree what Conrad called "the gift of familiarity." The eagerness of his manner was flattering and there was the warm timbre of his voice, but I am at a loss to say just what it was that created such an atmosphere of intimacy so that you felt almost at once that you knew him better than the few hours spent with him justified.

When we left the Brevoort those of us who were not ready to go to bed came up to my apartment to finish the night. I had been given a case of Chambertin, so we drank wine and ate cheese while *contre-pèteries* (the French counterpart of our limericks) flew back and forth like shuttlecocks. There was a lively competition as to who could remember the most. Everyone laughed a great deal. I did too, though my French was not always able to keep up with the lightning speed of the word-juggling.

The next afternoon Varèse returned with a bunch of those white roses that remind one of the thick, creamy skin of certain lucky women. While I was arranging them Varèse prowled around looking at my pictures—a Monticello, a Corot, a drawing by Marcel Duchamp, and an uncle's watercolor of peaches. When I brought over the roses and put them on a table under the peaches, Varèse said: "Roses and peaches are in the same mode—*même saveur grasse et succulente* (same fat, succulent savor)—and rum is, too." I said, "Peaches are out of season but I have a bottle of rum. Let's test your theory." But when Varèse saw the label—some light cocktail rum—it wouldn't do. Only dark Jamaica rum was in the rose-peach category. After burying his nose in the roses, he made a face. "Your American flowers, like your magnificent fruits, are only good to look at—no smell, no taste." He spoke of the luscious pears and peaches *en espalier dans les jardins de curé* and he actually drooled over the recollection of the little peaches in Italy when he was a boy that were not much to look at but—oh the taste! . . . and we laughed as he took out his handkerchief to wipe his mouth.

Although Varèse later used to say that between him and New York it had been *le coup de foudre,* he was really homesick for Europe and, though he talked a great deal about Berlin, for Paris. At that time, when pointed toes were the fashion in New York, he made me go to a shoe shop called the French Bootery, for only there were to be found round-toed shoes like the ones "*les poules de Paris*" were wearing when he left. For Varèse, all girls who were not "constipated bourgeoise" or "society bitches" were "*poules.*" He often called me "*ma jolie petite poule,*" though *poule* (chicken) had usually not a very flattering implication; with Varèse, unaffected by usage, it was affectionate.

That winter, though our intimacy progressed, it was still casual and remained in Stendhal's third category of love, which, as Santayana commented, "turns the vital element into laughter and delight." And it was certainly very unsuitable that our love affair should finally have turned into something so much deeper and lasting. Music had not entered into my life. (I discount my mother's early attempts, which failed, to make me musically cultured by taking me to concerts that bored me.) I knew poets, writers, painters, journalists, but not a single musician. I had no conception of what a realistic politician you had to be to succeed as a conductor or in the official music world, and I knew nothing of the terrible creative passion. I was frivolous and a little bookish (but books, after all, are "nobler and less garrulous than life," Malraux has said). At that time, I was enjoying the sensation of being as free as the sparrows of New York.

Although Varèse must have told me with enthusiasm and pride of the Berlioz *Requiem*, I was too ignorant, as well as too indifferent to public recognition, to appreciate the joy of it to him and the importance. Since then, thanks to Varèse, music has become a necessity to me (only one of the many ways Varèse enriched my life). Very slowly, I also learned what consecration to an ideal means. *Non si volta chi a stella e fisso.* However, even after almost a lifetime with Varèse I feel alien to the music world. My love of music has not changed my temperament, which is the opposite of the extrovert, gregarious temperament of musicians. I was, in other words, useless to Varèse in his exterior musical life and once, at least, I was a serious hindrance.

In 1918 Varèse was invited to conduct the Cincinnati Symphony Orchestra. Its regular conductor, Ernst Kunwald, being German, had been interned and the board of directors were inviting guest conductors to choose another permanent conductor from among them. As well as conducting a concert in Cincinnati, Varèse was to take the orchestra on tour to several of the Southern cities. "Why don't you come with me?" he suggested. "Wouldn't you like to see me conduct?" It seemed to me a delightful idea and, without a thought for the proprieties, I went. Varèse, ignorant of our tribal taboos, was excusable, but I, being a native, was not. Unfortunately, at that time I lived as though the rest of the world, if it didn't, ought to think as I did about such things, otherwise one simply ignored them. Not an attitude susceptible of aiding someone who, in spite of his determination to have a career as a conductor, was all too prone to act on the same inexpedient principle.

A girlhood friend of mine had married into Cincinnati society and as soon as she knew I was there asked me to stay with her. I dislike visiting, it makes me feel confined to other people's rhythms, so I stupidly declined. I didn't even have sense enough not to go to the hotel where a room had been engaged for Varèse, only just enough to take one far removed from him. As we were about to sit down to luncheon in the hotel restaurant, a gentleman (was he the manager?) hurried toward Varèse. He had missed him, he said, and now Varèse must come and lunch with him and others who were already seated at a table in the dining room waiting for him. Varèse foolishly excused himself saying that he was just about to lunch with his friend Mrs. Norton and introduced us. The gentleman, ignoring me, said that in that case he would see Varèse later and, showing quite plainly his displeasure, left. Varèse said, "Stuffed shirt!" (he was beginning to delight in American slang) and we proceeded to eat quite unconcernedly.

I suppose, though I don't remember, that after lunch the same gentleman escorted Varèse to the Music Hall for rehearsal and introduced him to the orchestra. The next thing I remember is the concert itself. It took place the following afternoon, March 17, at 3:30. It was one of a series of Sunday afternoon "Popular Concerts," though the program Varèse had chosen hardly measured down to the ideals of that category. As one critic remarked, "The program was considerably heavier than patrons of the Sunday events are accustomed to." How that once prevalent locution *heavy* dates the musical period!

Although German music by that time was generally ostracized, Varèse had had the temerity to open the concert (after, of course, the national anthems, American and French) with Wagner's *Prélude* to the first act of *Lohengrin*. Then followed Bizet's *Pastorale* from *L'Arlésienne;* Borodin's *In the Steppes of Central Asia;* the two *Gymnopédies* by Satie, orchestrated by Debussy; Debussy's *Prélude à L'Après-midi d'un Faune; L'Apprenti Sorcier* by Paul Dukas. The soloist chose her own arias: *Ah, fors'è lui* from *La Traviata* and from *Louise,* inevitably, *Depuis le jour.*

I remember how vigorously (in spite of the heaviness of the program) the audience applauded and at the end of the concert streaked down the aisles and went on applauding until Varèse had taken I-don't-know-how-many bows.

As for the critics, the *Cincinnati Commercial Tribune* reviewer wrote:

> Edgar Varèse, the young Parisian orchestra leader, appeared as guest conductor of the season in Music Hall, Sunday afternoon. An immense audience was present and greeted the program with interested attention and received the program with the most enthusiastic applause. . . . Mr. Varèse, who is evidently a well-routined conductor, was warmly applauded and repeatedly called to the box, the audience lingering at the conclusion to express its appreciation.

The *Cincinnati Times* spoke of "the very cordial greeting given Mr. Varèse. . . . Varèse attracted much attention to his own personality." Varèse had not exaggerated when he said after the *Requiem,* "*Le public m'adore.*" Audiences always did. Unfortunately, audiences do not choose conductors.

The critics all stumbled over the word *Gymnopédies*—from the Greek words *pais* (child or boy) and *gymnes* (naked)—which were danced by naked boys at Greek festivals. One critic said they were "dances performed by nude Spartan babies, infants in that sunny clime, unlike those in our own, doubtless being given this form of terpsichorean activity in sufficient numbers to inspire a composer to rush into music." Another critic, not bothering to consult a dictionary or even Carl van Vechten's program note, also invoked naked babies. (What age, I wonder?) Another said that they might be literally translated, *Three-foot Gymnastics.*

After the concert my memory is a blank. Did Varèse meet the great lady and president of the board Mrs. Charles P. Taft? Was he given an official reception? I think not. He must have added to his official unpopularity by spending all his free time during our stay with the young orchestra players of German parentage, who, though not interned, were nevertheless restricted to certain bounds. One was the son of the former conductor, Mr. Kunwald. Varèse enjoyed speaking German and talking about his friends in Berlin.

I remember two dinner parties given in Varèse's honor, one by my friend Ruth and the other by friends of hers. None official! When Ruth came to say good-by to me at the hotel, she scolded me for being so stupid and causing a scandal which could so easily have been avoided if I had stayed with her. Too late, I agreed with her.

The unfortunate result of the scandal was that Varèse's tour with the orchestra was cancelled. When he went to get his music, as he walked along the corridor he heard the voice of the manager shouting to Mrs. Taft, who was deaf: "No, Mrs. Taft, no— they are *not* on the *same* floor."

So ended my first lesson in the art and politics of music and in how a conductor should not behave. What astonishes me as I look back is that Varèse did not blame me as he should have. He never even expressed regret for his cancelled tour. He treated the whole thing as a joke and blamed only *"cette conasse de puritaine!"*

The New Symphony Orchestra

> *On ne plaisante pas impunément avec la règle du jeu. N'être pas comme tout le monde comporte des agréments; mais cela se paie cher.*
> *Alexis Curvers*

Not long after the Cincinnati adventure, those plans for a new "organization," mentioned by Varèse in his discouraged letter of May as cancelled because of the war, were resuscitated and implemented. A new orchestra was organized along the lines Varèse had proposed, to be devoted to the most advanced contemporary music, called in those days "futurist"; and it was to be co-opera-tive—a decision that was to prove fatally foolish. The organiza-tion was incorporated as The New Symphony Orchestra of the New York Federation of Musicians. It was a body with two heads; one of them was The New Symphony Orchestra Society with its own officers, its president, Mr. Walter J. Salmon (who was also one of the sponsors), and its own executive committee which consisted of three prominent women: Mrs. Newbold Le Roy Edgar, Mrs. Charles Guggenheimer, Mrs. Harry Payne Whit-ney. There was also a large Ladies' Committee to do whatever ladies' committees do. The other head was The Musicians New Orchestra Society with its own officers and its own executive committee made up of three musicians from the orchestra. The music director was to be Edgard Varèse with *complete autonomy over the programs* (italics mine). With hindsight one can see that such a hydra-headed organization might well expect trouble.

There were to be three pairs of concerts in the spring (April 11–12, April 25–26, May 9–10) after the season of the other orchestras was over and their musicians free to join the new group.

Varèse prepared three programs, each to be performed twice. He had suggested giving occasionally a classic work that was not being played to death by the other orchestras, so on his first pro-gram he included Bach's *The Heavens Laugh, the Earth Rejoices*. It was followed by: Debussy's *Gigues*, No. 1 of *Images* for or-chestra; Alfredo Casella's *Notte di Maggio;* Béla Bartók's *Deux Images* for orchestra, Op. 10; Gabriel Dupont's *Le Chant de la Destinée*. They were all marked, "First time in New York."

The second program: Emerson Whithorne's symphonic ballet, *Ranga,* Sibelius's symphonic fantasy, *Pohjola's Daughter,* Charles Griffes's *Nocturne,* Charles Martin Loeffler's *A Pagan Poem.*

The third: Vincenzo Tommasini's *Chiari di Luna,* Erik Satie's two *Gymnopédies,* Ferruccio Busoni's *Berceuse Elégiaque,* Al-bert Roussel's *Évocations,* Maurice Ravel's *Daphnis et Chloé.*

When I returned in the fall of 1918 from a summer with my

son in Nantucket, the orchestra was in the process of organization and Varèse almost breathless with anticipation and activity.

A curious scene had occurred between Varèse and the two
sponsors, Mr. Lewisohn and Mr. Salmon, an incredible scene as
Varèse told it. After one of the many dinners more or less or-
ganizational of that time, the two men approached Varèse saying they must speak of his salary. Varèse, according to his story,
told them that, being above all interested in the success of the
orchestra and as it was co-operative, he, too, like the men, would
be content with a modest salary, and he named a sum. What it
was I don't remember but to those two multimillionaires it
evidently seemed so ignominiously small they were convinced that
a man who held himself as cheaply as that could not be first rate,
and, Varèse said: "They turned their backs on me." The truth
of the matter is, I am sure, that they came to tell Varèse (not to
ask) the salary that had been decided on for the music director
of the orchestra, commensurate, no doubt, with that of other
conductors of that period (which is what I believe he eventually
received) but that Varèse, in an excess of zeal and carried away
by his enthusiasm, had not given them time to name. Varèse
never learned when not to be impulsive. He lacked in the cir-
cumstance what Conrad called, "the polished callousness of the
man of the world." Where his deepest feelings were involved
he was as uncalculating and impetuous as a little child. Only
indifference at times gave him the proper air of cool callousness
which those two old men would have understood.

Varèse being occupied with multitudinous activities—organiza-
tional, musical, and time-consumingly social (the price conductors have to pay for their jobs)—he had much less time for me.
Consequently, I saw more of other friends. Varèse objected to
some of them and in general objected to our dancing, drinking
habits; I objected to and resented his assumption that he had
the right to dictate to me. So we quarreled. That was some time
in January when Varèse was in a highly nervous state. I should
have understood the strain he was under; instead I lost my
temper, he lost his temper, and we both said unforgivable things
and parted forever. That eternity lasted until early in the follow-

ing March. We happened to meet at Walter Arensberg's when, having really missed each other, we decided on reciprocal forgiveness and the resumption of relations.

There were then only a few weeks before the final concert, and I saw that Varèse was worried though he said very little. He made a few caustic remarks about the laziness and venality of orchestra musicians, the smug ignorance of the rich. He also spoke of rumors that the manager was trying to discredit him. I however was so inexperienced, so ignorant of the music world and its politics that I had no idea that the situation was as grave as it turned out to be.

From the first, luck was against Varèse. It poured the evening of April 12 and the lobby of Carnegie Hall was a wet and dreary sight. It was enough to damp the spirits of the keenest music lovers, to say nothing of music critics. One of them, James Huneker of the *New York Times,* pointed out: "The weather was against him. His orchestra sounded like a wet hen."

As I looked around the hall I felt happy that in spite of the weather the audience was large and to my inexperienced ears the applause sounded enthusiastic; the critics went only so far as to say that it was "cordial" and "very cordial." On the size of the audience they did not see eye to eye either but all laid stress on its distinction. One said: "The audience, although not large was select." Another wrote: "The hall was well filled in spite of the weather and the toilettes of the first circle unusually elegant." And another, after commenting, "Last night's audience was not only numerous but contained many persons well known in fashionable and musical circles," went on to give a long list of celebrities.

Poor Varèse, at this most decisive juncture of his career—he who cared nothing for society and even less for their clothes—found himself and the music rivaled by the brilliance of the audience and the elegance of their "toilettes"! However, since at that time an audience for new music was not even small but nonexistent, it was just as well that society in the boxes made so brave a showing that the critics had something to be positively enthusiastic about.

As for the music, scarcely a good word was said for it and there was no agreement as to which composers deserved a modicum of praise, which damnation. Henry Krehbiel of the *Tribune* was the most sweeping and energetic in his denunciation of all of them, and he fairly expressed the majority opinion:

It [the concert] began with the instrumental introduction to an Easter cantata composed by Bach two hundred years ago, yet it was the freshest and most refreshing piece of music on the programme arranged by Mr. Varèse. Long before the list of pieces was brought to an end the wish obtruded itself that it might have been preserved as a postlude instead of having been spent as a prelude. After an hour of music by ultramodern composers it would have provided a much needed ventilation of the room, the artistic atmosphere of which had been made stagnant and oppressive by unrelieved and dissonant clashing of keys, re-iteration of unmeaningful rhythmical figures, paucity of melody and monotonous striving for unwonted combination of instru-mental timbres. All the other pieces, not excepting the first of Debussy's *Images* (y-clept "Gigues"), seemed to have been com-pounded of a little of everything that the composer could think of in the way of harmonic and instrumental oddity.

Perhaps it was Béla Bartók who fared the worst. Krehbiel wrote:

Béla Bartók, a Hun and a rival of Attila in his capacity for in-spiring terror . . . When he reached the theme of his village dance he convinced us that we liked Sir Arthur Sullivan's treat-ment of Miya Sama better in the original package—so to speak.

Another said:

The Béla Bartók dullness may be dismissed as imitative common-place.

Another:

All one needs to compose such stuff as the Bartók things is paper, pencil, time and no conscience.

His music was referred to by another critic as "Hungarian futurism."

The critics were also unanimous as to the impossibility of passing judgment on the orchestra and the conductor until they heard a performance of a standard work in the repertory of other conductors. Here are some examples:

In the opinion of the reviewer for *Musical America:*

> Nearly all the music was so new as to bar comparison of Mr. Varèse's work with other conductors.

Mr. Krehbiel deplored that:

> the instruments had so little opportunity to speak in the idiom native to them that one hesitated to pronounce an opinion on their native quality. A phrase or two from a work by Mozart, Beethoven or Weber might have resolved our doubts.

However, he threw one small sop to the leader of the orchestra:

> It [the orchestra] had been subjected to able and energetic training by the conductor.

Another SOS for Beethoven:

> Some may have said to themselves, but we would like to hear the New Symphony Orchestra play the Fifth Symphony of Beethoven. . . . Nor can we tell what the conductor amounts to until he tries something we know.

After reading these reviews and realizing the bewilderment of these sheep without a shepherd, one understands why a conductor who has a jealous regard for his career should avoid presenting composers whose status time has not blessed and whom other conductors, either through caution or distaste, have not performed. These musical sages of the press who had, unhappily, the taste of the public in their keeping—to say nothing of the career of a young conductor who was, at the least, venturesome—

New York Varèse, Conductor

chose to ignore the purpose for which the New Symphony Orchestra had come into being. One, it is true, admitted: "It is
good to have in New York an orchestra devoting its energies
to produce new things," but then hastily went on to talk about
the eminent members of the audience and to give a long list of
celebrities; and the *Journal*'s reviewer wrote: "One personally
applauds the programmatic bent. The breath of novelty is always refreshing," then proceeded to help demolish the one conductor willing to jeopardize his career in order to bring such
refreshment to New York and to run the gauntlet of critics'
embattled conservatism.

It is quite true, as another critic observed, that Varèse was
nervous. For weeks before the concert he had felt around him
an atmosphere of hostility. He had felt it in the manager from
the beginning, but much more alarmingly during rehearsals in
the unco-operativeness of most of the musicians, who grumbled
among themselves not too discreetly. Their attitude had come as
a rude shock to Varèse, whose past happy experience had led
him to expect cordial relations with his men and an effort on
their part to give him their best.

When Varèse took up his baton on the evening of April 12 he
felt that he was facing disaster with this body of sullen men he
was about to conduct. He knew also that if the critics proved to
be against him, as was likely, he was doomed.

Varèse was living at the time of the concert with our friend
Witold Gordon, a Polish painter and designer, at his apartment
on 110th Street. I had gone with Witold and Franca, his wife,
to the concert and back to their apartment afterward to wait for
Varèse. Only when I saw Varèse's face with that closed, keep-off
expression, did I know that the concert had not been the success I had supposed. He did not need the thumbs down by the
critics the following day to know what to expect.

As soon as the reviews seemed to prove that they were right,
the players came out boldly with their demands for a change
to more standard programs. They had their eyes on the box
office besides looking forward to less strenuous work playing
music they practically knew by heart. The sponsors and the

officers of both the boards eagerly agreed with them. Of his executive committee, Mrs. Guggenheimer was also of the opinion that it would be advisable to make some changes. Mrs. Edgar wrote Varèse the following note:

> Dear Mr. Varèse:
> I have tried several times to reach you on the telephone but without success. I want to tell you how very deeply I regret the trouble which has arisen. The opinion and attitude of your musicians completely took me by surprise. I am only sending you these few lines to say that the wisest course to pursue at present is for you to conduct another pair of concerts, for your own good and your further career. I hope you will take this piece of advice in the manner that it is given, which is one of friendly interest in you.

At the tempestuous meeting that followed the Sunday afternoon concert, Varèse was told that it had been agreed upon that the programs would have to be modified. Angrily he pointed out the stupidity of starting a new orchestra on the same pattern as the two which already only aped each other. An entirely different orchestra, such as he had proposed and which they had *accepted,* would gradually form its own audience of people sick of always hearing the same programs and who would come to the concerts eager to listen and learn; who would be indifferent to the opinions of a handful of men with frozen ears and minds; and of course musicians would have to be found who would not sabotage the new works. He was too angry and too shocked to be either tactful or persuasive and refused to popularize his programs (as he said in private to me, "for a bunch of lazy, ignorant performers, smug rich men, and smugger critics"). He resigned. Immediately Mrs. Whitney, disgusted forever with music, as she said, also resigned from the executive committee.

Rachmaninoff was approached; he declined to take the place of his friend, Mr. Varèse, a fine musician, he said, whom he admired for his undaunted courage. Then Mr. MacMillan, the manager, at once proposed Artur Bodanzky, whom he had wanted in the first place. Bodanzky took over.

Grandpère: Claude Cortot

Claude and Célinie Cortot at the time of their marriage

Oncle Joseph, Grandpère's brother

Tante Marie, his wife

Blanche Cortot soon after her marriage to Henri Varèse

Romanesque church next to the Prieuré

Front part of Grandpère's house in the Prieuré

Abbatial church of Saint-Philibert, Tournus

Varèse in Turin with his two younger brothers, Maurice and Renaldo, and Corinne, the older of his two sisters

Bergeggi on the Mediterranean near Savona, where Varèse spent many summers as a boy (photograph taken in 1955)

Varèse in Italy

Charles Bordes

Vincent d'Indy

Albert Roussel

Paul Le Flem

Armande de Polignac-Chabannes

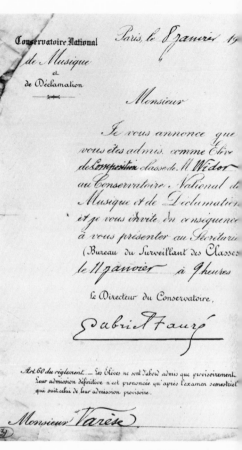

Announcement of Varèse's admission to the Conservatoire de Musique

Charles-Marie Widor, Varèse's teacher at the Conservatoire

René Bertrand and his dynaphone

Leon Deubel

Fernand Léger

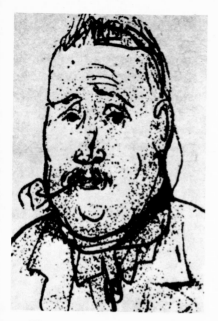

Picasso's Apollinaire

Ricardo Viñes

Claude Debussy

Erik Satie by Alfred Frueh

A Sunday evening at Cipa's (Cyprien Godebski): Ravel (leaning on the piano); Viñes (at the piano); Godebski (seated); Florent Schmitt, Déodat de Séverac; Calvocoressi; Albert Roussel; Godebski's son, Jean

Romain Rolland

Rodin

Varèse with his baby
"Claude *adorée*"

Suzanne Bing Varèse with Claude

Ferruccio Busoni

Busoni's dedication to Varèse on his
Berceuse Elégiaque

Richard Strauss

Hugo von Hofmannsthal

Karl Muck

Varèse with the manager of the
Prague Philharmonic, Urbánek.
Prague, May 1909

Varèse when he conducted the
Prague Philharmonic, 1914

Varèse in uniform, 1915

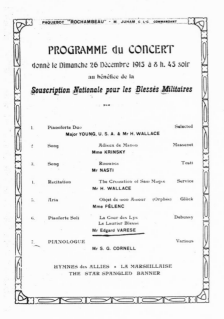

PAQUEBOT "ROCHAMBEAU" · M JUHAM C L-C COMMANDANT

PROGRAMME du CONCERT

donné le Dimanche 26 Décembre 1915 à 8 h. 45 soir

au bénéfice de la

Souscription Nationale pour les Blessés Militaires

1.	Pianoforte Duo		Selected
	Major YOUNG, U. S. A. & Mr H. WALLACE		
2.	Song	Adieux de Manon	Massenet
	Mme KRINSKY		
3.	Song	Romance	Tosti
	Mr NASTI		
4.	Recitation	The Cremation of Sam Magee	Service
	Mr H. WALLACE		
5.	Aria	Objet de mon Amour (Orphée)	Glück
	Mme FÉLENC		
6.	Pianoforte Soli	La Cour des Lys	Debussy
		Le Laurier Blessé	
	Mr Edgard VARESE		
7.	PIANOLOGUE		Various
	Mr S. G. CORNELL		

HYMNES des ALLIES · LA MARSEILLAISE
THE STAR SPANGLED BANNER

Program of concert on board the
Rochambeau at which Varèse played
Debussy on his way to New York

Varèse, summer of 1916

Varèse (wearing the "green hat") in Scranton to rehearse chorus for Berlioz's *Requiem,* 1919

THE SCRANTON REPUBLICAN, THURSDAY, MAR

C OMMITTEE of the Scranton Oratorio Society Which Greeted Director Edgar Varese
  He Reached the City Yesterday.

Joseph Stella and Marcel Duchamp

Francis Picabia

Head of Varèse by Gaston Lachaise

Silverpoint drawing of Varèse by Joseph Stella

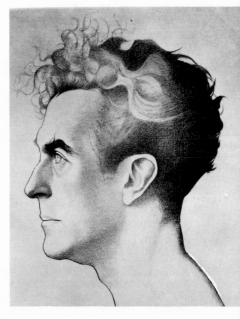

Varèse made this design for a pos
but the concerts that season w
given at the Vanderbilt Theatre
the Little Theatre.

Varèse and Louise Norton, 1921

A pictorial feature that appeared in *Musical America* to publicize the
International Composers' Guild concert. Top, left to right: Ruggles,
Torpadie, Varèse. Bottom, left to right: Salzedo, Casella, Schmitz.

arlos Salzedo at the piano rehearsing
ngers for Stravinsky's *Renard,* which Sto-
wski conducted

1922 - NEW YORK· EXPERIENCES
FIRST PERFORMANCE OF VARÈSE'S
"HYPERPRISM." ─

ver with Stella's painting pro-
sed for printed score of *Octandre*
t not used

Varèse's drawing in ink and red cray-
on, title page of his manuscript

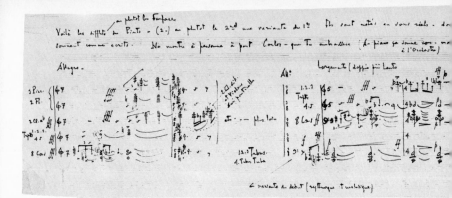

Varèse's description
of his dream and the
Fanfare he had dreamed

New York Varèse, Conductor

Not long ago I came across the following paragraph in *Beyond Good and Evil* and I thought of Varèse:

> Independence is for the very few; it is a privilege of the strong. And whoever attempts it . . . proves that he is not only strong but also daring to the point of recklessness. He enters into a labyrinth, he multiplies a thousandfold the dangers which life brings with it in any case, not least of which is that no one can see how and where he loses his way, becomes lonely, and is torn piecemeal by some minotaur of conscience. Supposing one like that comes to grief, this happens so far from the comprehension of men that they neither feel it nor sympathize. And he cannot go back any longer. Nor can he go back to the pity of men.
>
> (Translated by W. Kaufmann)

Often when Varèse was his fiercest, most unapproachable, it was to ward off demeaning pity. He refused, as Eisenhower once said of Churchill, "ever to show a defeated face publicly."

There were, however, not a few people who after the debacle comprehended very well that Varèse had "come to grief" and did not offer him pity; they congratulated him with complete understanding and sympathy. One of them was Lawrence Gilman, who wrote him this note:

> Dear Mr. Varèse:
> I want to send you my word of salutation for the inspiring achievement of last night. You must realize that you have been the one to turn a new and engrossing page in the musical history of New York—a page novel and stimulating. To be the means of revealing a fresh and beautiful phase of art seems to me to be a public benefaction. The chorus of envy and belittlement should not surprise or daunt you: it was to be expected. For me, it was an evening long to be remembered. . . . These obstructionists we have always with us like the Poor. Thank you from my heart. With best wishes . . .

Lawrence Gilman later took Krehbiel's place as principal critic on the *Tribune* and was for years the most openminded and generous of the critics in New York, as well as the most schol-arly. If he had reviewed the April twelfth concert, Varèse would have had at least one strong ally.

From Mr. Francis Coppicus of the Metropolitan Music Bureau there was a more formal letter but none the less warm:

> Dear Mr. Varèse,
> Please allow me to send you my heartiest congratulations upon your success. . . . I enjoyed the new compositions very much. Please don't worry about the New York "Beckmessers," and with my very best wishes for your artistic endeavors . . .

And from the painter Boddington:

> Dear Varèse,
> I have just this moment heard of your difficulties in the matter of the New Symphony Orchestra and you may believe me when I say that I am very, very sorry. I am sorry that a conflict of ideals has made it necessary for you to forego the benefits of what appeared to be an excellent opportunity. Ideals, my dear Varèse, often take on the appearance of impediments to success, but from what little I know of this matter, you have every reason to hold your head high in the consciousness of your uncheapened artistic integrity.

The New Symphony Orchestra—no longer new in any sense—at once modulated to orthodoxy. We got some bitter satisfaction out of one critic's review of its first concert of the season the following October:

> The New Symphony Orchestra came into being last spring with the ostensible mission of presenting to New York audiences un-familiar music, principally "music of the future," to say nothing of futuristic music. Edgard Varèse, an avowed apostle of the tonal art to come, was the conductor chosen. The opening concert took place a Thursday evening in April in Carnegie Hall, and it is safe to say that many of those who were present will never forget it. I believe this concert was repeated the following after-noon. Then the plans of the orchestra suffered a modification.

New York Varèse, Conductor

The reviewer went on to say that Artur Bodanzky of the Metropolitan Opera Company suceeded Varèse and gave one pair of concerts in the spring: "The music of the day after to-morrow was represented by Debussy's *L'Après-midi d'un Faune,* dating from 23 years ago yesterday." And ended: "Well, the New Symphony Orchestra, still directed by Mr. Bodanzky, launched for the season a series of ten pairs of concerts whose programs as already announced would scarcely trouble in his slumber the jealous guardian of a museum of antiquities or a morgue."

After that one season the old New Symphony Orchestra folded its wings and silently stole away. Just as Varèse had said, there was no place in New York for a third conventional orchestra.

That Varèse ever got his nonconformist proposal accepted was a miracle of stubborn conviction and extraordinary persuasiveness. He had momentarily hypnotized a certain number of ordinarily orthodox and practical musical people into the belief that a symphony orchestra for the exclusive performance of unknown music was a cultural necessity for New York. But even before the first concert, doubts were being insinuated from the second division of the two-headed body to the first. Varèse had lost his army before the battle. The big guns of modern music had made cowards of them all. One wonders what the result would have been if Varèse had followed Mrs. Edgar's advice and conducted a second pair of concerts. Instead, incapable of doing "a diplomatic egg dance," he had seen red and resigned. I find myself asking questions which never occurred to me at the time. Was the insurance of Varèse's autonomy over the programs written into his contract? Had he legal rights he might have invoked? How he reacted to this appalling disaster—for it was nothing less—I do know: by hiding his hurt in the deepest, darkest corner of his heart and putting on his pride-mask which he kept for zero hours. The blow to his pride must have been almost unbearable, remembering all the congratulatory letters from colleagues in Europe. He had been so pleased and proud to include on his program Roussel, his old teacher; Debussy, who had been such a moral support in his young years; Busoni, to whom he felt he owed a debt of gratitude; as well as his friends and colleagues, Satie, Casella, Ravel, Béla Bartók. Besides, he had been rejoicing at the thought of being able to provide a carefree future for his Claude.

Before our quarrel he had also broached the subject of our getting married now that his situation was assured and considering the despotic puritanism of "your" country. I had by then obtained a divorce and rejoined that I was willing to risk it if he was. Though I spoke lightly the risk was serious; our backgrounds and temperaments were too different and I was totally unsuited and unprepared for the hardships of a conductor's wife, being somewhat antisocial, not very robust, and not able gracefully to endure boredom—to say nothing of living on the slope, so to speak, of a live volcano. However, Varèse's abrupt resignation had settled the question for the moment.

That fall, I moved from my one-room apartment on Eleventh Street to a somewhat larger one on Fourteenth Street, west of Seventh Avenue. My aunt was getting rid of her old Steinway upright piano and I had it brought to my place for Varèse, knowing that he liked to have a piano to pound on for sound when he was composing, or else occasionally to play Bach. That was a period when Bach was the composer who seemed to be in his fingers more often than any other. Varèse used to come down from 110th Street and almost every day would work on his score, and, working late, would sometimes spend the night. He finally moved in altogether, still keeping his uptown address for the formal world. The apartment was far enough west so that as he worked, all the river noises entered his room and he discovered the music in the foghorns, whose nostalgic ghosts walk so poignantly through *Déserts* composed over thirty years later. He listened to the "parabolas and hyperbolas" of the fire-engine sirens with their haunting music, which he had, thanks to Helmholtz, discovered so long ago. He now elevated one to the rank of musical instrument in the score he was working on, to which he was to give the title *Amériques: Americas, New Worlds*.

In the early spring Varèse's work was once more interrupted and this time by what seemed to us a somewhat antic interlude but one which was not only profitable but proved very enjoyable. Varèse had met the Barrymore clan—John, Lionel, Ethel, and Uncle John Drew—soon after arriving in New York. He had got to know John quite well, and one day that winter when he went to see him he took me with him. Barrymore asked him what he was going to do now that he had given up the orchestra. Varèse said it was a problem. As a matter of fact Varèse had been offered a very lucrative job conducting the orchestra of a new motion picture theater, the Rialto, but with a shudder of his European musical pride he had declined. I noticed that Barrymore was scrutinizing Varèse intently. Finally, he said: "If you want to make some money, I can put you in a picture I'm doing in Chicago." Varèse protested that he was not an actor and Barrymore rejoined that he did not have to be. Fortunately, in those days the movies were still silent. So, in April, Varèse went to Chicago for two months. I cannot remember the name of the film, which I never saw, or what the flashback in which Varèse appeared had to do with it. The scene in the still which I saw showed a long banquet table gorgeously set, Hollywood quite outdoing the extravagant Renaissance in lavishness, and Varèse looking stunning in the part of an Italian nobleman, his hair combed forward in a bang, wearing a sixteenth-century costume which suited the Italian in him. That must have been what Barrymore was seeing when he had sat looking at him. Varèse's role was that of a cuckolded husband sitting between his young wife on one side and her lover on the other in the act of putting poison—from a poison ring, of course—into the lover's goblet of wine. After the Chicago picture was finished, Mr. Robertson, the director, offered Varèse another bit part in a Billy Burke film he was to direct in New York. Mr. Robertson, the extreme opposite of our ideas of a Hollywood character at the time, was a Scottish-Canadian gentleman with charming manners. When we dined with him and his wife at their hotel in New York he brought out some stills in which Varèse appeared. One of Varèse in the Billy Burke picture showed him wearing a cap and holding a knife which he seemed about to throw—his role that of a young roughneck or gangster demonstrating the technique of knife-throwing to the heroine, Billy Burke—what the story was

I don't know. And that is all I remember of Varèse's movie career. It had served its double purpose; his spirits and bank balance rose (he even invested some money and, as I remember, disastrously) and for good measure he had enjoyed himself immensely.

It also gave him more time to "look around." But where he looked during that reprieve was rather within than around. There he found the same importunate idea that had launched the New Symphony Orchestra, the same doggedly entrenched idea, but now of necessity more modestly conceived and free from any practical context of ambition, pride, or gain. It was not many months before the obsession materialized in the first society for the exclusive performance of modern music: The International Composers' Guild. Carlos Salzedo became his first accomplice.

Carlos Salzedo was widely known and is remembered principally as a remarkable harpist and teacher—a preposterous neglect of all the other astounding gifts stored up in his protean musical make-up. At the Paris Conservatoire he had won first prize in harp and piano on the same day. Varèse used to say that if Carlos had chosen the piano instead of the harp he would have had a career rivaling any pianist of his generation. The harp repertory had been trivial and trashy before Salzedo enriched it with his own compositions (concertos—one with six harps—songs with various instrumental combinations, a sonata for harp and piano that belied the generally held belief that the two instruments were antipathetic), as well as with his skillful, tactful, faithful arrangements of other composers, Debussy notably. He also invented technical means for providing his instrument with innumerable new sounds and colors. Later I shall speak of his lavish generosity of all these musical gifts.

Varèse, who had met Salzedo casually, said in one of his hasty judgments—misjudgments—to their common friend Alfredo Sidez, who wanted to bring them together: "That little harpist—he doesn't interest me." However, Sidez finally succeeded, and after an evening, or rather a night into morning, spent together, they discovered they were friends. So it was to Carlos Salzedo that Varèse first presented his ideas for a modern music society, and with enthusiastic acquiescence Carlos became Varèse's collaborator and cofounder of the International Composers' Guild.

It was not long before Varèse gained another important ally, Mrs. Julianna Force. Red-haired, vivacious, efficient, with inexhaustible vitality, it was Mrs. Force, through Mrs. Whitney, who made it possible for Varèse to start his new society. She was Mrs. Whitney's art secretary and confidante and director in succession —as they changed their name and scope—of the Whitney Club, Whitney Studio Club, Whitney Studio, Whitney Studio Galleries, and finally Whitney Museum. The Whitney Studio when we first knew it in 1921 was housed at 8 West Eighth Street; as Mrs. Whitney acquired contiguous houses it spread into numbers 10 and 14 and finally in 1929 into number 12 when, soon after, it became the Whitney Museum. Mrs. Force's own apartment was, as I remember, in number 14, where she loved to give parties in her high-ceilinged drawing rooms whose furnishings, selected by one of her painter friends with aesthetic taste, in the very modern Victorian vogue were, nevertheless, strangely un-Victorian in their overall effect of elegant frivolity.

At 19 MacDougal Alley directly behind the Studio, for some years Mrs. Whitney (or Gertrude Vanderbilt Whitney, sculptress) had had her own studio, which, like all the other studios in the alley, was a converted stable. She had connected it with the Eighth Street house, installed kitchen and dining room, and gave luncheons for her artists to which she invited for their sakes art patrons, dealers, and critics. Varèse was a friend of most of her painters and sculptors, and after she became his patroness and a sponsor of the ICG we too were often invited.

It seems to me fitting that I should say a further word about this good, beneficent friend to Varèse, both during and after the ill-fated New Symphony Orchestra. Of all the patrons of the arts I have ever heard of, she was the most understanding of the artist and the most self-effacing. She avoided thanks by letting the manna of her munificence fall on the artists from the hands of her spirited and indefatigable collaborator, Julianna Force, who brought their needs to her attention as she did in Varèse's case. Mrs. Whitney had a quiet charm and, though I knew her only formally, I sensed a warm, sensual artist's nature through her dignified social graciousness—a nature craving an artist's life and denied full development through the exigencies of her birth. Her senses' needs, I felt, were for art and artists. Her flights to MacDougal Alley must have given her something of a child's feeling of happy defiance playing hooky. I remember her Fifth Avenue mansion where I went with Varèse to tea and thinking how depressing its heavily rich Edwardian décor must be after the large white simplicity and provocative plastery smell of her sculptor's studio, and its freedoms. Surely her sculpture suffered from the dual nature of her life, as did that of her friend Jo Davidson, who also chose to divide himself and became a very successful society and VIPs' sculptor, never an artist's artist. It was that equivocal road he urged Varèse to take, but Varèse had learned from his experience in 1919 that he did not have the right kind of equipment for such a safari. He was incapable of compromise and unable to endure boredom.

When Mrs. Force heard of Varèse's plans for organizing a music society entirely devoted to the performance of contemporary composers ignored by musical officialdom, she responded with enthusiasm, for they seemed to her to parallel Mrs. Whitney's efforts to help young painters and sculptors who had no uptown dealer. The result was that Mrs. Whitney, in spite of her vow never to have anything to do with music again, became one of the principal sponsors of the ICG.

Although for the present Varèse had no monetary worries, the future looked uncomfortably blank. He believed that the New Symphony Orchestra fiasco was the final checkmate to his career as a conductor. Musician friends, among them Fritz Kreisler, tried to persuade him not to give up. They pointed out that it was the music, not his conducting, that had brought about the revolt of players, backers, and critics. He must get a manager. But Varèse had been too hurt by his treatment at the hands of his men, besides feeling a disgust that amounted to nausea for the official music world and its Atlas, the society of wealth, to listen to sensible, or any, advice. He said that he would get a job that had nothing to do with music and compose for himself. A friend of ours, Benjamin Glazer, taking him at his word, found him such a job. It was related to music only very platonically, for he was invited to become a salesman of pianos at Wanamaker's, a department store which used to be located on Broadway between Eighth and Ninth Streets. After that Varèse lived on two emotional levels: the one euphoric since his score, progressing well, was giving him joy and there was the stimulation of planning his new society with Salzedo; the other, the looming piano nightmare! How could he compose, how could he organize and carry out this project he had set his heart on if those "damn pianos" (he resented pianos anyway for having chained music to the tempered system) kept him in prison all day? I was beginning to understand Varèse's ambivalent moods, going from exhilaration to unpredictable fury, and I was worried. Salzedo and I went to see Glazer. I told him that the thought of taking that Wanamaker job was making Varèse ill, and Carlos insisted that it would be a crime to let a valuable musician like Varèse stagnate for eight hours a day, that with all his dynamic urges curbed, the boredom would kill him.

Glazer asked me, would I, if it became urgent before something suitable could be found, be able and willing to keep him going. I said that I had a very small income that one could live on fairly comfortably; two, uncomfortably, but that I was willing to do anything to keep Varèse working and stop his corroding anxiety. The only trouble was I knew Varèse would not consent to such an arrangement and Carlos said Glazer would meet with resentment if he proposed it. Glazer, however, did find a solution. He went to Mrs. Force, who said she understood the predicament and that something must be done. She thought that Mrs. Whitney, who was indignant at the treatment Varèse had met with, admired his courage, and was, moreover, interested in his society, would very likely come to the rescue. Not long after when I met Mrs. Force at the Studio she asked me to come to her apartment, that she had something to tell me. Mrs. Whitney, she assured me, by giving him an adequate allowance, would make it possible for him to go on with his plans.

Of course I rushed home to tell Varèse that he could throw all those pianos out of his mind. At first he was inclined to be annoyed with me that I should go begging to Mrs. Force, who knew of our unmarried marital state. When I explained that it was all Glazer's doing he decided, in that case, he could give in to the relief he felt, hugged me, and said, "Let's celebrate." So he went out to buy wine and the makings of his *boeuf bourguignon*—no, that would have required overnight marinade— it must have been *veau marengo*. At any rate, that night we ate and drank and got a little drunk and made love and afterward Varèse talked and talked—then *magic blazed,* to steal the words of a poet, not having any of my own to describe the power Varèse had to cast radiance over being alive. And it had nothing to do with the stimulation of our erotic moment, more gay than passionate. It was Varèse's seriousness that was passionate, as when he talked about his grandfather and his little Burgundian village as he did that night, holding my hands pressed tightly against him or lifting them to his face, his inevitable gesture of tenderness, saying, as if it had suddenly occurred to him: *"Tu sais je t'aime comme j'aimais mon grandpère."* I was infinitely touched. Sometimes Varèse's way of saying something had the quality of ingenuousness, the simplicity and freshness of poetry. Even his rages were wild dithyrambs. At least they were not prose.

All winter I had been living in the whirlwind of Varèse's organizing fervor, which in the spring alternated with storms of gloom that blew into our apartment from Wanamaker's piano department. I was exhausted. I went to our doctor to beg for a restorative elixir—there were as yet no magic pep pills. He said the stimulant I needed was a complete change and advised a sea voyage. "Nothing like the sea for tired nerves." I decided to take his advice. I would go to Paris, where I had never been, and thus combine sea air, a mission for Varèse collecting music, and falling in love with Paris.

Before I left, Varèse was the recipient of a mysterious tribute. A letter came from a lawyer asking him to come to his office. Varèse went and returned with a large check—how large I don't remember. It was, the lawyer explained, the gift of admirers who wished to remain anonymous. Varèse never discovered their identities. By way of thanks, when his score of *Amériques* was finished, he dedicated it: *To my unknown friends of 1921.*

So, my mind at ease, in March I sailed for Paris on the *Rochambeau*, the ship that had brought Varèse to New York.

In his first letter, remembering certain moments of extreme irritability, contrite as usual, he wrote:

> 4 P.M. Thursday, 10 March 1921
>
> *Petite Gosse,* I wanted to wait till the boat had disappeared but they forced me to leave the pier—I came home my heart heavy and a lump in my throat—realizing that I had sometimes been brusque with you and not always *très gentil*—Forgive me. . . . *Te gobe—Baisers.*

At that time our friend the Italian painter Joseph Stella was living on Fourteenth Street near our apartment. Stella and Varèse were very fond of each other, in spite of occasional breaches in their friendship due to Stella's neurotic susceptibility. He was easily offended, one never knew why, and for months he would sulk. That spring, however, relations were extremely warm and he and Varèse were often together during my absence. Stella was born on the toe of Italy's boot and never got over his peasant superstitions. After a loved brother, who had been one of Caruso's physicians, died, Stella would never mention him by name but always referred to him as *"L'Autre* (the other one)." He was very fat and loved to eat. A gargantuan capacity. At a Greek restaurant on Sixth Avenue near Eighth Street where we often ate together, known unappetizingly as "The Dirty Spoon," Stella once ordered a "family steak." When the waiter, expecting the arrival of the other members, failed to bring it, Stella shouted: "Hurry up! *I* am the family." With no difficulty at all, half a leg of roast lamb would disappear into his enormous belly. For all that, he was as sensitive as a poet and loved poetry, especially the poems of Edgar Allan Poe, which he often read aloud to me. Though he bellowed when he talked, he used to sing in the sweetest, softest tenor, and his favorite song was not, as one might have expected, *O Solo Mio* but *My Wild Irish Rose!*

Stella and Varèse had a kindred—a creative—passion for New York and Stella's five paintings, *The Skyscrapers, White Way, The Port,* a second *White Way,* and *Brooklyn Bridge,* are its magnificent multiple portrait. These are reproduced in a brochure Stella gave me, dedicated *To My Brother, Dr. Antonio Stella* and titled, *New York, Five Oils.* Stella's introduction, called *Brooklyn Bridge, A Page of My Life,* was written during the war years. It is a triumphant paean and a prayer of thanksgiving. Here are a few all-too-brief excerpts.

> During the last years of the war I went to live in Brooklyn, in the most forlorn region of the oceanic city near the bridge. . . . For years I had been waiting for the joy of being capable to leap up to this subject—for BROOKLYN BRIDGE had become an ever growing obsession ever since I had come to America. . . . To render limitless space on which to enact my emotions, I chose the mysterious depth of night. . . . Many nights I stood on the bridge—and in the middle alone—a defenseless prey to the surrounding swarming darkness—crushed by the mountainous black impenetrability of the skyscrapers—here and there lights resembling suspended falls of astral bodies or fantastic splendors of remote rites—shaken by the underground tumult of the trains in perpetual motion like blood in the arteries—at times ringing as alarm in a tempest, the shrill voice of the trolley wires—now and then strange moanings of appeal from tug boats, guessed more than seen, through the infernal recesses below—I felt deeply moved, as if on the threshold of a new religion or in the presence of a new DIVINITY.

And here is a less apocalyptic Stella in a letter I received from him in Paris:

April 4, 1921

Dear Louisiana,

Varèse has made me read your praises of Paris. It couldn't be otherwise—I am sure that your health will put out the best blossoms of this spring—Drink good wine, to my health, too. I am taking good care of Varèse—I force him to go to bed early and eat force and milk morning and evening—In order not to make him cry, I took a pledge to do him the best portrait that ever was silvericed since humanity first began to gasp—I will send you a photo when it will be finished. I hope to meet you over there in a year—I can't tell you how your letter has sharpened my homesickness for dear Paris—You know very well that I love you. Embracing you lovingly and brotherly (I have to write down *brotherly* because Varèse is making eyes)—I wish you a world of joy—Yours, Stelloncino

Of the beautiful silverpoint I have a photograph, not, I regret, the original.

Varèse added a postscript: *"Crapaud*—Leaving for Philadelphia tomorrow about the society . . ."* This trip was for the purpose of consulting Maurice Speiser, a Philadelphia lawyer and Gleizes's brother-in-law. He was one of the ICG's two legal advisers; the other, a little later, was Charles Recht, an attorney concerned with Russian affairs in New York.

Crapaud means "Toad," so this is perhaps the moment to speak of Varèse as an inveterate inventor of odd nicknames. Over the years mine were many, most of them temporary—just popping into Varèse's head, onto his tongue and out, others lasted. In the taxi on our way to the boat, for some reason, he began talking to me about one of his many animal lovers, a toad in his grandfather's garden in Le Villars. "As soon as he saw me," Varèse said, "he would hop toward me and let me pick him up. He had beautiful yellow eyes." So, though I do not have yellow eyes, in his letter, before the memory of his Burgundian pet faded, I became *Crapaud*. In other letters I was *Gobette: gober* means literally "to gulp, to swallow whole"—like an oyster—and from it is derived *"Je te gobe,"* slangily speaking, "I love you" and which Varèse and I preferred as less commonplace. Hence Varèse invention *Gobette.* More lasting was *Pinto* or *Pony* because for a long time I wore my hair in a straight bang which Varèse liked to pat or pull like a pony's forelock; also *Toto,* borrowed from

one of our favorite clowns. The connection? I don't remember. I
have forgotten most of the others, except *Canari* for no reason except that his ear enjoyed its sound, but all these nonsensical pet
names were a nice change from the rather plethoric *darling*s and
*chéri*s of lovers' language.

After a month of endless enchantment in Paris, I went south
to see Varèse's Claude. She was living with her grandmother at
Beausoleil, high above Monte Carlo. As I came from Varèse,
Mme Kauffmann was particularly kind and insisted on my leaving
my hotel and moving into her apartment for the rest of my stay.
Claude at that time was eleven years old and a very pretty little
girl. At first she was quite shy with me, though I am sure she
must have laughed to herself and with her grandmother at the
way I mixed up the sexes of French words (and still do—and no
wonder: they are as confusing as the sexes themselves are today).
She had a keen sense of mockery and was already very critical—I
say "already," for she told me the last time I saw her that it is
still her besetting sin. Being a practicing Catholic, however, she
is luckier than we unbelievers who have other words for our
unpardonable offenses to ourselves, but no father confessor to
shrive us.

Claude and I used to take walks up the broad road to the
gray green olive orchards where the ground was garnished with
the neat little droppings of goats. We talked about her *père
chéri* who, not quite forgotten, was to his small daughter an almost legendary figure thanks to her grandmother's fond praises.

Before leaving for the Midi, I had met Mme de Chabannes,
who, as Armande de Polignac, had been a classmate of Varèse's
at the Schola. She had asked me to come to have lunch with her
and her husband as soon as I returned to Paris and when I wrote
Varèse of her invitation he replied: "Give my love to Alfred de
Chabannes, a jolly good fellow, clean-cut and human. Ask Mme
de Chabannes if she will let us have one of her works for the
ICG. She's a peach of a girl like my Pony."

Of course I saw Juliette and Albert Gleizes, who had returned
to Paris after the war and in their apartment met their friend the
Chilean poet Vicente Huidobro, who became our very dear

friend, too. He gave me some of his poems and, as I liked them, I sent them to Varèse, who chose *La Chanson de Là-haut* as the text for one of his *Offrandes* (originally called *Dedications*), the first of Varèse's works to be played by the International Composers' Guild.

In June, Varèse sent me a letter of introduction to Erik Satie, in July one to Paul Le Flem and told me that Carlos had written to Florent Schmitt and that I should get in touch with him. Of the three interviews I remember only the one with Satie. Memory is unaccountable. It behaves like Indian hemp, which always leaves out parts of whatever it presents to you. Like dreams and drunkenness.

Satie came to see me at the apartment a friend had loaned me on the noisy rue Notre-Dame de Lorette and, warned by Varèse, I had provided a bottle of cognac. He was the image of the person Varèse had described to me: pointed beard, derby hat, stick in one hand, gloves in the other, and the most mischievous eyes I have ever seen, behind crooked pince-nez. He stood his cane in a corner by the door, put his gloves in his hat, and sitting down, placed them on the floor beside his chair. Then he said: *"Oui, oui. Et comment va ce brave garçon?"* He was full of his recent travels. He had gone to Brussels! Then he talked about *Alice in Wonderland,* which he adored. He wanted to make a ballet of it. Would I write it? He was the only Frenchman, he said, who understood English humor (his mother had been English—or Scottish?) and the only composer whose music "understood Alice." I sincerely agreed with him. Besides the *Gymnopédies,* I had heard some of his piano pieces which Carlos played and had read the Satie nonsense that enlivened every page. He promised to have scores sent to Varèse and he did.

Another interview I recall only because of Varèse's reaction to it. I had been told that the person above all others I must see was Roland-Manuel. When I went to see him, though extremely courteous, he was not very helpful. He recommended especially works by *les Six* and suggested that I see their publishers. Varèse wrote: "Darling, don't bother. I don't want them for the ICG." Paris was in that particularly frivolous period of the *Boeuf-sur-le-toit,* which Varèse disliked and called pure "Parisianism," one of the worse adjectives in his vocabulary. However, in the end he programmed Milhaud, Honegger, and Poulenc and became friendly with Milhaud in New York and later with Honegger in Paris; also in New York with Germaine Taillefere—though never with her music.

My meeting with another former friend of Varèse's, Jean Cocteau, upset me. Jean Crotti, whom I had known in New York with Yvonne, his first wife (later he married Susanne Duchamp, Marcel's sister), arranged a luncheon at Prunière's for me to meet Cocteau. But a perfect sole au beurre noir and a splendid Pouilly-Fuissé were spoiled for me when Cocteau said in a tone that to my very partisan ears sounded condescending: "*Un garçon charmant,* Varèse—a charming fellow, Varèse; I remember him going about everywhere with an enormous score under his arm that was perfectly unplayable." In a French that must have been quite incomprehensible to Cocteau because of my stammering zeal, I told him that, quite the contrary, that score (which was certainly *Bourgogne*) had been performed in Berlin in 1910, recommended by Richard Strauss, and that Busoni had got up out of a sickbed to hear it. Varèse wrote in reply to my indignant letter: "Don't worry about people's opinion. As soon as I am in contact with them, they change it," which may sound conceited but was, as I had occasion to observe, simply true.

Pertinent to this remark of Cocteau's, which so incensed me, are the following comments by André Billy, one of the same coterie of prewar literary friends, written after Varèse's death. He writes:

I open the *Figaro Littéraire* and a photo of Edgard Varèse illustrating an article by Claude Rostand elicits from me—But who is that? Straightaway the caption tells me: *Edgar Varèse, prophet and precursor* of the music of today. Oh, but he has aged, Edgard Varèse. . . . Yet it is a fact that to the end he had kept his magnificent leonine head. A real musician's head, and a musician of genius, a head worthy to hang beside that of Berlioz! All that mop of hair! And those eyes! As I contemplate his photograph I finally recover the Varèse of 1910. Yes, it is really the same but with fifty years added. . . . I used to meet him at that time in the neighborhood of the Panthéon at the house of friends where we would gather evenings to drink tea, for in those days we knew nothing of whiskey which would, in any case, have been too dear for us. A little later I took Varèse to Louise Faure-Favier's on the île Saint-Louis and there he got to know Apollinaire and the whole crowd, unless perhaps he had already met them around the Vieux Colombier. . . . The last vision I have of him is that of a Varèse in blue soldier's coat and red trousers: it must have been in 1914 or a little later. He had been drafted. . . . But what I really want to point out is how wary one should be of youthful judgments. I say frankly we did not take Varèse seriously. He had composed a symphony, *Bourgogne,* and seemed unable to go beyond it. He talked about it too much. We used to say that he'd never do anything else. And here is Claude Rostand saluting him as the prophet and precursor of the music of today! Alas, he is dead! It is the photo of a friend of my youth who looks at me across half a century of years.

The doubting Thomases of Varèse's youth were all writers. They were also French and naturally skeptical. Music did not interest them unless it was connected with the theater. As Cocteau said, Varèse was a charming *camarade,* but his ingenuous enthusiasms about his score was to them boring and proof of impotence. None of the musician friends of the young Varèse would have been surprised by Rostand's article.

Of the letters Varèse wrote me that spring and summer I have found only five. There must have been many, for after being convinced that one had gone astray, Varèse began numbering them. One of the five is numbered 12, and another 33. It is a great pity that I let so many vanish, for in them I am sure Varèse wrote in detail on the progress of the ICG and of his score *Amériques,* as he did in his letter of June 22, in an English that was his very own:

> The score is progressing in a magnificent way and if I say so you shall believe it. You know I am not easy satisfied. And after this others—one always better—and full of joy and sun.

Another letter of June 28 was in the same happy vein:

> Gobette—Just to say hello to you and tell you that I have one
> of the most beautiful periods of work I have had in my *putain
> de vie*— . . . for what people think of me, I don't give a
> damn. . . .

And the letter ended:

> Score a little slow it may be, but progressing strong and healthy
> and tremendously rich.

In July he was beginning to copy, still satisfied with his work:

> I enjoy myself working. I think you will be proud of the score—
> Don't tell anyone but you shall see for yourself and judge—I
> am much better than the others and full of sun and life.

Joy, Sun, Health, Life. How Varèse longed to be Zarathustra!
Sadness was the skeleton in his closet. The door was seldom
opened even a crack, even in his depressions. *They* made him
not sad but furious. He hated himself. So I knew when he was, as
he said, "brusque" and *"pas toujours très gentil"* that he was not
angry with me but with himself. Not that I enjoyed his violent
outbursts. Violence unnerves me—an angry voice, a cutting tone,
a look in the eyes . . . If only he could have had physical relief
in blows as in those bloody fights with boys in the streets of
Turin. Instead of being stunned, I should have been violent too.
Then we might have thrown things at each other, like those two
mad, wonderful lovers, Caitlin and Dylan Thomas. There are
worse pains than a black eye, or a bloody nose. Chou Wen-chung
has written of Varèse that he was "a man full of sun," and when
he was, how he radiated! He warmed others and the warmth
was reflected back to him and then he believed the closet was
empty. One might compare his need of conviviality and human
sympathy to a drunkard's need of alcohol. In *Beyond Good and
Evil,* Nietzsche has written:

Men of profound sadness betray themselves when they are
happy: they have a way of embracing happiness as if they wanted
to crush it, suffocate it, out of jealousy.

It was in much the same way that Varèse hugged those hours
that brought him relief, when he forgot that bastard, sadness, he
refused to acknowledge. Like Spinoza, he felt that "sadness is
the passage of man from the greatest to a lesser perfection."
Varèse fought his demon of darkness. He was a fighter, never a
whiner. Unfortunately a great deal of energy was wasted in the
struggle. But he did know at times unqualified happiness in his
work, felt "the proved illusion that his achievement had almost
equaled the greatest of his dream" for which, Conrad also says,
we should not grudge him. Only when he really liked his work
did he really like himself. He would rush upstairs from his
workroom to tell me in an ecstasy of joy: *"Ça marche! Ça marche,
nom de Dieu!"* and rush down again. But more often he had to
fight it too. How many times I heard him say: "And they talk
about the joys of creation!" So it may be imagined how elated I
was when I received that succession of contented letters.

Since sometime in June, Varèse had been writing to me on the
new letterhead of the International Composers' Guild. It bore
the handsome and ingenious seal Witold Gordon had designed;
the address, 120 East 40th Street (that of Moritz Jagendorf,
Varèse's dentist, also a folklorist-lecturer and author of children's
books); Director, Edgar Varèse; Secretary, Mary Reed; and a
heterogeneous Executive Board: Adam Gimbel, Benjamin Glazer,
Moritz Jagendorf, Louise Norton (myself), Charles Recht, Carlos
Salzedo, Mrs. William Shepherd (wife of Professor Shepherd,
historian, then at Columbia), Maurice Speiser, and Joseph Stella.

All this was only a temporary scaffolding. There were many
changes over the years. But, in spite of Mrs. Reis (briefly the
executive secretary), who did not believe in hierarchies, Edgard
Varèse remained its "despot" director during the six years of its
existence, together with his staunch and invaluable lieutenant,
Carlos Salzedo.

Although since April Varèse had been receiving a monthly

allowance of $200, he was still feeling uncertain about the future, for in June he wrote: "I hope next month, *if* my allowance continues, to be able to send you $100. I have saved some money." It was not until late fall that his mind was set at rest after a reassuring talk with Mrs. Force.

I spent the last weeks of my stay in France in Marly-le-Roi with our friend Mad Turban (Madeleine, later married to Pierre Trémois) at an inn opposite its magnificent forest, which still displayed some of the king-made orderly beauty of a royal park with broad grass avenues and trees uncluttered by underbrush. There I received the Manifesto of the ICG. It was a joint effort of Varèse and Salzedo and in true manifesto tradition flew flags and rolled drums:

> The composer is the only one of the creators of today who is denied direct contact with the public. When his work is done he is thrust aside, and the interpreter enters, not to try to understand the composition but impertinently to judge it. Not finding in it any trace of the conventions to which he is accustomed, he banishes it from his programs, denouncing it as incoherent and unintelligible.
>
> In every other field, the creator comes into some form of direct contact with his public. The poet and novelist enjoy the medium of the printed page; the painter and sculptor, the open doors of the gallery; the dramatist, the free scope of a stage. The composer must depend upon an intermediary, the interpreter.
>
> It is true that in response to public demand, our official organizations occasionally place on their programs a new work surrounded by established names. But such a work is carefully chosen from the most timid and anemic of contemporary production, leaving absolutely unheard the composers who represent the true spirit of our time.
>
> Dying is the privilege of the weary. The present day composers refuse to die. They have realized the necessity of banding together and fighting for the right of each individual to secure "fair and free presentation of his work." It is out of such collective will that the International Composers' Guild was born.
>
> The aim of the International Composers' Guild is to centralize the works of the day, to group them in programs intelligently

and organically constructed, and, with the distinguished help of singers and instrumentalists to present these works in such a way as to reveal their fundamental spirit.

The International Composers' Guild refuses to admit any limitation, either of volition or of action.

The International Composers' Guild disapproves of all "isms"; denies the existence of schools; recognizes only the individual.

PART III

The International
Composers' Guild
1921–1928

The man who started something.
W. J. Henderson,
music critic, 1923

WHEN I returned to New York I found Varèse, after
a long hot summer of work, ready for a vacation. *Amériques* was
finished and he had started on his songs. The ICG had been incorporated. Varèse had been offered the Greenwich Village
Theatre on Sheridan Square gratis for the Guild's three Sunday
evening concerts, and he had already collected enough scores from
which to make up his first program. To Salzedo was left the responsibility of finding musicians and fixing dates. So, with
Barney Glazer we went to Nantucket, where a house my mother
had rented for the summer and which she, with my young son,
had just vacated was still available. It was in the town off the

169

cobbled Main Street with its old colonial houses, two of them fine brick mansions which Varèse duly admired, refusing, however, to grant me that the white frame house we were occupying was also admirable. "But" he said, "it's made of wood!" just as if it were nothing but a shed. He did not like "white painted planks," as Henry James put it. For Varèse frame houses were not properly dwellings to be considered aesthetically but only temporary shelters.

In those Arcadian days no automobiles were allowed on the island. A drive across the moors, behind a leisurely nag, to Siasconset on the open ocean was an excursion. There were no weekend trippers. It was pre-Revolution colonial England. A lovely place. The smell of the sea and the charm of the island roused Varèse to the peak of enthusiasm, which in him was very high indeed. He even decided to stay on for another week after Barney and I had to leave—I to attend to arranging our new quarters. Varèse, in spite of the eager hospitality of a handsome and strenuous Boston woman who had enlarged and renovated a boathouse on the harbor which she kept overflowing with guests, became bored. After a few sailing parties, beach parties, dinner parties he longed for New York. And later his remembrance of Nantucket was not of his senses' first delighted response but of intolerable boredom for which, ever after, he blamed the charming island as if it had let him down.

Back in New York we settled in our two one-room apartments in an old brick house on West Eighth Street near the Whitney Club, and Varèse returned to the composition of his songs and to the hard work and the fun of organizing concerts. The fun was mostly mine, the hard work that of the team, Varèse-Salzedo. In the perfect concord of the two friends' division of responsibilities and in the appreciation of each other's talents, the ICG began its pioneering first season.

Now that Varèse had been receiving a monthly allowance from Mrs. Whitney since May and was assured by Mrs. Force that it would continue, he felt rich and, as my income did not exceed his, with all male prerogatives preserved intact, we got married at City Hall. Afterward to Carlos's apartment on Riverside Drive, where Mimine Salzedo gave us a "wedding breakfast" prepared by her devoted Janet with the Salzedo collie dog, Flux, barking congratulations. Then Varèse gave up his room, moved upstairs to my larger skylight studio and, with City Hall's sanction, we openly cohabited.

To obviate the ticket tax, the Guild had been incorporated as a nonprofit membership society, admission to the concerts by subscription only. All of us folding, stuffing, stamping, and licking, we sent out subscription blanks to lists obtained from various friendly sources, enclosing with them, and also distributing to all the city newspapers—which, incredible as it seems today, numbered seven or more, besides several Brooklyn papers—the following announcement:

> The International Composers' Guild will give three concerts during the present season. The first will be held on Sunday evening, February 19, 1922, the remaining two on dates to be fixed in March and April respectively. Admission to these concerts will be by membership card only. Your membership application must be mailed before February 8th in order to entitle you to admission to the first concert.
>
> The first concert will be given with the co-operation of: Greta Torpadie, Louis Gruenberg, André Polah, Carlos Salzedo, and the I.C.G. String Quartet, presenting the following:

Program

1. Three Greek Impressions
     for string quartet   Whithorne
         (The I.C.G. String Quartet)
2. Polychrome (Pieces for Piano)   Gruenberg
3. (a) Songs   Malipiero
         with piano accompaniment
         Greta Torpadie
         Carlos Salzedo
    (b) Three Songs with string quartet   Honegger
         Greta Torpadie and the
         I.C.G. String Quartet
4. Sonata for violin and piano   Goossens
         André Polah and Louis Gruenberg

171

Varèse: A Looking-Glass Diary

The concert was a success, the audience expressing its entire approval in the long sustained applause and the tone of the anxiously awaited reviews the next day was one of encouragement and praise for so brave a venture. There was a party at the Whitney Club after the concert attended by practically the entire audience. The program being as mild as milk (and to unmusical me as boring) provoked none of the reviewers' jests about the music as in 1919. Possibly because the critics of the principal daily papers did not attend, only the friendly *Villager* reviewer and *Musical America*'s critic, who was also a composer. The program was hardly revolutionary, though four of the composers represented what was considered ultramodern music in their respective countries: Malipiero and Casella in Italy, Goossens in England, and Honegger, of *les Six,* in France. The Guild was praised by one critic for its restraint: ". . . it can do valuable work if it does not overdo it. . . ." In later years the consensus was that the Guild and especially the composer Edgard Varèse did overdo it, going far beyond the critics' endurance. For the moment all was approval. *Musical America* had studied the audience and found in it the society's justification:

> The coteries turned out in full force for the opening concert of the International Composers' Guild . . . but also present were musicians of dignified standing who heard the program with interest. The character of the audience was indicative of the significance of the enterprise.

And the Greenwich *Villager,* claiming Varèse for its own, wrote:

> The first performance of our Edgard Varèse's creation, the International Composers' Guild, is a historical event of the first magnitude in the world of music this side of the Atlantic, it was a complete success as to program, execution and management.

I can find nothing in my memory to say about the second concert. The same two critics continued to be encouraging and even benevolent and this time it was the Greenwich *Villager* that offered congratulations on the Guild's moderation:

> We have to be grateful to Messers Varèse and Salzedo and the other artists of the group that they are not bound for sensationalism but are tactfully and slowly leading us into the world of the new musical art.

They could hardly have found the music of Florent Schmitt and Ravel, or any of the others represented on the program, revolutionary. The *Tribune* after mentioning "another unusual concert bristling with first performances," added: "Eva Gauthier wearing an appropriately strange costume was the principal soloist singing four Stravinsky songs." Over the years Eva Gauthier appeared many times at Guild concerts. She had been for some time devoting herself to contemporary composers, especially to a William Watts and she made up for the mediocrity of his music and the limitations of her voice by the flamboyance of her gowns. Someone said that whenever Eva Gauthier sang, anyone bored by the music always had something to divert his eyes.

I come to the third and last concert of the first season—a very different matter both for Varèse and for me. Varèse was to hear music of his performed for the first time since 1910 and I for the very first time ever. My memory has cherished it, or rather the rehearsals, at which my dormant music sensibility was shaken awake. Although for almost two years I had been hearing snatches of chords and phrases on the piano as Varèse worked on *Amériques* and then on his songs, I had no idea of the extraordinary sounds he was creating for instruments. He had often talked to me, as he had been talking for years, of the need for, as he called it, "liberating sound," and for instruments freed from the tempered system. Without my understanding clearly what was meant by the tempered system, he produced in me the conviction of the urgency of his needs. As usual he made me *feel* so intensely that I failed immediately to realize that I did not understand. I think he had this same effect on many people whom he convinced often without—in his impatience—ever bothering about logical sequence, only, you might say, by the authority of temperament.

It was when Salzedo was rehearsing the instrumental part of *La Croix du Sud* without the voice that for the first time I was listening not with my unmusical ears but with my whole body. Always before music had seemed to slither off me as though I had been covered with feathers; this time it penetrated. I do not admit, what many might conclude, that this sudden musical awareness was due to my emotional attachment to Varèse, though, of course, I must have been more keenly attentive and expectant than when I listened passively to other music. But Varèse's music *forced* my attention as it has that of others as unmusical as myself. This moving power came that time from the instruments alone, for later when the voice joined them I resented it—it was in my way just as at the theater one is irritated by a bobbing head in front interfering with one's view of the stage.

La Chanson de Là-haut, on the other hand, enchanted me as a whole. The brooding joyous instruments and Nina Koshetz's gay, sweet voice intensified the mood of Huidobro's lovely little poem of Paris and its bridges. Poem, instruments, and voice were one. Varèse had written it for Nina's voice and she sang it as I have not heard it sung by any other singer.

The audience was vociferously enthusiastic and shouts of *encore* brought Salzedo back to conduct it a second time. Mrs. Force gave a reception at her place on Eighth Street after the concert and there has never been a happier, gayer party. Varèse's pioneering venture had passed the test of the anxious first season.

Musical America summed up the songs: "Fascinating rhythmic color is achieved in a little battalion of percussion in which the composer managed the big cymbal. [I forgot to mention this.] Carlos Salzedo conducted the pieces with skill. There was great enthusiasm and recalls for composer, singer and conductor. The first, *Chanson de Là-haut,* was redemanded." This was the last time for many years that Varèse's music would be greeted with unprotested enthusiasm.

I cannot finish with that first year of the ICG without recording some memories of Nina Koshetz and her husband Sasha

International Composers' Guild 1921–1928

Shubert, with whom Varèse was able, completely and content-edly, to relax. They were my first Russian acquaintances and a very special charming couple at that. Besides, after hearing a great deal about the prima-donna temperament, I now had a chance of witnessing it in action when, Carlos rehearsing with Koshetz Varèse's songs for the first time, they clashed. Carlos, knowing exactly what Varèse wanted, became more and more determined and insistent and Nina more obstreperously obstinate on her right as a great singer to her "interpretation." Stalemate. Varèse came over to me and said: "Take Nina to lunch and let her blow off steam. I can't get away. I'll be able to tackle her when she calms down."

So Nina and I had lunch together at a restaurant around the corner and I listened, as I was supposed to do, to her angry pro-testations. She could not possibly sing if Carlos Salzedo con-ducted. How dare he tell her how to sing Varèse's beautiful songs. "After all . . ." and there followed an impassioned description of every role she had sung in opera, every song in concert, and the applause, and the reviews, and the praise of all the conductors, and so on, and so on. When we got back Varèse was there ready to tackle her. "Let's go over this together, Nina. You are a great artist but also, thank God, unlike most singers, a fine musician (and he meant it). We'll take it from here. . . ." I don't know by what abracadabra of his own Varèse succeeded not only in mak-ing Nina sing the disputed part as he wanted it sung but he made her believe that it was the way she had always intended to sing it. This was not the only time that I saw Varèse, the hot tempered and impatient, exercise an extreme of patience and Machiavel-lian ingenuity in getting his own way at rehearsals and quieting all opposition. It must have been the Italian in him. When Carlos came in, Nina turned to him triumphantly; "You see, Varèse agrees with me!" followed by a peal of that joyous laugh of hers, as liquid as a gurgling brook.

Nina's was not a powerful voice but so fresh, so tender with the sensuality of a five-year-old child. It had a quality heard in some untrained voices that usually gets trained out of them. She moved Varèse as no other lyric singer ever did and that in spite of what he never forgave in any other singer, a slight vibrato. I know that when Nina sang, *"Je vois tourner la terre et je sonne mon clairon vers toutes les mers,"* Varèse had a lump in his throat. At the final rehearsal after Nina's half-spoken, half-sung, incomparably charming *"Dans ma tête un oiseau chante toute l'année,"* he rushed up to embrace her. "Nina, you sing like an angel," he said and held both her hands, kissing them over and over again.

As for Sasha, he was the most perfect gentleman of czarist Russian tradition, with gallant hand-kissing manners and long white fingers. He was altogether unsuited not to have money. He was helpless. He was a painter. Not having been able to take out of Russia the many canvases he had painted in the Crimea, he now began painting the same pictures from memory! He talked of nothing but the imminent downfall of the Bolsheviks and his return to his beloved Mother Russia. Their household was taken right out of Chekhov. At one time the cook was the wife of a high-ranking Tibetan general and the apartment overflowed with refugee White Russians. It consisted of a floor in a remodeled Riverside Drive mansion of the millionaire period. The entrance door opened into a small dining room between bedroom and living room, with a round table that almost filled it, covered with a lace cloth over pink, an exact replica of one in a scene of Chekhov's *Cherry Orchard,* which I saw when Stanislavski brought his Moscow Art Theater to New York.

Though Varèse and Salzedo were well satisfied with the favorable reception their new society had received and the interest it had aroused, there were many problems to be solved for their second season. They would have to find another hall. The only satisfactory thing about the Greenwich Village Theatre was its gratuitousness. It was too small to accommodate the larger audience which the packed house of the last concert gave them every right to count on; it was too inconveniently far downtown for both subscribers and critics and, as a final musical drawback, it was built over the subway. The friendly Greenwich *Villager* had expressed the hope that "future concerts of the Guild may be given in a less noisy place, where the subway does not rumble so tactlessly during the most poetical pianissimos." Then there was the very urgent need of finding someone who would take over the practical end of the organization, that is, an executive secretary. Louis Gruenberg, the pianist and composer whom Varèse had known in Berlin and who had played something of his own at the first concert, proposed a friend of his, a Mrs. Arthur Reis, who had been managing concerts at the Cooper Union. So Varèse and Salzedo went to see her and she eagerly accepted. Mrs. Reis began by finding an auditorium uptown for the concerts. Her affiliations were many and moneyed. She obtained the Klaw Theater for three Sunday evenings at a very moderate rate, as she tells in her carefully misleading (not to use a less euphemistic word) account of the ICG in her book. The Klaws were friends of hers. She also added other friends to the executive board: Mrs. Alma Wertheim, who was a daughter and sister of the Morganthaus, and Stephen Bourgeois, a picture dealer. She was indefatigable. She took over. The musical guidance of the Guild was to be left exclusively to Varèse and Salzedo. She was a treasure—or so we thought.

Early that summer Varèse heard that Busoni was ill. I think it was from a pupil of Busoni's who had come to New York and who made Varèse so homesick for Berlin that he decided to go there that very summer. He would not only renew his friendship with Busoni but he would stop long enough in Hamburg to see Muck, who was then conductor of the Hamburg Orchestra. As he would not be back until November, he cautioned Carlos to keep an eye on their "new foreign element" now in the innermost circle of the Guild. Already he sensed in his admirable executive secretary, a tendency toward tentacular proliferation.

Late in July of 1932 we sailed for Hamburg, where we stayed with friends for a few days, and Varèse had a long visit with Muck. It must have been an emotional meeting for them both, taking them back to their wonderful Berlin, before the war had separated so many German and French friends. Varèse left after a long good-by embrace at the top of the stairs. Muck watched him going down, and when Varèse turned to wave and call

"Aufwiedersehen," Muck leaned over the banister and said: *"Ach, Varèse, wir kennen uns so lange!"*

In Berlin an old friend of Varèse's, Rita Boetischer, had taken a room for us at a pension. Varèse called Rita Boetischer "Busoni's Rigoletto"; she was slightly hunchbacked and had the privileged role of king's jester. She may also have been his secretary. In any case she was his accomplice, abetting him in his mocking gibes and adding her own malicious witticisms to his. Together they could be quite dreadful and dreaded by the timorous. The first morning as I sipped my café au lait (the milk was extra) I tasted only milk and kept pouring in more coffee. Still no taste of coffee. No wonder—it was not coffee but some lamentable ersatz. I was gradually to become aware of the tragic, the unbelievable poverty of the majority of Germans as they were swamped by the relentless tidal wave of inflation. After trying to eat one of the pension's meals, we gave up and Varèse found a delightful Russian restaurant (not Italian this time) called the Domino, where the Wiener schnitzels were the best I have ever eaten, and a charming young Russian woman sang sentimental Russian songs. We could easily afford to pay for this double set of meals while we stayed at the pension, since the inflation which impoverished the Germans made us rich. Varèse's old friend, Jóska (now married to a charming niece of the brilliant Hungarian violinist Jenő Hubay, Szigeti's teacher) soon found us an apartment of two rooms, kitchen and bath furnished, including linen sheets and silver; the rent was the equivalent of two American dollars a month! It was "modern"; that is, it had radiators, a completely equipped kitchen, and bathroom. Unhappily there was hot water only every two weeks and when autumn turned wintry you had to sit on the radiators to feel any warmth at all. Other apartment houses had hot water once a week, some even twice a week, depending on how much the assembled tenants were able to pay for coal—for it was the tenants who had to keep themselves as warm as they could afford. It became the fashion to bathe around; if you were invited to friends for dinner on the right day you went early for a bath. As we sat shivering in our apartment we envied the lucky people who lived in old houses that still had old-fashioned wood-burning stoves with their gentle pervading warmth and where we would have been independent and could, rich as we were then, buy plenty of wood. The poverty of the Germans was heartbreaking. One day Varèse and I were in a little grocery store on Kurfürstendamm near our apartment when an old lady came in and asked the price of *one* egg. The price was beyond her means and she left without that bit of protein to add to the everlasting diet of cabbage and potatoes. When Rita's mother came to have a light Sunday evening supper with us, probably nothing more than cold cuts, salad, and a bottle of wine, she became violently ill after she had eaten. She was unaccustomed to such a banquet! Rita often ate at Busoni's, but her mother lived on *one* meal brought from the pension where we had been unable to eat for more than a day. Her small income had been wiped out by inflation. There were expensive night places in Berlin at that time with a clientele of rich foreigners including Americans, as well as a horrible young cousin of mine who talked about the gaiety and cheapness of Berlin with a *hah hah* that made me want to kill him, remembering all the misery in Berlin when he was there.

The first time we went to Busoni's on Victoria-Luisenplatz a few days after arriving in Berlin, he was in his dining room drinking milk—doctor's order. One could see that he was not well but still very handsome though rather unkempt, and with his long white hair he looked like Liszt. With him was the composer Bernard van Dieren, who was the most persistent stream-of-words talker I have every encountered. Even Busoni was unable to stem the flow. So leaving Varèse to van Dieren, he turned to me and talked about the young Varèse he had known before the war. I have told how Busoni described Varèse. In addition I find in a notebook among scattered notes about our stay in Berlin, the following: "Today B. talked about V. again and became almost lyrical: 'Je me rappelle un jour de pluie. Je le voyais qui passait dans la rue; il était pâle, il était beau, il courrait dans la pluie." As soon as van Dieren left, Busoni turned to Varèse questioning him about his music, his activities. Eagerly Varèse began to talk about the ICG and finally, inevitably, with his passion for starting things, suggested that they form a German ICG. Busoni liked the idea. However, he said that he was not well enough to take an active part in such a project but would give Varèse the names of composers and others who would certainly be interested. He also consented to be named president of the society. The result, a German Internationale Komponisten Gilde was founded with a board of directors consisting of: Ferruccio Busoni, president; Heinz Tiessen, vice-president (Tiessen had been one of the founders of the music magazine *Melos*); Alois Hába; Philipp Jarnach; Constantin David, manager; Dr. Fritz Kalischer, treasurer; and Varèse's former pupil Ernst Schoen, secretary. There was also a committee of eleven composers: Alfredo Casella, Bernard van Dieren, Eduard Erdmann, Alois Hába, Paul Hindemith, Philipp Jarnach, Ernst Krenek, Arthur Lourié, Felix Petyrek, Heinz Tiessen, Edgar Varèse.

Of all these men, I remember only the ones who during our stay in Belin became our friends, Casella and Lourié and, of course, Ernst Schoen. Lourié had been a commissar of music in Russia and was Varèse's companion on long midnight walks and talks. Varèse used to question him about Russia with all the passionate interest he felt in the new regime, which held our high hopes at that time. I also remember the composer Heinz Tiessen because he sat beside me at several rehearsals, a palish blond young man who smelled of pound cake.

The concert which took place the evening of November 1 held a disappointment for Varèse. Busoni was not well enough to attend. His *Gesang vom Reigen der Geister* for small ensemble was played; also a string quartet by Hindemith, works by Lourié and van Dieren, and Varèse's *Dédications,* which Koshetz had sung so movingly in New York that spring. In Berlin it was sung by Nora Pissling-Boas, that poor Frau Pissling who had once been the butt of Busoni's punning humor. The audience, which had not been too responsive before, with Varèse's *Dédications,* came alive. Reviewing the concert on November 30, the *Musical*

International Composers' Guild 1921–1928

Courier wrote: "Varèse was enthusiastically applauded by the international audience and achieved the chief success of the evening."

The next concert was announced on the program with works by Jarnach, Ravel, Schoenberg, Tiessen, and Miaskowsky. I don't know how many concerts followed, but I do know that the Berlin branch of the ICG did not last long. The group lacked a leader to hold it together and was superseded by the newly formed International Society of Contemporary Music, a matter, no doubt, of musical politics and personalities.

Henry Mencken, whom Varèse had met in New York, was in Berlin and Varèse invited him to have dinner with us at our little Russian restaurant. When he arrived at our apartment and Varèse introduced him to me, I had a shock. I had imagined him looking like what he was, an intellectual, and at that first glance I thought: But he looks like a butcherboy! I soon found, however, that he had a mind as sharp as a butcher's knife. He and Varèse enjoyed each other, saw mind to mind, especially about democracy, a subject that lasted through several courses. I remember only the tenor of their conversation, but it surely followed Mencken's written thinking in a *Mercury* editorial in which he compared democracy to a cancer and wrote: "The aim of democracy is to destroy, if possible, and if not, then to make ineffective the genetic differences between man and man." I remember that Mencken particularly liked Varèse's quotation of Clemenceau's definition of democracy: *le nivellement par en bas;* that is, the equalization of everyone on the lowest intellectual, artistic, and spiritual level.

There were several American acquaintances in Berlin during our stay: strange, intense, talented Marsden Hartley, one of Stieglitz's painters; Isadora Duncan's sister, Elizabeth, and Eva Gauthier. I met Tzara, the Dadaist poet, for the first time and the cubist sculptor Archipenko, who had opened an art school in Berlin. For a funny reason I remember an afternoon at the Kreislers' apartment, where we had gone for tea or rather, more likely, coffee. We sat with other guests around a table in one corner of the large drawing room—not a low coffee table, as in

181

America, but a sturdy round table with comfortable armchairs drawn up around, a Berlin custom at that time which I found very *gemütlich*. Among the *Kuchen* on the table was a dish of chocolates. I saw Kreisler's hand dart out toward it and another stretching hand pounce down on it. Kreisler had been forbidden chocolates and Mrs. Kreisler was seeing that he obeyed doctor's orders. I was shocked by Mrs. Kreisler's disciplinary gesture in public. When Varèse, determined to reduce a growing paunch, gave up bread he would say to me before we went out to a dinner party: "Please don't let me eat bread tonight." So, if I saw him helping himself to a piece of bread I would say, if I could catch his attention across the table: "Taboo!" Whereupon he would give me a dirty look and stick a piece defiantly in his mouth. The next day blaming me, he would say—with shameless inconsistency—"Why did you *let* me eat bread?" I gave up!

While in Berlin, Varèse took advantage of the exchange to have his enormous score, *Amériques,* copied. And that reminds me of an incident that occurred at customs when we arrived in Hamburg and which made Varèse say to me: "You see, it's still true what I told you about Germany. The serious composer is everywhere respected—not like your country!" Varèse was carrying a large portfolio which contained his score of *Amériques* —the first huge version. The inspector, curt and overbearing in the manner of officialdom the world over, asked: "What's that?" pointing to the portfolio. "Music," Varèse answered. "Whose?" asked the man. "Mine," said Varèse, opening the portfolio that held his manuscript. The inspector looked at the score and then at Varèse, seeing him as a person for the first time. *"You* wrote that? *You* are a composer!" From boorish he became almost servilely respectful and our luggage passed without further questioning.

As soon as we returned to New York in the middle of November, Varèse, as chairman of the ICG, called a meeting and, as naturally as breathing, resumed leadership. This, it was soon to become evident, was resented by Mrs. Reis and her clique, who, during his absence, had assumed that theirs was the power and the glory to come. They began, not yet frankly, but with the determination of pique, working *democratically* to dethrone him.

However, before war was actually declared, the Guild's second season opened at the Klaw Theater on December 18 with a concert that had the honor of being the first to arouse vociferous audience participation, as one might call it. One critic wrote that "the audience was equally divided between the jeerers and cheerers." It should, however, be said that the jeering and cheering were caused by one piece only, Carl Ruggles's *Angels* for six muted trumpets. Though the music may have been too dissonant for the ears of 1922, the hilarity of the audience derived more from sight than sound. Six trumpet players, all extremely stout, as trumpeters are apt to be, marching on in single file and sitting down in a row at the front of the stage in full view of the audience (in an orchestra, the brass section is happily less prominent) and blowing with inflated cheeks into their muted trumpets would have been laughable even if they had been playing a revered classic. If I had not resented the titters for interrupting Carl's music, I should probably have laughed too. Afterward the applause was thunderous and the now grinning trumpeters filed back and played it all over again. There was a wit present who was heard to say that he would have preferred six muted strumpets.

Only one critic, the perceptive Paul Rosenfeld, wrote well of the concert in the *Dial:*

> the fragment of Ruggles' suite is distinguished by the loveliness
> of the sound of the six close dissonant, silversnarling trumpets;
> and by an inner homogeneity.

The rest of the program was mild enough. Honegger's sonata for violin and piano and Ravel's for violin and cello were approved by the critics and were, as they said, superbly played. The songs by Lazare Saminsky and Marius Gaillard were warmly applauded, being histrionically presented with gestures by the spotlighted Mme Georgette Leblanc Maeterlinck, the same Georgette Leblanc who had caused a rupture between Maeterlinck and Debussy when Debussy rejected her as his Mélisande, and she now in New York almost caused another in the peaceful Jane Heap-Margaret Anderson ménage—but that is literary, not musical, gossip.

Just how or exactly when Varèse discovered Carl Ruggles I don't remember, but when he came into our lives he came to stay, together with his handsome, heroic Charlotte. He was a priceless and preposterous addition to the ICG and later when the Guild was splitting in two, the most uncompromising and the most vociferous of Varèse's supporters. There were very few, *perhaps* a handful, of contemporary composers who met his high standards of musical integrity. Schoenberg and Varèse came first. Carl was a man who inspired friendship and his own principle of loyalty to his friends was as remarkable as one peculiar use he made of them when he needed an authority to bolster an argument. To Varèse he would say: "You know what Seeger (or some other eminent friend) says?" To Seeger and others, "Do you know what Varèse says?" Carl had a fund of scatological limericks and bawdy stories which he would tell with a histrionic sense an actor might envy. Then with that characteristic gesture of his hand to his mouth he would laugh with purehearted joy. He also liked to recite poetry, and he, Stella, and Varèse could recite without spoiling the poems for me as the poets themselves mostly do. Carl had a musician's ear and a perfect sense of timing which few poets possess. His caesuras were a joy and his pressures just right. His great love was Walt Whitman. But he also, like Stella, often recited Poe. Surprisingly for anyone with his conversational abandon, Carl had great dignity. He could also pay compliments in the style of a *grand seigneur.* Anyone, that is women, will remember the felicity of his *"My dear,"* when he said: *"My dear,* you are beautiful!" or *"My dear,* your legs are musical." Carl was a master of style whether in profanity, scatology, bawdry, or flattery, even in his special greeting to his best loved male friends: "Jesus Christ, you son of a bitch, I'm glad to see you!" Carl was utterly helpless and completely useless in any practical capacity. He looked dazed if you asked him to hand you a cup of tea and, of course, was no assistance in the affairs of the Guild; in fact he was the most awful gadfly to Varèse at rehearsals. When his music had been rehearsed he would keep following Varèse (beset by innumerable emergencies), saying and repeating, "Wasn't that glorious, Goof! (our one-time nickname for Varèse)"; and Varèse, exasperated, would rejoin, "Yes, yes, Carl—why don't you go over there and talk to Louise?" There were also days when Carl, having nothing to do, would come to the house when Varèse was particularly harassed and would sit for hours needling him with unhelpful criticisms, till one day Varèse's famous temper swept him out of the house: "Get out, Carl, and *stay* out." An hour later the telephone rang. Carl: "This is Carl." Varèse: "Well, what do you want?" Carl: "I told Charlotte what you said to me. And you know what Charlotte said? She said you were right." Impossible after that to stay angry with Carl, so Varèse laughed and said: "All right, Carl, come on over with Charlotte and we'll have a bite to eat here."

Another of Varèse's difficulties with Carl was getting a score out of him in time for a performance. I find this letter from Carl, unfortunately undated:

> The choral work is going slowly, just about a 3rd done. Yes, it's for brass, trpts & Trombones. I think you will hear some new sounds in it. Now for God's sake don't make me promise you when you can have it. We almost wrecked our friendship over that once. And it's not going to occur again if I can help it.

So there was a certain amount of *Strum und Drang* in their friendship, but it was solid and it endured.

I have never heard anyone say that Carl was handsome. But I do. What can you call anyone with that long, beautifully designed, clever nose; those straight-looking, sea-captain, blue, blue eyes (Carl was descended from the masters of New Bedford whaling vessels); and that noble bald head!

Activities that season tended to center around Mrs. Reis's house: the folding, stuffing, licking, stamping, and the meetings (if not at Mrs. Wertheim's) and the after-concert receptions, which Varèse ungratefully called "those delicatessen parties," ostensibly on account of the mounds of mayonnaise which covered chicken salad that he happened not to like, but really because of what he felt as an alien atmosphere. He missed the gatherings at Mrs. Force's or at the Whitney Club of the year before. *For us* something had gone out of the Guild—something for which, lacking an English word, I fall back on that precious overworked *Gemütlichkeit*. I stress "for us," as probably for Mrs. Reis and her followers everything was as cozy as possible.

For the most important première of the second concert, Varèse had planned to give Schoenberg's *Pierrot Lunaire*. Varèse wrote Schoenberg, who first replied with a cable asking the aims of the society. The manifesto was sent him. Then came an indignant and insolent letter: The society calls itself international and has not played a single German; it announces *his Pierrot Lunaire* for a certain date without knowing if he will permit them to perform it; have they an adequate woman speaker, conductor; in Vienna he had 100 rehearsals and a perfect ensemble under his direction; how many rehearsals will they have; have they any idea of the difficulties, the style, the declamation, the tempi, the dynamics . . . and he is supposed to co-operate! and so on, and so on; if they can satisfy him on all these points he will give them his blessing. He ends with the hope that at some other time he will have occasion to be more friendly. (That occasion came many, many years later and in, of all places, Hollywood.) After a further exchange of letters and explanations the rights were obtained and the date of the concert set for January 21, 1923.

As Louis Gruenberg the previous autumn in Berlin had attended rehearsals and the concert conducted by Schoenberg himself and had studied the score, he was chosen to conduct the difficult work. It was still a controversial work in Europe though it had been performed in every important city. Gruenberg soon foresaw that he could not have the work in shape by January 21 and the opening was postponed to February 4. After twenty-two rehearsals, which had been conducted in Mrs. Reis's music room, he still insisted he needed more, but even Mrs. Reis agreed that the concert should not be postponed again. The charming and dauntless Swedish-American singer Greta Torpadie, beloved of "modern" composers for her musical intelligence and complete reliability, even though her voice lacked the beauty of timbre, bravely took on the *Sprechstimme* role of Pierrot.

Mrs. Reis and Miss Mina Lederman—publicity girl for the Guild and later the excellent editor of the magazine *New Music* —bent all their enormous combined energies toward getting advance publicity, and succeeded; also, they arranged an ICG-sponsored preconcert lecture on the work by Carl Engel, at that time chief of the music division of the Library of Congress, with Louis Gruenberg illustrating it on the piano, and Greta Torpadie assisting.

Most critics, respecting Schoenberg's distinguished reputation, did not in general allow themselves really derogatory remarks and gave much space though little praise. Pitts Sanborn was more discerning: ". . . a painstaking performance," he wrote, "of one of the most typical and significant compositions of one of the most important of living composers." The vinegary and honest Mr. Finck of the *Post,* who had walked out during the performance, terminated his uncomplimentary review headed "Musical Tomfooleries": "A queer little bubble on this planet is this 'futurist' gang. Judging by the size of the audience last night the number is limited."

This brought an indignant rebuttal from the Guild's executive secretary, who, having worked hard to assure a packed house, particularly resented Mr. Finck's summing up. Mrs. Reis wrote:

> The fact that Mr. Finck after hearing exactly one third of a new work chooses to describe the music of Arnold Schoenberg— the renowned scholar and composer—as "musical tomfooleries" is unimportant as an issue but when a hall is sold out and the few vacant seats are already subscribed to, then Mr. Finck is attempting to deceive the public.

Mr. Finck stuck to his guns and wrote a stout rejoinder accusing her, as she had accused him, of garbling and misrepresenting the other critics' remarks. Critics always have the last word and the best part of wisdom is to silence them with silence and let time settle the issue. Who today knows who Mr. Finck was, and is there anyone who does not know who Schoenberg was and is?

To the performance of Greta Torpadie and Louis Gruenberg the reviewers did ample justice and, as many of them also pointed out, "an audience that included Alfredo Casella, Georges Enesco, Darius Milhaud, Willem Mengelberg and Leopold Stokowski could be called distinguished." The concert was a great success and it was just that which fanned the smoldering animosity of the two factions of the Guild, the old and the new, into a cathartic blaze.

Mrs. Reis, with enough energy to split atoms, had been a paragon of executive secretaries. It was a great pity for Varèse that she could not have remained in the role for which she had so great a talent. She stepped out of these prescribed limits only to come to the defense of the composers who were her friends, being bullied by a dictatorial chairman, as she herself has candidly explained:

> As the executive director I tried to remain on the sidelines. I saw, however, the point had been reached where what was regarded as Varèse's domination of the Guild was no longer acceptable to some of his colleagues. I did think that because he was European and rather new as a leader among colleagues of equal artistic and intellectual stature, his attitude might stem from a misunderstanding of the democratic method expected of the chairman of an organization in this country.

This, of course, was the kind of democratic cant Varèse (he would have used a different four-letter word) could not stomach. Mrs. Reis was quite right; Varèse, though as democratic as it is possible to be in his human relations, was an autocrat in all musical matters. As for the ICG, Varèse in his Zeusian pride felt that he had created a full-grown musical offspring that was in no need of wet nurses. Mrs. Reis quotes Salzedo, loyal and very much worried, as saying: "This is Varèse's society; it must belong to him." A very generous statement from the one man who was indispensable to Varèse and the Guild. Carl Ruggles was also Varèse's staunch ally and the most vituperous and disruptive voice at the stormy meetings that followed *Pierrot Lunaire.*

The ostensible reason for the final quarrel, though reason enough, was not the real one. That was simply, as in most divorce cases, a matter of incompatability. If it hadn't been one reason, it would have been another. Mrs. Reis and Gruenberg, supported by Saminsky, Jacobi, and Whithorne, voted for a repetition of Schoenberg's work. Their argument was eminently practical. The Guild needed money and the success of the first performance would, they argued, have aroused sufficient curiosity to insure a second crowded house. However, Varèse referred them to the bylaws of the organization which ruled out repetitions. The purpose of the rule had been to provide the broadest possible view of contemporary music and to give a hearing to as many qualified composers as possible. It was much too early in the life of the Guild to consider changing this rule. Many works of many composers, Varèse insisted, still remained to be heard. Varèse's opposition led to a heated quarrel between him and Gruenberg, with Ruggles on the sidelines crying, "Compromise," "Commercialism," "Catering to the public." To Varèse this question, involving the very *raison d'être* of the Guild, was not one to be argued coolly in parliamentary style (Mrs. Reis was a stickler for parliamentary procedure). Varèse felt too deeply. It seemed to him that the same elements that had disrupted his orchestra might once more defeat his purpose. He was at this point not arguing, he was charging. He wanted a fight—a fight to the finish. It came in the end when Mrs. Reis, even further overstepping her role, took it upon herself to call a meeting to be held at the gallery of her friend Mr. Bourgeois.

Varèse went at once to seek legal advice. I cannot remember which of the Guild's two friendly lawyers, Maurice Speiser or Charles Recht, found the solution in what, as it turned out, was a very lucky oversight on the part of the incorporators of the society. So, whichever lawyer it was had Varèse write a letter to Mrs. Reis in reply to her telegram, the meat of which was contained in the following paragraphs:

Upon further investigation I ascertained that at no time was there a meeting of the incorporators, which should have been done immediately after the filing of the Certificate of Incorporation with the Secretary of State in Albany and with the County Clerk in New York County, as required under the Membership Corporation Law of the State of New York.

That every act done or performed until this day has been entirely unauthorized, unwarranted and unsupported by the Membership Corporation Law, as I am advised. Accordingly, the first step to be taken is to call a meeting of the incorporators of the Guild, which I propose to do, in the very near future. Appropriate By-Laws will then be submitted for adoption, whereby it is contemplated that all the business of the Guild shall be conducted by an Executive Committee, consisting of five to thirteen members, and a Composers' Technical Committee, consisting of about ten members. That the musical policy of the Guild is to be exclusively entrusted in the hands of the Composers who shall, in turn, elect among themselves a Chairman, who shall be known as the Musical Director and who shall be entrusted exclusively with the power to direct the music policy of the Guild.

The administrative side of the Guild, that is to say, the functioning of the Guild, insofar as the procuring of proper places for the giving of concerts, the printing of tickets, and the distribution of same, shall be entrusted to a committee to be appointed for that purpose by the Music Director, whose office shall be equivalent to that of a Chairman or President of any corporation.

Until the appropriate steps are taken, outlining the functions and powers of the various men and women who originated the idea of the Guild, any act contemplated by the Guild as a corporate entity is null and void.

Accordingly, the steps to be taken for the proper organization of the Guild are as herein above outlined. Any other step taken by anybody else is not only without sanction and authority, but, as I am advised, is contrary to the Corporate Membership Laws of the State of New York and therefore null and void. Finally, I most respectfully submit to you the inadvisability of doing anything further by you at the present time, until appropriate steps are taken by those authorized to take them, as specified in the Certificate of Incorporation.

The document from which I have quoted is obviously a rough draft, but whatever the changes may have been in the final version, the message was the same and Mrs. Reis understood it. She threatened Varèse: "What if we start a society of our own?" to which Varèse replied in so many words: "Go ahead, just so you stop interfering in mine."

There was great rejoicing among us. The whip of the law had restored homogeneous peace to the ICG.

Now I must retrace my steps, for between the beginning of the quarrel and the final solution the third concert intervened on March 4 when little *Hyperprism* (that is, very short) caused a very big commotion. There had also been lectures sponsored by the Guild; the first by Casella on those contemporary Italian composers who were trying to get away from Verdi and Puccini: Malipiero, Pizzetti, Castelnuovo-Tedesco, and Casella himself; the other with three speakers, Ludwig Lewisohn on the response of critics and audience to contemporary music, Alfred Swan on Scriabin, and Saminsky on Béla Bartók.

Varèse had begun *Hyperprism* in November after we returned from Germany. He decided to conduct it himself and began rehearsing the percussion section early in April. There were sixteen different instruments, many never before heard in a concert hall, including a siren and a "lion roar," which Varese preferred calling a "string drum." As it would have been impossible to find sixteen professional percussion players willing to give the amount of time required, Varèse appealed to Margaret Heaton, at that time head of the Dalcroze School of Eurhythmics, with the result that her entire school collaborated, each member taking on one or two instruments. In addition Salzedo's wife Mimine played the triangle and tambourine. Carlos, the Guild's Jack-of-all-trades and *master of all,* harpist, pianist, conductor, this time was in the percussion section playing the snare drum, and that other protean musician of the Guild, Julius Mattfeld, I don't remember what other instrument, perhaps the siren.

This last concert of the 1922–23 season marked the first of many tumults aroused by Varèse's music at the Guild's Sunday evenings but was, as I remember, the most tumultuous of all. A broadside on bright orange paper which appeared the next day gives a cartoonlike picture of the event:

[SPECIAL SUPPLEMENT TO MANUSCRIPTS NUMBER 5]

They played a quartet by *Bela Bartok;* someone sang; Marie Miller and Charles Salzedo presented Mr. Salzedo's sonata for harp and piano; someone sang; and Leo Ornstein played beautifully his own sonata and something of Haydn as an encore; and then

EDGAR VARESE

Conducted His "HYPERPRISM" (*First Performance*) For Flute Clarinet 2 Trumpets 3 French Horns 2 Trombones

It All Happened At The Klaw Theatre Sunday Night March 4, 1923

AND PERCUSSION

Played by the Faculty and Pupils of the Dalcroze School of Eurythmics

at the International Composer's Guild

Just as we are going to press so we thought we'd

MENTION IT

He played it once: W I L D   E N T H U S I A S M
A gentleman jumped up on the stage and said:

This is A Serious Work   Those Who Don't Like It

PLEASE GO

A gentleman in the front row orchestra gave him some B A C K   T A L K
Some gentlemen in the G A L L E R Y   SAID:

GET OUT   GET OUT

MR. VARESE Began to repeat "Hyperprism" B U T SOMEONE   L A U G H E D
MR. VARESE TURNED AROUND AND GLARED while the orchestra stopped and waited
SILENCE HAVING BEEN RESTORED   MR. VARESE PERFORMED

"HYPERPRISM" A SECOND TIME

With *Hyperprism* the critics began to enjoy themselves thinking up witty insults. One compared *Hyperprism* to the "burlesque band in the big circus when clowns with broken-down
trombones and kindred instruments set up a discordant din of
grunts and groans."

Another wrote: "Every sound, animal, vegetable and mineral,
was there." And still another spoke of the "two frantic camps
one of which hissed, the other hissed the hissers." Even a whole
week later Mr. Henderson of the *New York Herald* had not yet
got *Hyperprism* out of his hair, so to speak, and going over it
all again, wrote:

> Mr. Varèse's work asked for much industry of trumpets and trom-
> bones. It employs mutes. All these works do. It makes use of
> casual pause and this appears to have been its undoing, for in
> the intervals of silence the ribald ones in the audience began to
> hiss.

Coming back to *Hyperprism* later in his article, Mr. Henderson continued:

> it remained to Edgard Varèse (more power to him) to shake the
> calm of a Sabbath night, to cause peaceful lovers of music to
> scream in agony, to arouse angry emotions, and tempt men to re-
> tire to the back of the theatre and perform tympani concertos
> on each other's faces. . . . The name of Edgard Varèse will go
> down in musical history as the man who started something.

I remember that the policeman in the theater hastened to the
rear to prevent serious casualties and even took two of the most
belligerent off to the station house.

Instead of being depressed by the hissers and the hooters and
the facetious critics Varèse was exhilarated. He now felt sure
that he had a following. There were a few people at least who
were willing to fight for his music. As Varèse always said—and
how many others—there has never been an unrecognized genius.
In that respect, whether Varèse was a genius or not, he followed

the same pattern. From the very beginning there were fanatical partisans, and they kept on turning up unexpectedly for years in odd corners of the globe.

One of the most vigorous applauders in the audience that evening was a visitor from London, Kenneth Curwen, music publisher, and in his luggage when he returned to England was a copy of *Hyperprism*, which J. Curwen & Sons, Ltd. published the following year. A few years later in the *Sackbut* (published by his firm and edited by Ursula Greville) Kenneth wrote a charming tribute to the Guild and to Varèse:

> I believe I have never met a band of musicians working together with quite the spirit of the INT Com Guild. . . .Edgard Varèse, their president, has I believe the strongest sense of direction of any man I have known. He will do any work however invidious if it sets him forward towards the goal he has envisaged and will occupy no position, however prominent, that seems to him to interfere with his progress. . . . I met those who told me Varèse had had his chances and had refused them. I believe a man's career lies in the chances he refuses even more than in those he accepts. . . . He has the crudity of genius in the making, and combines with it the subtlety that is given only to the very sincere. And he is a good cook—which I find is regarded in New York as one of the acid tests of musicianship. . . . And if *Intégrales* is as beautiful as his steak and peppers, it will do. . . . He has his own standards of value, and is accustomed to do his own thinking. And when such a man bases himself not on a contempt for his predecessors, but on encyclopedic knowledge of the past and an intense appreciation of its beauties, it is idle to say, "This is not music."

That summer—a very happy one, Varèse having won the battle of the ICG—Mrs. Force, the artists' *dea ex machina* for Mrs. Whitney, appeared as a kind of juggler, with one hand paying the rent of a painter's apartment so that he and his wife could go to Europe, with the other giving us the key so that we could live free of rent for a few months. The gift of a four-room apartment came, I may truly say, at a "psychological moment."

Since February we had been living in a studio—a large one—but nevertheless just one room, and though it had given us an opportunity of testing our self-control, grit, and stamina, it is a question how long before two nervous breakdowns might have occurred. Comfortably housed, we weathered the tropical heat of a New York summer by going for a couple of weekends to Mahopac, where a friend had a house on the lake. It was more rural then and in a way farther from New York than it is today, for you had to take two trains to get there; the second, reminiscent of a Toonerville Trolley of cartoon fame, was smoky and poky and had the fussy wobble of a conceited octogenarian. In these streamlined days when transportation is impersonal, clean, and smokeless, having given over to the hapless cities the prerogative of choking us to death, one remembers with affection those ridiculous little trains. They had personality.

Though Carlos had been urging us to visit him and Mimine at Seal Harbor on Mount Desert Island in Maine, where he at that time had his school for harpists, Varèse declined. "There are too many musicians," he said. Adjacent Bar Harbor had for several years been the summer resort of a famous colony of musicians, in fact the most brilliant virtuosi of their time: Josef Hofmann, Harold Bauer, Gabrilovitch, Povla Frijsh, Godowsky, both Walter and Frank Damrosch, Kreisler, Stokowski, and Muck spent one summer in the colony. Though Varèse's relations with the many fine performers who played for the Guild was extremely friendly, he felt a resentment toward the great virtuosi who all without exception performed the same works of old masters—and only a limited few of those—over and over again, ignoring completely contemporary composers who wrote in a new idiom, unfamiliar and unpopular. "They don't give a sh—— about music," he said, "only their 'careers'—their 'interpretations.' They still think I'm a circus freak." I, however, by August had had enough of sticky New York heat and longed for the sunny coolness of Maine, so I accepted Carlos's invitation and went to Seal Harbor for a couple of weeks.

Late in 1922, Varèse had sent *Amériques* to Stokowski, who had acknowledged it saying: "I am eager to study it as soon as I am less busy." Not hearing from him, Varèse sometime in the summer wrote pressing him for an opinion, but when by August he had no reply—as usual if an action of his did not start an immediate reaction—Varèse was fuming and wrote to me at Seal Harbor complaining: "Stokowski, the swine, hasn't answered my letter. I don't think I have a chance with him." In his next letter he asked me to tell Carlos: "Stokowski is back but takes good care not to answer my letter. Better not say anything. No use pestering him. I myself will ask Stokowski to return the score—and *merde pour lui.*" On the seventh of September Stokowski wrote Varèse a very nice note explaining that he had not written sooner because he had sailed for Europe two weeks earlier than he had expected, and that he would work on Varèse's score at the earliest possible moment. Then a letter of November 17 brought the final fatal negative answer. Reason: economy and prior commitments. "I fear it will be a long time," Stokowski wrote, "before I shall be able to come to your work. . . . Personally I regret this very deeply but the Committee is not able to give me a free hand in this matter for financial reasons." Varèse immediately made up his mind that "a long time" meant "never." He was wrong. It meant, as it turned out, three years and five months.

I wonder if anyone still remembers Romany Marie. Perhaps her legendary Village fame has been handed down from ours to later generations. For years her restaurant was Varèse's café in New York where, continuing his incorrigible Paris-Berlin café habits, he could go to find concordant spirits or argumentative minds in Marie's friendly ambiance. Marie encouraged her habitués to turn her restaurant into a café by lingering on into the late hours of the night, even into the early hours of morning, in endless talk over her innocuous Turkish coffee (no alcohol). A Rumanian Jew and self-styled gypsy, dressing the part in bright colors and beads and telling fortunes in coffee grounds, Marie was a handsome, dark woman with so deep a voice that when she telephoned I invariably mistook her for a man. She had several particular pets among the habitués whom she distinguished above the rest as *geniuses*. Of these the explorer Stefansson was one, Varèse another. I was cast in the minor role of wife of a pet. She was all human with a love for the expanding vistas of gossip. She was a matchmaker, always hoping for romance between her pets of different sexes. But above all, Marie was kind. She had a big, soft, sentimental heart and she loved artists. Her extraordinary generosity kept many a poor artist alive and working.

Marie moved her place several times over the years, but they were all alike—dark and smoky and you sat on hard benches. There were candles that kept their drippings for the sake of atmosphere. Her husband, Marchand, sometimes mysteriously wore spurs, "to chase the cockroaches," Varèse said. He also told fortunes. He was a chiropractor and almost killed his cat.

In 1924 Marie closed her place (temporarily as it turned out), and on May 10 Bernardine Zold in her column in the *News* wrote:

> One of the most piquant figures among the real characters left to the artists who want back the Village of their work and play is Romany Marie. In a fortnight she will close her café at 39 Christopher St. where for seven years she has fed and clothed and sheltered from entreating families and irate landlords every artist who owned a smock, if she believed in his or her talent. Among the who's-who at Marie's are Edgar Varèse, head of the International Composers' Guild and Charles [*sic*] Ruggles, the modern composer. . . . John Sloan, President of the Independent Artists, comes in daily with Mrs. Sloan, who is called the tiniest wife in New York.

It was mostly painters, writers, and sculptors living in the Village who took advantage of Marie's hospitable café-restaurant. There were also uptown sightseers, but they usually came only for dinner, a fortune, and a stare. I met Theodore Dreiser there with Kira Markam and found him as heavy as his novels, which were in those days highly praised for their "daring." We often ate at Marie's with the Salemes, beautiful Betty and Tony, a sculptor (who was doing a more than life-size nude of physically magnificent Paul Robeson, the black singer and actor who was such a moving Emperor Jones in Eugene O'Neill's play), and with John Sloan, of the so-called ash can school, and his tiny Dolly.

The Sloans also took us to dine at a little French restaurant connected with a pension where his friend John Butler Yeats, father of the poet, lived. It was called Petitpas, the name of the three French sisters who ran it and must be known to all those who have read the life of J. B. Yeats or of John Sloan or, for that matter, of other well-known writers and painters, who often dined there and always sat at Mr. Yeats's table in the garden as we did. Mr. Yeats, a white-bearded patriarchal figure, was a portrait painter, a poet, a philosopher, a critic, and a famous conversationalist. There were several of his friends at his table the evening we met him whose names I have forgotten. Dolly, ever a quick and kindhearted little manager, went to get Varèse at the other side of the table and made him change to her place so that he could talk with her wonderful Mr. Yeats. They were soon absorbed with each other in what Varèse told me was an extremely entertaining conversation, and Mr. Yeats, who was not at all interested in music, told John that Varèse was the only musician he had ever met who could talk about anything besides music and that he knew more about painting than most painters. He died the following February and we were shocked. Remembering his vivid youthfulness and a kind of childlike expectancy, his death at eighty seemed premature. In John Sloan's diary there is an entry which describes his early impression of J. B. Yeats: ". . . a fine unspoiled old gentleman. His vest is slightly spotted; he is real. I went to dinner at his boardinghouse at 29th St. West of 300 plus. Three French women run the home—a good dinner" Was it the spotted vest that made him real, proved that he was not "bourgeois," for John was a zealous socialist and liberal who had been connected with *The Masses* as a cartoonist when it was a magazine dedicated to social causes, women's suffrage, workmen's compensation, safety for miners, and so on, and Dolly, for a while, was its manager and treasurer. John was a friend of its editor, Max Eastman, also of "Big Bill" Haywood, one of the organizers of the Industrial Workers of the World, whose initials, IWW, humorous capitalists said stood for "I Won't Work." John had severed his connection with *The Masses* when it became too politically leftist for his socialist liberalism. He painted a very bad portrait of Varèse.

Several years later Gaston Lachaise (first met at Romany Marie's too) also did a head of Varèse—a beautiful likeness, though from one angle almost too faunlike to be the Varèse of those strenuous, stirring, indefatigable years. Did Lachaise sense the inner solitary Varèse, leaner than the exuberant extrovert. Or perhaps, that being the summer of 1927 when Varèse, suffering again from an old infection (so the doctors said), may really have been as leanly handsome as Lachaise's portrait. Varèse must have had chameleon blood. When in 1930, Georgette Lupasco, wife of Stephane Lupasco, Rumanian philosopher, asked Varèse to sit for her, she soon gave up in despair: "One day you come to me with a long face, next day it is short and broad." Years later Murabito's meditative head of Varèse was criticized by many of our friends for not being rugged and forceful enough, to which Murabito might have replied, what he said to us at the time, that he could do half a dozen heads of Varèse each different and each one like him. So no painting or sculpture could have been true to everybody's Varèse, and not many photographs either. The photographs that are the nearest to the living Varèse are those by Thomas Bouchard, whom Varèse called "the poet of photographers." All those taken by commercial photographers for newspapers or magazines are more severe than Varèse really was. He had a sovereign contempt for the professional smiling politicians, so that often in his photographs he seems to be saying: "Just try to make me smile if you can."

Romany Marie loved to bring her great men together. So when she introduced Edgard Varèse and Georges Ivanovitch Gourdjieff to each other, she stood beaming over them expectantly. This time she was disappointed. Varèse took an instant dislike to this conceited, posturing man. *"Quel m'as-tu-vu!* What a ham!" Varèse said. And I have read since that Gourdjieff did indeed admittedly take on roles, which he would change according to the person he was trying to affect. He chose the wrong one with Varèse. Gourdjieff reciprocated Varèse's aversion.

Gourdjieff had a school in Fontainebleau, which he called "Institute for the Harmonious Development of Man." His system of instruction was based on esoteric Oriental philosophies and religions with a salutary emphasis on physical co-ordination and control. He saw himself as an irresistible guru. He was probably not as phony as he seemed to Varèse—only vain. We attended a demonstration he gave at the Neighborhood Theatre on Grand Street—I think it was in 1924—and in spite of Varèse's dislike of the man, he found the ritualistic exercises, expertly performed by Gourdjieff's pupils in leotards, beautiful, and more stimulating than any Russian ballet or modern dance. Gourdjieff's pupils had certainly profited physically from his teachings and perhaps also spiritually enjoyed scrubbing his floors and planting his cabbages for the good of their souls. After the exercises Gourdjieff sat in the audience and "transmitted" numbers submitted to him in writing by members of the audience to his pupils on the stage. Invariably the numbers were given back to him quickly and correctly. Was it one of his "tricks" or "half tricks," as he called some of his maneuverings; or was it "supernatural," as he called others? It was not, he said, mental telepathy so it must have been the magic of harmonious man. The miracle is how anyone could have endured the man. Evidently he exercised his hypnotic powers more successfully over his pupils than over Varèse. One of the most ardent was Margaret Anderson, the clever, charming editor of the *Little Review,* one of the first (or was it the first?) of the intellectual little magazines in this country. In it appeared, in installments, James Joyce's *Ulysses* even before gallant and intrepid Sylvia Beach published it entire in Paris. Uspenski, whose *Tertium Organum* was for a while the book of the hour, a book of revelation and a best seller among intellectuals, after he had met Gourdjieff in Moscow became interested in the principles on which Gourdjieff's teachings were based, systematized them, and helped him found his Institute.

In those days it was not unusual for painters and poets to make the rounds of the Village hawking their wares. One evening a girl came in to Marie's selling her poems. As she was very attractive, Varèse held her in conversation over a cup of Marie's fortunetelling coffee, which failed, however, to reveal her identity or the true author of the poems. They were by Henry Miller and she was his wife, June. If you like, you may meet them both together, with all their intimate intricacies, analytically unraveled by Anaïs Nin, with her habitual skill, in the first volume of her prodigious *Journal.*

At Marie's, Angna Enters, at the very beginning of her career as a mime, or rather before it had begun, would ask Varèse's advice about her project and talk to him about her problems. Varèse used to say: "Why should girls always take me for their Father Confessor?" He was wondering, not complaining.

Occasionally Georgia O'Keeffe, looking claustral in her long black cape, would come in with Stieglitz. It was at Marie's too that "Bucky" (as he was habitually called) Fuller showed us plans for his Dymaxion house turning on its pole to meet the sun, his first "dwelling machine." Since those days when his projects provoked indulgent smiles, manifest symbol of the skeptics' superiority to crackpots, Mr. Fuller has been honored by his peers, and his fantastically *practical* geodesic dome has made many of the condescending belittlers change their tune. No longer a crackpot, Buckminster Fuller is now an "inventor of genius." Everyone who is hopelessly bogged down in the morass of political and ecological pessimisms (that is, all of us) should read his lectures, which have been collected under the propitious but premonitory title: *Utopia or Oblivion.* With a big IF, they propose a brighter future to come. Personally I thank my lucky star that old age will exempt me from ever having to live in a Utopia of cities under domes with artificially salubrious atmospheres and skyscrapers as tall as Mount Fuji!

Among Marie's early habitués were also the painters Niles Spencer and Mark Tobey; the sculptor Zorach; and Holger Cahill, who later, when consultant for the Newark Museum of Art, did so much to make contemporary American artists known. In the early thirties, before they were married, Cahill brought Dorothy Miller to Marie's and she in turn at the Museum of Modern Art, where she was Curator of Collections for over thirty years, organized exhibitions of the painters Niles Spencer, Noguchi, and Gorky, all of them first met at Romany Marie's.

Sometimes hard benches, smoke, and too many voices reverberating in those low-ceilinged rooms would drive me home soon after dinner to the quiet and upholstered comfort of our apartment. Later in the evening I might return to Marie's to pick up Varèse for one of our late night rambles in the silent downtown streets or west to the river and its whistles and foghorns.

In the winter we would often go to Walter Arensberg's in the Sixties near Central Park West, where you might meet anyone from poets and painters and scholars to musical comedy dancers and Hollywood stars. One evening in particular I remember because it was the night Walter lost his front teeth. Walter and Lou were out when we arrived but the elevator man said there were others already in the apartment and took us up. We found Isadora Duncan lying on a large couch which two of her strong *cavaliers servants* were carrying nearer to the burning logs in the huge fireplace over which hung Gleizes's "woman with the ether mask," as we called her (now at the Philadelphia Museum of Art, with the rest of Arensberg's collection of modern paintings). The day was some sort of an anniversary for Isadora, perhaps her birthday, so Varèse and one of her young men went out to buy champagne. Isadora drank an amazing quantity during the evening and that had much to do with the subsequent loss of Walter's teeth. Soon our hosts arrived with Marcel and a little later Wallace Stevens, looking more like the businessman he practiced being than the poet he really was, and Charles Sheeler, painter of Pennsylvania barns, and their two wives, followed by, why or from where I don't know, the Dolly sisters, perhaps they were interested in art, for Walter took them through the apartment upstairs and down, showing them his whole collection of modern paintings from Cézanne and Douanier Rousseau to Brancuşi, Braque, Duchamp, and Picasso. That was in the twenties, and the collection, though already large, was small compared to what it became over the years. When we left with Isadora and her attendants, Walter, always the charming host, took us out to the elevator. Ample Isadora, in an excess of affection and with the instability of champagne, threw herself on her (by comparison) frail host and bore him to the tile floor. Isadora was unhurt but Walter lost two front teeth. In compensation his dentist replaced them with much handsomer ones.

Walter's apartment was spacious enough for different groups to form in different rooms and corners but with Lou invariably at the piano, paying attention to no one and no one paying attention to her, playing over some new score, mostly opera, which, having studied singing, she preferred. However, one evening (it was before I knew Varèse) when I had come with Allen, who was, as usual, playing chess with Marcel in another room, I found myself, contrary to custom, *hearing* what Lou was playing. I asked her what that extraordinary piece was that sounded to my unmusical ears like an intricate shower of loud rain drops. It was Schoenberg's *Six Piano Pieces*. My ears had pricked up at the sound of my first modern music. They were quite ready for my musical future with Varèse.

We would sometimes have dinner with Stella, now married to his friend Mrs. Waltzer and living in a house on Twenty-fourth Street, west of Ninth Avenue in old Chelsea, which still had the delapidated charm of former gentility. Stella's wife, who catered to her husband's fabulous appetite, used to make mountains of spaghetti covered with rivers of meat sauce. She would place the huge platter in front of Stella and, leaving him to serve, would return to the kitchen to see to her roast. But food-minded Stella, whose painting was more remarkable than his manners, after helping himself to a heaping plateful, would look up with his mouth full and, waving his fork, inquire: "Why don't you eat? EAT! EAT! It's good." Stella had a dog as fat as himself whom he called "Fat Darling" because he was both. Fat Darling always sat by Stella's chair and never begged because he didn't have to. Stella enjoyed stuffing him with choice morsels, as he stuffed himself. Varèse used to tell how one day, arriving at Stella's, he found him in high spirits. He had spent the morning at the aquarium, where he often went to gloat over the gorgeous colors of the tropical fish. He pointed to the fish he had been painting. "Look," he said, "you know what I did?" and he chuckled. "I changed all his colors!" He had played a good joke on the fish. Stella's wife had a young daughter of an unusual beauty who gave Stella many hours of aesthetic joy painting her surrounded by strange flora. Stella had a taste for exotic and erotic-looking flowers.

Early in September Varèse wrote to Arthur Judson, the manager of the Philadelphia Orchestra:

> We are planning to give Stravinsky's "Renard" at our first concert this season (a Sunday evening in December before Christmas). We should like very much to have the collaboration of Mr. Stokowski. Will you kindly transmit our request to him and ask him if he would be willing to conduct the above mentioned work?

Judson replied on the tenth that Stokowski was very much interested, provided the Guild should engage the Philadelphia Orchestra men.

Like Schoenberg, Stravinsky had been reluctant to give his approval of a performance of *Renard* by the ICG; but unlike Schoenberg's lordly letter to Varèse, Stravinsky's reply (June 17, 1923) to Salzedo's request, though discouraging, was courteous. He pointed out the special requirements of *Renard*, particularly that of a conductor familiar with his music after *Le Sacre*, and the only conductor, he said, who really understood his music was Ansermet. The letter ends: "I regret if my letter discourages you but I prefer not to have *Renard* played at all rather than to have it done under any conditions but those that would insure success."

Stravinsky had been "deeply disappointed," as he has written in his *Autobiography*, by the performance of *Renard* the year before by the Russian Ballet at the Paris Opera. However, permission was obtained and *Renard* performed by the ICG with hilarious success.

About the middle of October, invited by Stokowski, Varèse

went to see him at his house in St. Martins, a suburb of Philadelphia, and returned from his visit exultant: Stokowski had been friendly, had been charming, and that famous charm coupled with Stokowski's warmly professed interest in Varèse's score, which he was then studying, melted susceptible Varèse and there were no more angry animal epithets of dashed hopes. He also brought back an official letter from Stokowski stating that he would be happy to conduct *Renard,* since he admired the music and was in complete sympathy with the aims of the ICG. He also asked that the players be chosen from his orchestra to make rehearsing easier for him.

The first of October we moved from our eleemosynary apartment to the top floor of a small house on the corner of Eleventh and Fourth Streets, a surprising juxtaposition which is one of the eccentricities of Greenwich Village streets, having once been cowpaths.

Varèse and Salzedo reorganized the ICG along very simple and impregnable lines. There was a Technical Board made up of four composers and one conductor: Casella, Ruggles, Salzedo, and Walther Straram; and an Advisory Committee of twenty-two composers, European and American, who did no advising (the following year the name was changed to Committee of Composers). Julius Mattfeld, a founding member, continued and would continue for the life of the Guild, as treasurer. Musicologist, author of many books, organist, pianist, and at that time chief of the music division of the public library, Mattfeld, like Varèse and Salzedo, filled in when he was needed, playing stranger instruments than his own organ. Our new executive secretary, Esther Sayles Root (she also wrote music reviews for the *World*) left the Guild after one season and married Franklin P. Adams, or F. P. A., as he was generally called, who was for many years the *World*'s popular columnist of "The Conning Tower."

Although the Technical Board had five members on paper, only three lived permanently in New York, two active, Varèse and Salzedo, and one a militant partisan, Carl Ruggles. Walther Straram, who had recently conducted a festival of "ultramodern" music in Paris, must have been in New York very briefly and Casella, after his visit in the winter of 1923, did not return until 1925. Meanwhile Casella kept in close touch with Varèse by letter, having scores sent to him for the Guild and recounting the progress of his own modern music society in Rome, as in the following note of September 27, 1923:

> Carissimo,
> Malipiero's quartet has been sent to Ricordi where you can have it picked up. Have written to Vienna that you would like a complimentary copy of mine and hope you will receive it shortly. Our society is going along famously. d'Annunzio has joined with enthusiasm, and has baptized the society with the most beautiful name: CORPORAZIONE DELLE NUOVE MUSICHE. How do you like it? Our review is called *La Prora*. Enough for today. I'll write again soon. Thanks for everything. Warmest regards to you and Luisa.

One of the first acts of the new-old ICG—that is, of Varèse, Salzedo, and me—was the composition and distribution to all the papers of disavowal of any connection with a certain new society. Printed on bright red paper and headed, IMPORTANT, it proclaimed:

> The International Composers' Guild, Inc., wishes to make clear to its subscribers and other friends, that it is in no way connected with a society recently formed by six persons who were associated with the Guild during its second season, but whose unsuccessful attempt to impose changes incompatible with the aims of the founders of the Guild led to an inevitable separation.
>
> Although this organization has modeled itself outwardly along identical lines, its purpose and policy are fundamentally opposed to the progressive spirit of the International Guild.
>
> Confusion may arise from the fact that this new society is using the old office of the International Composers' Guild and has announced concerts for the season 1923–24 to be given at the Klaw Theater, which housed the Guild concerts last season.
>
> Moreover as it has apparently made use of the Guild's list of subscribers and mailing list, we ask all those who have heretofore shown their interest in our movement to carefully distin-

guish between this organization and the International Composers' Guild.

We also sent out a leaflet announcing the Guild's third season, 1923–24, giving its new address at 8 West Eighth Street, Mrs. Force having offered Varèse space in the Whitney Studio Club for its office. It listed the new Technical Board, the Advisory Committee, the names of the thirty-eight composers whose works the Guild had performed during its first two seasons, and it reaffirmed its policy of giving only the newest music.

Now that the third season of the International Composers' Guild was about to begin, its original pilot and copilot were more determined than ever to fly their passengers, willing or unwilling, musically all the way to the back of the moon. They had lost a competent stewardess but were willing and thankful to put up with a lesser one who would keep out of their cockpit. In other words the flight had been exhilarating and the schism was looked upon, at least by Varèse, as a complete triumph.

I began amusing myself writing my first program note—at the request, I should add as vindication, of two eminent musicians, Carlos Salzedo and Edgard Varèse, who should have known better. It was a case of fools rushing in. However, it did not need a musicologist to write the story of Stravinsky's *Renard,* which in concert form was to be the meat course of the first concert of the season. I also gave the Guild a slogan: NEW EARS FOR NEW MUSIC AND NEW MUSIC FOR NEW EARS, which I felt confident would make clear to recalcitrant listeners what was expected of them. Carlos and Varèse liked it too. In addition I chose, as epigraph for my program note, a quotation I had come across from Schopenhauer: "Art is ever on the quest, a quest and a divine adventure." I had not yet learned how indifferent musical people at concerts are to literary tidbits. That didn't matter anyway and it was all fun for me. I had begun helping Carlos in various capacities with his *Eolian Review,* which, though it had started as a magazine for harpists, became, after Salzedo's connection with the Guild, more and more a vehicle for the new music. I acquired an editorial name, John Perdrix (origin unremembered), who wrote a rubric called "Short Cuts" and edited articles. As soon as it was announced that the glamorous leader of the Philadelphia Orchestra would conduct the first concert of the Guild, new subscriptions kept coming in. While Stokowski was rehearsing the instrumental part of *Renard* in Philadelphia, Carlos prepared the four singers, two tenors and two basses (Fox, Cock, Cat, and Goat) in New York. It was not the only time that Carlos prepared in his masterly and modest way a work for Stokowski. His generosity in this respect was admirable. He was a great musician and knew it so well that he took it for granted and knew it much too fundamentally to haggle over how he used his gift, whether unselfishly for the benefit of someone else or more rewardingly to reap public plaudit for himself. And Stokowski knew that when Carlos handed over a work to him he could take it from there with perfect confidence.

It was a lively evening that December 2, 1923, at least after the uncontroversial piano pieces by Hindemith, Lourié, and Béla Bartók, played by Claudio Arrau. But Schoenberg's *Herzgewächse* (for soprano, harp, harmonium, celesta—a musical setting of Maeterlinck's *Feuillage du Cœur*) left no one indifferent and in spite of the protests of almost half the audience and the torture it must have been for the poor soprano, who had an ugly voice but one which could rise—in a way—to the F of the climax, Robert Schmitz, who was conducting, repeated it for the wildly encoring other half.

Lawrence Gilman was the only critic who saw some virtue in the piece and also insulted the jeerers with his usual literary elegance:

> It is curiously felicitous in its evocation of the mood of the poem and the singular combination of instruments (harp, harmonica and cello) weave about it an iridescent web of delicate poignant beauty. . . . There were Boeotians present who released their emotions in an ostinato of scarcely suppressed merriment.

The critic Finck quoted the critic Henderson, who, when his neighbor said that the climax sounded like a cat, rejoined: "A cat wouldn't do *that!*"

The pitch of the concert may be judged from this commentary by the *Times*'s reviewer:

> The success of the entertainment which the International Composers' Guild gave at the Vanderbilt Theatre last night was proved by the fact that at quite an early stage everyone became light-hearted and some became light-headed. Even staid newspaper reviewers had cast care aside before the second part of the program in which Stokowski conducted the music of Stravinsky's burlesque on Russian folk tales, and had been heard joining in the demand for a repetition of Arnold Schoenberg's *Herzgewächse*. When newspaper reviewers call "encore" it is a sure sign that the temperature has been raised above the normal of the ordinary concert room.

Then came *Renard* and the whole audience forgetting their aesthetic differences gave themselves up to complete uncritical enjoyment like children at the circus. In fact, I belive, Stravinsky had said he would like *Renard* to be played in a tent with acrobats and clowns. He called it "a Burlesque to be sung and acted, arranged for the stage from Russian folk tales." To the familiar fox and cock is added a goat.

Stravinsky had both wit and humor; he was a comedian, a clown, an intellectual Charlie Chaplin. He was the only composer who could make listeners laugh like children; not that forced laughter of Wagner and Rossini audiences politely recognizing the composers' intention. Stravinsky's humor seemed to me very Russian, having the gusto and the cruelty of children's with the added consciousness of a cool and clever intelligence. *Renard* like our *Alice* is a classic of nonsense. Too bad we do not have the opportunity of hearing *and* seeing it sometimes.

The last words of *Renard* are spoken:

> And if our story pleased you
> Then pay me what is due me

and everyone concerned that night was royally paid by the uproarious applause that forced a repetition.

A few weeks after the concert a journalist from the *New York*

Times came to interview Varèse about the ICG. In the interview, which was published December 22, the journalist himself comments:

> This lusty young organization has created something of a furore in metropolitan musical circles—indeed some say it has thrown no little sound and fury into a previously harmonious musical atmosphere—and promises to be an important and perhaps noisy factor in the musical life and development of this country. At first, the subject of acrimonious discussion and derisive comment, the Guild is now accepted as a fact and a force that must be reckoned with.

He then quotes Varèse as saying:

> "One wrong impression about our work which I would like to correct is that we are 'experimenting.' Quite the reverse is the case. The compositions played at our concerts, instead of being experiments, are realizations of the composers' dreams and ideals."

Though Varèse spoke as the head of the ICG, his statement had its source in his resentment at his own music having been treated as experimental. There would seem to be a contradiction between the view he expresses here and that in the third season's announcement which stated:

> The International Composers' Guild accepts and proclaims *experiment* as a valid and indispensable artistic principle of all historic periods in which music is at present and that those who oppose this principle serve a dead rather than a living art.

This apparent inconsistency is the result of Varèse's failure to take into consideration the ambivalence of the subject. All inconsistency disappears when one learns that Varèse also said, and many times and in different ways:

> I have always been an experimenter. But my experiments go into the wastepaper basket. I give only finished works to the public.

And:

> I do not write experimental music. My experimenting is done before I write the music. Afterward it is the listener who must experiment.

Still quoting Varèse, the interview continues:

> "There is a lot of absurd talk about there being no form or method in the new music. It is just as much subject to plan and logical development as the old masters: The difference is that rigid conventional rules are done away with, allowing for a free and spontaneous development of ideals in a wider field. The new composers have not abandoned melody. . . . There is a distinct melodic line running through their work. . . . But the line in our case is often vertical and not horizontal. This is what causes confusion and distress to people who have been used to listening to music in the old manner. . . . Wagner was berated as cacophonic in his early days by critics and public just as Stravinsky and Schoenberg are today. . . . Well, the day is coming when the present modernists in music will be found as simple as we now find Schubert and Chopin. It's all in the point of view and in the training of the ear, therefore our slogan, New Ears for New Music and New Music for New Ears."

The next program of the Guild, on January 13, was made up of the works of the four composers of the Technical Board: Salzedo's *Préambule et Jeux* for small ensemble, which Carlos himself conducted; three songs from Ruggles's cycle of seven, *Vox Clamans in Deserto* for voice (Greta Torpadie) and small orchestra, also conducted by Salzedo, Casella's *Five Pieces* for string quartet; Varèse's *Octandre* for seven wind instruments and string double bass, conducted by pianist Robert Schmitz. Schmitz had lately organized the Franco-American Society that later became Pro Musica, with Salzedo as his vice-president and Varèse on the board together with the Metropolitan bass Rothier; the violinist Tinlot; composers Marion Bauer, Vladimir Golschmann and Richard Hammond (of the Hammond organ family) —strange boardfellows for a Varèse. The society, though contemporary, did not aim to be as prophetic as the Guild.

Varèse: A Looking-Glass Diary

The Vanderbilt Theatre was crowded with the usual mixture of pros and cons—many enthusiastic artists and amateurs, the usual professional scoffers, but also several critics in sympathy with the ICG and with Varèse, and many who had become subscribers in order to enjoy the entertainment, if not the music. For instance (I don't know at which concert), one subscriber, Otto Kahn, called an usher and underlining the fire department's injunction printed in the program: "WALK, DON'T RUN," sent it across the hall to a friend.

In this connection I should like to quote a torn fragment of a review—from what paper, by what critic, I do not know. I found it astray in one of the Guild's clipping books, whose disintegrating pages, at a touch, rain down a shower of paper "dandruff."

> we went to the International Composers' Guild. It was interesting and amusing but I don't see why they don't call it a party instead of a concert. While their own numbers were not being played composers and musicians were running up and down the aisles, greeting friends, chatting loudly, clapping one another on the back. But perhaps I am in an old-fogish error in this matter: perhaps handclapping, footsteps, bustle, laughter, and general buzz are the music. This might well be, for Edgard Varèse had a refreshing piece scored for instruments whose sounds were made to imitate buzz-saws, rasps, flat-wheels, bronchial trouble, babies' rattles, and exhaust pipes. Most of the twelve piano studies by Karol Szymanowski I thought were exceedingly [illegible] and E. Robert Schmitz's playing of them seemed to me such mastery as I have seldom heard. I liked too the piece by Carlos Salzedo, Préambule et Jeux and the five pieces for string quartet by Alfredo Casella. During the intermission I talked to Archipenko, the Russian sculptor; Covarrubias, the gifted young Spanish caricaturist; Han Stengle, Varèse, and Dr. Henry K. Marks. Whatever may be said about these modern concerts, they are never tedious or boring.

In spite of the exaggeration, humorous in intent, it gives some notion, though caricatural, of the friendly, informal atmosphere of our Guild concerts which, to a certain extent, made them as popular with the cons as well as the pros. Who doesn't like parties, as the unknown reviewer called them, or at least gaiety rather than solemnity? Art should raise one's spirits and all great art does whether serious or even tragic. Not that the Guild offered nothing but "great" music—quite the contrary, for in spite of my complete loyalty to the purpose of the Guild, I admit, and Varèse admitted, that much of the music was inevitably mediocre and extremely boring. After all, no matter what Varèse said about the music, the concerts were certainly experimental—testing ground for the new music.

The review by the unknown critic also betrays the caliber of most of the criticism. Fatuous and cocksure, with a lack of originality, all the critics chose the same flippant similes from barnyard, zoo, or factory. When Slonimsky in 1951 was collecting such howlers for a book, I sent him many from the Guild clipping book. In a postcard to Varèse he commented on them:

> The samples are marvelous! The comparisons with menageries are not new: Oulibishev wrote that the Scherzo of Beethoven's Fifth was the caterwauling of a demented cat. You are in good company.

But much more important than all this facetiousness was the serious attention given to Varèse's music by a few critics. Because of Winthrop Tryon of the *Christian Science Monitor,* Lawrence Gilman of the *Tribune,* Paul Rosenfeld writing in the *Dial* and the *New Republic,* and an anonymous critic for the *New York Review,* Varèse could shrug off the insulting witticism of the others. Moreover with each new work his music gained new supporters among the listeners.

In the March *Dial* of 1924, after reviewing *Octandre,* Rosenfeld wrote:

> Last month, in this space, we demanded to know who was the man destined to lead the art of music onward from Stravinsky's into fresh virgin realms of sound. One answer came quickly.

The critic of the *New York Review,* after saying of *Octandre:* "It provides us with a decided stimulus and we are able to grasp something of its design and purpose," continued with this encouragement to the Guild:

> One thing is certain; the only way for the enduring to be separated from the ephemeral in "new" music is for as much as possible to be performed and as often as possible. . . . Thus the Guild is justifying its existence through its concerts, and the more it gives and the more largely they are attended, the better it will be for music as a whole.

Varèse was particularly pleased with this comment in an article by his friend and colleague Carlos Chávez:

> Here is the gold of pure music. . . . His technique is the essence of his nature. Varèse creates music, he does not make harmonized melodies or melodious harmonies. He has an all-embracing, sonorous concept which comprises all possible material means—a phenomenon common to all musicians of genius.

The last concert of the season, on February 3, was not sensational and I have no recollection of it. I know from delving that Marya Freund, one of Paris composers' favorite singers, sang songs by Schoenberg, Castelnuovo-Tedesco, and Pizzetti, that there was Malipiero's *2nd String Quartet* on the program, *A Fantasy* by Casella, a sonata for a few instruments by Milhaud, and strange to say, songs by Samuel Barber!

By the spring of 1924 the ICG was notorious enough to have the honor of being spoofed by the youthful Grand Street Follies at the Neighborhood Playhouse. These Follies, much more amusing than the grown-up Broadway ones, were a yearly affair satirizing everything and everybody from themselves to politics, theatrical personalities, and theater critics. William Lea in the *New Leader* wrote:

> One of the most amusing numbers—"the Sinfonica Domestica Triangula, performed for the first time (presumably without rehearsal) by the International Composers' Guild." Lovers of modernized music will rejoice to learn that at least such devices as the hammer and pan, the glass and mixing spoon, the carpet

sweeper and the typewriter have been added to the resources of the symphony orchestra.

We missed it, having sailed two weeks earlier (May 13) for France on the *Suffren*, formerly the *Bismarck*. It was the slowest boat on the ocean—once it took eleven days to go from New York to le Havre (the good old days). "*L'escargot de la mer* (snail of the ocean)" Varèse called it. It was also the steadiest. The water taps were marked *Kalt* and *Warm*, and the smoking room, though a large portrait of France's valiant Suffren hung on the dark paneled walls, had the heavy German coziness of a *Weinstube*. Much of our time was spent in it with shipboard companions, mostly musicians of the Boston Symphony and also Gwen Le Gallienne (sister of the actress Eva Le Gallienne) and the violinist Polah. The most delightful person on the ship was Longy, the well-known clarinetist and father of Renée Longy, who has taught so many exceptional and grateful musicians, Leonard Bernstein for one. Because of his passion for poker (his wife's despair, for he always lost), we saw less of M. Longy than we would have liked. Varèse was in splendid form that trip and there was always laughter around him. His own was really happy—as rich as Rabelais—not forced, not willed as it sometimes was in darker periods. Nietzsche would have loved him as everyone on the ship did. So the *Suffren* joined the *Rochambeau* as one of our pleasure words to be repeated to each other now and then for their mesmeric potential.

It had been over eight years since Varèse had left France and, in spite of all the derogatory things he had said about Paris and Parisianism, I saw that he was very much affected the day he arrived in his native city. Pilgrimages to his old haunts began at once and before leaving Paris there was not a street where he had lived, nor a café nor a bistro once frequented, that I was not shown. Varèse also pointed out Widor's house, where he used to go for extra lessons, and a particular corner of the Luxembourg Gardens favored by himself, Bernouard, and their cronies in their students days.

Varèse: A Looking-Glass Diary

Like so many American artists of one kind or another, we stayed at the Hotel Jacob on the rue Jacob until Varèse found us rather strange quarters for the summer in a large studio on the rue Notre-Dame-des-Champs on the way to and not far from the famous Closerie des Lilas. In the winter it was an art school where Léger was one of the principal teachers. As there were far too many Léger paintings around—most of them Léger at his most indurate and uncompanionable—we put them in a corner of the enormous room with their faces to the wall. There was hardly any furniture, a few chairs, a table, cupboards, and a narrow cot-couch which became Varèse's bed. When Varèse first took me to see the place, with a histrionic gesture he waved his hand toward another smaller room and said: "The royal boudoir for Her Majesty." The room and I were flattered. About as bare as the studio, it was where I bathed in a large round tub until I discovered that the curtain that went only part way up the high windows, sheltering enough from ordinary traffic, did not hide me from the tall lorries that occasionally passed with curious drivers. If not palatial, our summer home was spacious, and if not American-comfortable, it was at least memorable for being the birthplace of *Intégrales*. When a piano was brought in, the studio came alive and Varèsian sounds soon began their work of smashing the atoms of tradition to make new ones.

His work was interrupted by two brief trips. Goossens had invited him to come to London when he conducted *Hyperprism* at a concert of the BBC on July 30. In June, Varèse went to London for a couple of days to talk matters over. This preliminary visit was the occasion of a good deal of curiosity and newspaper comment. Kenneth Curwen had seen to it that the principal critics received scores of *Hyperprism* and a young American journalist Walter Anderson, secretary for a time of the Guild and a fanatic of Varèse's music, also made sure that Varèse would not be ignored. Having been, or planning to be, a publicity agent, he thought that the sensational, bad or good, was good, and believed, as Picasso once said to Varèse, that "it doesn't matter what people say just so they talk about you." It was therefore, in some measure thanks to Walter that everybody knew that *Hyperprism* had caused a near riot in New York. Headlines read: *Noise Wizard Arrives, Shocks for Music Docs, Making Music Snappier.*

It often happened in those years that writers, on meeting Varèse, would express surprise at finding the composer himself very different from what they had been led to expect from his reputation as a wild iconoclast and from the jocular remarks about his compositions. One London interviewer was no exception. Having read such comments, as well as the score of *Hyperprism,* he wrote:

> Thus prepared I anticipated fairly confidently that I should find Edgard Varèse a young man out primarily to attract attention. . . . Instead, however, of the expert publicist, I found myself face to face with a man of culture and refinement, thoughtful and above all undoubtedly in earnest. He seemed to be entirely unaware of the courage involved in the challenging of institutions. . . . Some of us may decide to accept the new music and some will certainly reject it. But I am convinced it will prove easier to damn or praise Edgard Varèse than to ignore him.

An article by Varèse also appeared which, I believe, he had dictated to a reporter of a London paper and was then copied by papers in other cities reached by the BBC radio. In it Varèse briefly reviewed some of his most tenacious musical tenets:

> There has always been a misunderstanding between the composer and his generation. The commonplace explanation of this phenomenon is that the artist is ahead of his time; but this is absurd. The fact is the creative artist is representative in a special way of his own period; and the friction between himself and his contemporaries results from the fact that the masses are by disposition and experience fifty years out of date.

Then inevitably Varèse made his appeal for new mediums that would allow the composer to get away from the limitations imposed by the piano. "Just as the painter can obtain different intensities and gradations of color, the composer could then obtain different vibrations of sound, not necessarily conforming to the traditional half-tone, full-tone, but varying from vibration to vibration."

After speaking of the encouraging response to the concerts of the ICG, he continued: "I am convinced that our audiences do not consist of novelty hunters . . . to use a colloquial expression, *they sit up and take notice.* But after all, people desire to be kept alive just as surely as any real composer desires to prevent them from falling asleep. This is not a comatose age."

He expressed another of his pet ideas that music would be saved only by the purely instinctive listener and the aristocratic intelligentsia but that "there is little to be hoped from the bourgeoisie. The education of this class is almost entirely a matter of memory and at twenty-five they cease to learn and live the remainder of their lives within the limitations of at least a generation behind the times."

He returned to Paris until the twenty-ninth, when he again crossed the channel for the BBC concert broadcast the following day. Goossens had entitled his program, *From Bach to Varèse;* in between there were two hours of music, classical and contemporary—the latter Elgar, Bax, and Stravinsky. As before, the headlines were jocular: *A Cocktail of Sound, Noise by Wireless, Slapstick Music, Pandemonium Broadcast, A New Name for Old Noises.* One critic, referring to the "near riot" in New York, expressed a doubt as to whether, through error, the New York riot was not being broadcast in place of the music itself. Several of the principal critics were out of town and I can only find one serious review, that of Mr. Hadden Squire, who made this valid observation which was really "ahead of the times": "Varèse uses the qualities of certain sounds as the units out of which to build his composition just as an ordinary composer uses notes of a score."

He also sharply rapped the knuckles of his own kind: "The men in the street . . . will understand *Hyperprism* much quicker than the critic who feels done out of a job if one work of art is not an imitation of another work of art."

And a noted London drummer, by name of Wheeler, who played in the BBC broadcast is quoted by an interviewer as having said, "The piece was full of the greatest interest to a percussion player and was written by a man who possessed an extraordinary knowledge of the resources of that department." After all, Varèse was the first composer to give percussion players the status of virtuosi. After reading Mr. Squire's intelligent remarks and Mr. Wheeler's appreciation, Varèse said that it was like coming into civilized company after being mobbed by a lot of mud-throwing guttersnipes. Sure that he was right and his lampooners wrong, he even enjoyed their nonsense.

Varèse returned to Paris much stimulated. Kenneth Curwen and his Ursula (Ursula Greville, a soprano, who came with Kenneth the following autumn to sing at the Guild's first concert of the season), Frederick Laurence (composer and manager of the BBC orchestra), and Goossens saw to it that Varèse was shown all the sights of their historic city. However, though Varèse did appreciate the charm of Old London, it was not the historic monuments that he recalled with the greatest enthusiasm, not the reception given in his honor; it was the London pubs. "The barmaids," he told me with all the warmth of recent remembrance, "are nice, and they are as quick in the uptake as a Paris *voyou*. The English might point to them as a challenge to Villon's claim that *il n'est bon bec que de Paris*"; then he added with amused pleasure: "You know, they all called me 'Deary.' "

Among the many American acquaintances who were in and out of Paris that summer was Mrs. Christian Holmes, who, after Mrs. Whitney, had recently become the second golden pillar of the ICG. Mrs. Force came over to spend a couple of months and, at her request, Varèse had found her a villa pleasantly situated on the river near Fontainebleau with a large garden and a good cook, where a weekend was cut to a night—for Varèse at least—by the insomniac country noises of the tireless tree toads and the matutinal roosters. Stokowski dropped in to see us in our barn of a *pied-à-terre;* did he or didn't he disclose his intention of conducting *Hyperprism* before the end of the year? Probably not, for that I would have remembered. Eugene

Varèse: A Looking-Glass Diary

Jolas came to interview Varèse for the *Chicago Tribune Sunday Magazine*. A few years later, I think it was in 1927, he founded *Transition*, the most interesting and radical review of those years. A friend and disciple of James Joyce, he published segments of *Work in Progress* (*Finnegans Wake*) in each number and also a great deal of Gertrude Stein—for *Transition* had started, I believe, as primarily a linguistic magazine—as well as all the most radical writers and poets (English, American, French, German). There were reproductions of works by modern painters, sculptors, architects, and part of a score of at least one composer, Edgard Varèse. The covers were by artists, since grown famous, such as Miró, Duchamp, Léger, and Stuart Davis.

Intégrales was once more interrupted early in September when Varèse became ill. Albertine and François Bernouard insisted on giving up to us their sunny apartment on the boulevard Saint-Germain where, as François said to Varèse to persuade him: *Ma petite cousine Peau-Rouge* will be able to nurse you more comfortably." Varèse's fever rose alarmingly and we thought it was a bad case of *la grippe* until the doctor who was called in spoke of an inflammation of the prostate, that precious gland that seems to be so much on the male mind. Varèse worried about his for most of his life.

He was soon well again and the last thing he did before leaving Paris the end of September was to buy his first corduroy hunting jacket, the kind worn by all the hunters in France. He had been coveting one for some time, and it was Witold Gordon who found out that they were to be had at La Belle Jardinière and took him there. After that Varèse was never without one and in spite of their ruggedness wore out three or four. The last one which he left behind I keep snugly in a bag in a closet and take out from time to time to feel its soft sturdy texture, sniff the ghost of his good smell and for a second Varèse is back again. He used to threaten to wear it on formal occasions—"and if they don't like it I'll send them my tuxedo."

Back in New York constant and varied activities took us busily and convivially through the rest of the year and the following winter. Varèse and Carlos were occupied with the coming concerts of the Guild, "John Perdrix" helped editorially with *Eolus* (*Eolian Review* renamed), and we were very sociable: parties at the Whitney Club, at Mrs. Force's, luncheons at Mrs. Whitney's studio, musicals at Mrs. Rossin's, and so on, and so on, besides a superabundance of concerts—solo recitals, the Philharmonic Orchestra, the Philadelphia and other visiting orchestras, the Franco-American Society, and, of course, the Guild.

After so much undigested music, suffering so much "melodized boredom" (to quote Miaskowsky after a Rachmaninoff concert), I came to the conclusion that I needed music lessons and naïvely asked Varèse to teach me the arcana of musicmaking so that I could listen more intelligently and suffer less. Varèse said intelligence had nothing to do with it and studying the rudiments of music was pure drudgery which I would never put up with (nor he, though he didn't say so, with the chore of teaching unmusical me the illogical science of scales and all the rest of it). Just listen, he said, be blotting paper, absorb, absorb and don't expect to enjoy all the music poured down your ears. Though he refused to teach me—he taught me. When Varèse talked about the music we had heard together, especially music that had exhilarated him, he said things (if only I could remember his words) that seemed to give my understanding a leap into the mystery. After that my ears seemed to open. I began to hear what I was listening to and even at times to experience that lift of the spirit which is art's holy gift that makes the consolation of myths unnecessary. I have not become a *mélomane* but I am forever grateful to my teacher-in-spite-of-himself for having released in me a responsiveness to the only art that offers a momentary reprieve from gravity and a most blessed relief from the tyranny of words.

It was in that year that Rosenfeld from being a formal acquaintance became a friend and his generous enthusiasms continued to be a contrast and a reproach to the myopic, or I should say, myauric, attitude of the other New York music critics. Friendly Winthrop Tryon, that dear, odd New Englander, was more and more intrigued by Varèse, though still often mystified, and Lawrence Gilman conscientiously attended rehearsals, studying the more difficult scores in advance.

On November 26, Ursula Greville arrived with Kenneth

Curwen for the first concert of the Guild, at which she was to sing. It took place on December 7 at Aeolian Hall. Gilman commented on the change of locale:

> The International Composers' Guild has so materially enlarged its public that it must needs give its concerts this season at Aeolian Hall instead of in the smaller auditorium of the Vanderbilt Theater, where for the last two years its stimulating exhibitions have been held.

To conduct the concert Goossens came down from Rochester, where he was engaged as conductor of their orchestra for half the season. Understandably the concert was quite a British affair—an amicable gesture on the part of Varèse toward his hosts of the previous summer. There was a piece for chamber orchestra by Frederick Laurence, four songs by English composers, including one by Vaughan Williams with accompaniment of two violins and a cello, all chosen by Ursula, and a *Fantasy* for instrumental ensemble composed by Goossens especially for this concert.

More interesting was Ruggles's *Men and Mountains* with an epigraph from Blake, "Great things are done when men and mountains meet." Carl had a taste for epic eloquence. The work is in three short movements: *Men,* "rhapsodic proclamation for horns and orchestra," *Lilacs,* lyrical and lovely for strings, and the majestic *Marching Mountains* for the entire ensemble.

Varèse, having "discovered" Carl, was delighted over his success with the more perceptive critics. Gilman, sometimes quite rhapsodical himself, wrote:

> Mr. Ruggles is well suited to set Blake to music. He is a natural mystic. . . . There is a touch of the apocalyptic, the fabulous about his fantasies. He is the first unicorn to enter American music.

The "unicorn" was overjoyed and so were we, and even more pleased by *Musical America*'s declaration: "Not the most prominent of American composers, he is easily the most significant."

Most of the other critics did not agree. The *Evening Journal* reviewer wrote: "A New Englander with an irrepressible fondness for trumpets and horns," and called the work "childish enough to be embarrassing," going on to damn the whole concert.

Closing the concert was Ravel's bravura piece *Tzigane* for violin and orchestra, which he had recently written for the Hungarian violinist Jelly d'Aranyi. A parody on gypsy-style fiddling.

Ursula Greville was warmly received—"noisily acclaimed," as one critic said—and she and Curwen seemed very well satisfied with her success, and that was very satisfactory to Varèse, too. The audience also gave Goossens an enthusiastic reception at this his first appearance as conductor in New York. One critic called him, "The salon-ist of the modernists," a designation which fitted him wickedly. Charm was Goossens's great asset.

In November, Stokowski performed *Hyperprism* with his orchestra in Philadelphia and Varèse attended a couple of rehearsals. On his return he received this note from Stokowski:

> We found a very good siren from the fire department which we used Friday and I am going to use it again tonight. You are right; it is much better. . . . *Hyperprism* went splendidly, and practically all the audience remained to hear it.

Varèse was now supercharged with enthusiasm for Stokowski and looked forward eagerly to the performance at Carnegie Hall on December 16. I did not. Knowing the strictly circumscribed taste of Stokowski's New York audience—subscribers who had locked their minds and lost the keys—I dreaded the mass jeering, ridicule, and laughter which, at the Guild concerts, were countered and mitigated by the enthusiasm of a majority. At Carnegie Hall, there would not be enough Varèse followers to count. I was wrong. There were plenty and as Olin Downes wrote the next day in the *Times:* "the disciples of the fearsome Varèse were in evidence. . . . They applauded long and loudly while the rest of the audience laughed." Stokowski had played *Hyperprism* between two of the composers Varèse admired most,

Varèse: A Looking-Glass Diary

Berlioz (*Faust*) and Debussy (*Nocturnes*). Even after the resounding volume of a full symphony orchestra, little *Hyperprism* with its seven brasses and woodwinds, its sixteen percussion instruments and its sirens, filled Carnegie Hall and spoke, if only for five minutes, with authority and apology to none.

The reviews were as expected. *Hyperprism* reminded Downes of "election night, a menagerie or two, and a catastrophe in a boiler factory." For Mr. Ernest Newman, "the thing suggested an uproar at a zoo," and Mr. Finck excoriated it not only in his review the next day but again days later when it took him two columns to vent his spleen, summing up: "The lover of art can only declare his faith that the time will come when all these compositions will be swept violently down a steep place into the sea."

Mr. Gilman gave his entire article to *Hyperprism* without a word about the other composers on Stokowski's program, except to apologize for not giving himself time or space to mention them. In part he wrote:

> Now the music of Mr. Edgard Varèse, high priest of the International Composers' Guild, is the pure milk of the word Modernism. Mr. Varèse makes no such disgraceful compromise with euphony as do his more conventional brethren. Hearing Schoenberg's notorious Five Pieces for Orchestra . . . you will remember that Wagner once lived; hearing Casella's "Alta Notte" you will remember that Schoenberg still lives. Hearing Varèse's "Hyperprism" you remember only Varèse. . . . It is lonely, incomparable, unique. . . . For us there is nothing exotic about Mr. Varèse's music, a riotous and zestful playing with timbres, rhythms, sonorities. . . . The audience tittered a bit during the performance . . . but after it was over burst into the heartiest, most spontaneous applause we have ever heard given to an ultramodern work.

Another less kind critic called the applause ironic, but Pitts Sanborn wrote: "It was evident that some of those present were eager to have it repeated."

Sometime later Charles Martin Loeffler, interviewed for *Musical America,* made these curiously contradictory remarks:

I was fortunate enough to hear the Philadelphia Orchestra when they played Varèse's *Hyperprism*. It would be the negation of all the centuries of musical progress to call this music. Nevertheless I seemed to be dreaming of rites in Egyptian temples, of mystic and terrible ceremonies which history does not record. This piece roused in me a sort of subconscious racial memory, something elemental that happened before the beginning of recorded time. It affected me as only the music of the past has affected me.

In January Varèse finished *Intégrales* and sent it to Stokowski, who was to perform it and three other works with picked men from his orchestra at the last concert of the season.

Meantime at the second concert, February 8, conducted by Vladimir Shavitch, two young Latin American composers were heard, one for the first time in New York, the other for the first time anywhere. The first was the Mexican, Carlos Chávez, now internationally well known, who was himself planning to give concerts in Mexico patterned on the ICG and the following October conducted *Octandre* in Mexico City. Reviewing the concert in the *Dial,* Rosenfeld wrote of Chávez's work: ". . . the *Tres Exágonos* of Carlos Chavez, on little Pierrot Lunaire poems by Carlos Pellicer, came like a whiff of Latin-American freshness and gaiety and dry sureness of means. . . ." The other was Acario Cotopos from Chile and vice-consul of the Chilean embassy in New York, who once called forth from Walter Anderson the exclamation, "Wasn't the Guild full of characters!" His *Three Preludes* were from an opera he was going to write, *Philippe l'Arabe,* a personage who became his alter ego, accompanying him everywhere until for us he became another member of the Guild. Of the *Preludes,* Downes wrote: "In the first and second . . . there was perceptible a degree of imagination and impressionistic suggestion which when the composer is more mature and master of his medium may evolve into interesting music." Besides having imagination Cotopos, as round as the *o*'s of his name, was a prodigiously funny mimic, keeping us entertained for hours. He was inventive and made up preposterous personal anecdotes which, with a solemn face, he told strangers for our delectation. I don't know whether he ever "matured" but I hope he never grew out of his sense of play.

Varèse: A Looking-Glass Diary

The curiosity of the program was a piece by Henry Cowell called *Ensemble,* in four parts for a variety of instrumental combinations including two whirring thundersticks, the ancient American Indian instrument which did not live up to its name but, instead, very softly purred. They were evidently hard to manage, for one of them slipped out of Cowell's hand and flew across the stage without doing any damage but causing much laughter in an audience which, in part at least, always came prepared for hilarity.

Salzedo was represented by felicitous musical settings of three Mallarmé poems for voice, harp, and piano—himself at the piano; at the harp his pupil Marie Miller; and voice, of course, Greta Torpadie, who won an enthusiastic personal success by her singing of the second one unaccompanied and was encored. Paul Rosenfeld commented: ". . . the second, *Feuillet d'Album,* rendered as an unsupported patter-song appeared a musical achievement in the veritable sense of the word." There were two piano pieces, a folklorish sonatina by Béla Bartók and one by Casella's friend the Italian Zanotti Bianco, who was the first to speak of Varèse's use of "sound masses in space" in his article on *Amériques* in *The Arts,* the magazine which Forbes Watson edited and which, he, as Lloyd Goodrich, wrote: "with the financial backing of Mrs. Whitney, turned into the country's most influential art magazine." Webern's *Five Pieces* for string quartet affected Rosenfeld as "music less heard than overheard," but I heard them with amazed delight, in the words of Paul Stefan, "glide by as if by magic—the very shadow of a tune." Witold Gordon, who was sitting behind me, leaned over and whispered: "I'd like to put them in the back of my watch."

Another composer played for the first time that evening was William Grant Still, a gifted Negro, well known for his orchestrations of musical reviews. He had been a student at Oberlin and was now studying with Varèse. His score, *Land of Dreams,* won him several adverse criticisms for his having fallen prey to the unorthodox precepts of Edgard Varèse. From an interview which I read many years later, I judge that he repented and repudiated those early deviations from the norm. However, after the concert he wrote Varèse: "That was one of the greatest moments of my life. . . . Through it all I never lost sight of the one who befriended me."

Still gave a dinner at his house in Harlem (wonderful fried chicken) in honor of Varèse and afterward a very large and formal reception with all the women in elaborate evening gowns. It was a very dignified and even solemn occasion. Varèse and I stood together and were introduced individually in an exactly repeated formula to each one of the fifty or more guests. Still, as well as many of his dark guests, had ceremonious and even courtly manners that would have graced any embassy or king's court—the genetic memory of ancestral pride and ritualistic formality.

At the last concert of the Guild's fourth season, March 1, Stokowski conducted four works: Schoenberg's *Serenade,* Satie's *Dances de Piège de Méduse,* Eichheim's *Malay Mosaic,* and *Intégrales.*

Lawrence Gilman was strangely inimical toward Satie and the grudging best he could say was: "He might have written music of substance and value, for he was an imaginative and venturesome harmonist in his younger days. But he preferred to clown his way into sterile old age, content with being the patron saint of adoring youngsters." The very antithesis of Gilman's crabbed view of Satie was that of Olin Downes. After finding Schoenberg's *Serenade* "excessively ugly and tedious," he went on into ecstasies over Satie and his dances: "The very first of the 'rascal's' pieces knocked the involved self-important music of Schoenberg on the head with an effect so astonishing and so felicitous in its devastating impudence that the audience first gasped and then roared." Downes had met Satie the previous summer and I wonder if Satie talked to him about *Alice* as he had talked to me in 1921, for Downes ended his accolade with two lines from the Jabberwocky.

Varèse, for once, wrote his own program note for *Intégrales,* plainly as a protest and in answer to monotonous questionings:

The music is not a story, is not a picture, is not psychological nor a philosophical abstraction. It is quite simply my music. It has definite form which may be apprehended more justly by listening to the music than by rationalizing about it. I repeat, what I have before written, analysis is sterile. To explain by means of it is to decompose, to mutilate the spirit of the work. As to the title of a score it is of no importance. It serves as a convenient means of cataloguing the work. I admit that I get much amusement out of choosing my titles—a sort of parental pastime, like christening a newborn child, very different from the more intense business of begetting. I find no fun in family names. I often borrow from higher mathematics or astronomy only because these sciences stimulate my imagination and give me the impression of movement, of rhythm. For me there is more musical fertility in the contemplation of the stars—preferably through a telescope—and the high poetry of certain mathematical expositions than in the most sublime gossip of human passions. However there are no planets or theorems to be looked for in my music. Music being a special form of thought can, I believe, express nothing but itself.

In a film made to honor Varèse after his death, Messiaen, talking about him with Scherchen, commented—or at least the implication was to the effect that, whereas Varèse loved the city and machine noises he, Messiaen, loved nature and the song of birds. Messiaen confused nature with the countryside of birds and bees. In the first place, Varèse loved, if not their song, the birds themselves and I have even seen him splint a broken wing. Varèse was "a poet of nature—not of landscape," as Santayana said of Lucretius. It was only domesticated nature, *la campagne,* and the "unspoiled" nature of campers and hunters that bored him. Varèse loved nature—the mysterious nature whose secrets scientists with the patience of research doctors and alchemists are forever seeking to discover and which, like his good friend Leonardo, he venerated. Nature in its most magnificent and terribly impersonal aspects moved him passionately— the sky with its speeding planets, its bursting novae, its galaxies and nebulae—the sky out of which come hurricanes as sudden and unaccountable as his own swift furies. Over his table hung a photograph of the eye of a hurricane so like a spiral nebula (spirals, symbol of the never-to-be-reached beyond, studied so intensely by Varèse in the later years of his life for his musical ends). Varèse used to hang all sorts of things over his table—long streamers of paper covered with staves and notes clamped together for future use, photographs—at one time both Muck and Furtwängler were there and always the drawing of Grandpère by Gonzales, sometimes a Christmas card that happened to please him, like Winnie Lansing's painted ones, especially her funny bird and for a long time brilliant ruby, green, and gold tin foil, and later many of the spirals he was always drawing, innumerable odds and ends that changed from time to time; he called it his "laundry line" and felicitously named the photograph of the hurricane eye, *"la rose des vents,"* from Huidobro's poem, *La Chanson de Là-haut.*

Forests cluttered up with trees, high mountains closing one in like a "prison," and lakes that lay unmoving, "dead," among them, all gave him a feeling of apprehension. The sea and the desert, like the sky, were boundless and seemed, like his spirals, endless. Though wind exacerbated his nerves and made him restless, he liked to watch its passage through the trees. I remember one windy day in Eindhoven, standing with him at the window watching a line of tall trees that rose above the low Dutch houses beyond our garden. The wind directed them "like a conductor," Varèse said. Varèse was noting their unmetrical rhythms. I thought of the little boy for whom the wild currents of the Zambezi were music, the young man *listening* to the aurora borealis. The nature that affected Varèse—scientific or apocalyptic—was amalgamated in his mind with the music in them waiting to be crystallized. Meeting Varèse on the ship that took him to the première of *Déserts* in Paris, the Canadian composer Gilles Tremblay remarked: "As for Varèse's sally, I don't like nature, it did not prevent his watching the movement of the waves and commenting on true rhythm and on the splendid chemistry of distilled sea water, the blue, green, white seaway."

And so, by a somewhat roundabout road, I do at last come back to *Intégrales* and the critics at its christening. Lawrence

Gilman this time was not convinced, though he did cautiously say that his "receiving apparatus may have been defective" (as it surely was in regard to Satie) and admitted that "it is something to be able to evolve music that pays tribute to no man, that is willing to go to the devil if it must." Mr. Henderson was facetious: "One hearer felt that he knew why there was an earthquake Saturday. It would have been a fool earthquake that would have come yesterday [Sunday] and brought itself into rivalry with Mr. Varèse's cataclysm." Paul Rosenfeld described it thus:

> The piercing screams, sudden stops, extreme crescendi and diminuendi are his own. . . . Varèse's polyphony is very different from the fundamentally linear polyphony of Stravinsky. The music is built more vertically, moves more in solid sound masses. . . . Even the climaxes do not break the cubism of the form. The most powerful pronouncements only force sound with sudden violences into the air.

Mr. Gilman, in all fairness, ended his review: "But the audience apparently had no doubts, for its applause was so insistent that Mr. Stokowski repeated the work to an audience plainly reluctant to call it a day."

Among the letters Varèse received after *Intégrales* was one from the painter Georgia O'Keeffe, in which she exclaimed about his music: "It is as good as Broadway at night and that is one of my great excitements." It was one of Varèse's, too. But that was when Broadway was still dazzling and literally the "Great White Way," before vulgar colored neon tubes made it dull and drab.

I cannot resist recounting a comically unfortunate episode connected with the performance of *Intégrales,* which, however, had one fortunate result, in that it cured Varèse of his amiable folly of trying to make his friends friends of one another. Mrs. Holmes had intended to give a party for Varèse after the concert but by that time, being in mourning, she asked him if he and I would simply come to supper with two of her most intimate friends, nameless in my memory. Varèse knew that Mrs. Holmes, who had come recently from Cincinnati, where she had been active and prominent in its musical life and an intimate friend of Stokowski, had never forgiven Stokowski for his abrupt departure after breaking (so I am told) his contract with the Cincinnati Orchestra to become the conductor of the Philadelphia Orchestra. Varèse persuaded her to hold out the olive branch by inviting him to her small supper party, where, according to Varèse's plot, they would become friends again. Varèse had not bargained on a maliciously puckish Stokowski, whom he had never encountered since their relations were serious and musical only and, though prankishness was certainly not foreign to Varèse's nature, where music was concerned he was intensely serious. I don't know if what happened was preconcerted, but at any rate Stokowski cavalierly imposed on Mrs. Holmes's helpless hospitality, his friend Arthur (known familiarly as "Arty") Carls, the colorful Philadelphia painter of gorgeous colors. As Varèse and Stokowski could not get away immediately after the concert, it was arranged that Carls should join Mrs. Holmes in her car, where she with her two friends and myself waited for the uninvited guest. He finally arrived and, without the least civil word to his hostess, and with deliberate awkwardness, drew his long legs into the car. He was not drunk but not ice-water sober either. The drive up Fifth Avenue was charged with Mrs. Holmes's silent resentment. That was the first act, brief but portentous. The second began when, Varèse and Stokowski having arrived, we were seated around a gorgeously appointed supper table with much jade in the centerpiece among the flowers, a handsome tablecloth of openwork embroidery, and crystal water goblets and champagne glasses, which had been blown for Mrs. Holmes in Venice. Varèse, on Mrs. Holmes's left, gallant as always on such occasions, immediately raised his glass: "To our hostess," which amiable toast Stokowski, on her right, ignored and interrupted with: "To Varèse." After that the atmosphere grew steadily chillier with Varèse trying unsuccessfully to warm it. After champagne had gone around many times, I heard on my right the musical tinkle of shattering crystal, followed by Carls's: "Good riddance—a damn bad shape." He had broken his champagne glass. Whereupon, unprefaced by an excuse, he proceeded to pronounce a dissertation on form with all the earnestness and eloquence of an incorruptible and alcoholically inspired artist, amorous of his art. He held up his water goblet with its "noble curves," comparing it disparagingly with the champagne glasses. Mrs. Holmes's Venetian glass blowers, ignoring tradition, had given them stiff slanting sides—neither aesthetic nor convivial, as Carls pointed out. He then turned his attention to the tablecloth. "It's full of holes," he said. "But not enough," and began lowering his lighted cigarette. Mrs. Holmes gasped, her friends half rose but already Varèse, again raising his glass, had diverted Carls's attention with a toast: "Long live Art!" he cried, leaving unpronounced the *y* for Arty. Then came dessert and the final act. Abruptly Stokowski left his seat beside Mrs. Holmes and, coming down to Carls at the other end of the table, whispered something in his ear. He returned to Mrs. Holmes and, holding out his hand unsmiling, said they would have to leave to keep another engagement. Then with a summary and the least thankful of thank-yous the two *enfants terribles* departed.

Their engagement was a party at Bob Chanler's—one of his famous or notorious (adjective according to temperament) parties in his double house, two having been thrown together, near Gramercy Park, where bad gin would replace Mrs. Holmes's Veuve Cliquot, and fun, formality. Besides being a painter, Robert W. Chanler was a somewhat blackish sheep of a famous family. He was a big shaggy man and had the biggest bed I have ever seen with the exception of the one Nina Koshetz—being like the queen in St.-John Perse's poem, *parfaitement grasse*—had made for herself in Los Angeles. Another, somewhat embarrassing oddity at parties in Chanler's house was a bathroom without a door. He painted portraits of many of his friends, including Varèse, and in his will directed that at his death they should be given to his various sitters. On his portrait of Varèse, painted in 1927, he left margins which Varèse filled with a list of his scores on one side and on the other a chord from his score *Amériques*—or is it *Arcana?*

Varèse, characteristically overdoing gratitude toward anyone who not only appreciated his music but forwarded it—like an obsessed lover who cannot do enough for anyone who forwards his mistress's career—was always giving presents to Stokowski: a shirt he admired, a scarf, a book of fine color prints of Brueghel's paintings, which Stokowski found "naïve and interesting," adding in his letter: "Thank you for your kind thought in this and so many other kindnesses." Varèse also took a good deal of trouble looking up music for him, or even new players. That winter Varèse thought it would please Stokowski to have him send a present to Sonia, Stokowski's little daughter. As Stokowski was of Polish origin, Varèse asked Franka Gordon to dress a large doll in Polish costume. It was Miss McGinty, Stokowski's secretary, who wrote in Sonia's name to thank Varèse, quoting the little girl's exclamations of delight when she "took the wonderful Polish doll out of the great big box." Some time later we were at a luncheon for the Polish ambassador at Stokowski's house at St. Martins, near Philadelphia. After lunch everyone went up to Stokowski's study and there on his desk was Sonia's doll. To our amazement we overheard Stokowski, quite unconcerned that Varèse, though in another group, might be within earshot, saying as he held up the doll to show the ambassador: "Was it not charming, the people in my family's village sent me this wonderful doll—an authentic costume, is it not?" Too bad that print cannot speak with Stokowski's almost too *dolce* accent. Stokowski delighted in mystifications.

That was the summer we used to go to all the out-of-the-way theaters in New York: Chinese, Italian, Yiddish, with Maurice Speiser, who loved the theater and with Barney Glazer, his brother-in-law. At the Yiddish theater on Second Avenue, founded and directed by the great Jewish actor Maurice Schwartz, we saw the Dybbuk, and because all the actors were blessed with the racial gift of dramatic expression and aided besides by Glazer's whispered translation, we enjoyed a few *Doppelgänger* shivers. Varèse went mostly for sociability, for he never took much interest in plays. He used to say that there was just one moment which was never boring at the theater and that was when the curtain was rising and one felt a thrill of childish anticipation. Afterward we usually went to a Hungarian restaurant to finish the evening with goulash and *czardas*. It was a merry atmosphere to which that summer Varèse failed to respond with his usual zest. He was not well. Many of his friends became concerned. In July he received two warmly solicitous letters—each very characteristic of its author. Paul Rosenfeld wrote from Lake George, where he was staying with Stieglitz and Georgia O'Keeffe:

> Let me tell you how sorry I was to hear from Kreymborg that you have had a bad spring. When I think of your music, and feel the clearness and courage behind it, it acts like strychnine; you can therefore understand that my hope that you are on your feet again has a very personal core.

The other letter was from Stokowski:

> I am distressed to hear you are still not feeling well. I think probably you need a change of scene. You have been in New York all winter. Try to go somewhere in the country . . . and try to forget about everything. Try to play games like a child.

Stokowski was continuously preoccupied with health regimens and often gave Varèse advice. (I once noticed on his piano a package of a new health food.) His care of his own health has paid in an active longevity so that, well on his way to the Biblical fourscore years and ten, he is still the master of an orchestra.

During the winter Varèse had begun complaining of constant backache. By May he was suffering from sleeplessness and was becoming more and more nervous and irritable. He consulted his doctor, who, besides giving him treatments, advised more exercise, suggested handball and swimming at the YMCA and early morning walks in the fresh air. Perhaps New York air was not country fresh even then but not yet poisonous. For a few weeks Varèse conscientiously followed the prescribed regimen, got out of bed before seven every morning—a Spartan act for him to whom morning was for sleeping, night for living— and walked across Brooklyn Bridge. With the hope of getting better he lost some of his apprehension. I used to go with him occasionally, and one of those early morning walks has remained in my memory like an exceptionally vivid dream. As we paused on the bridge to look down at the harbor traffic, back at the misty towers of New York, Varèse's mood suddenly became one of intense exhilaration, which, as usual, at such times by some psychic osmosis passed into me, and I felt a euphoria as enveloping as champagne but with clearer focus, which was Varèse's ebullient talking. What a very great pity that it is my own sensations I so perfectly remember, not Varèse's words at a moment when, uninhibited, his thoughts had peremptory power over them. Pasternak in one of his "glittering phrases" has expressed what I often felt about Varèse, that his "thoughts were like other people's songs." At least that morning on Brooklyn Bridge grace notes were singing around all his words. I suppose one thing he must have talked about was his feeling for New York, its vital, its portentous quality, because I do remember that, pointing toward the skyscrapers, he exclaimed (as he would exclaim many times over the years), *"Ça c'est ma ville*—That is my city!"* Such eloquently unrestrained moments were not common, but even when Varèse was willfully reserved and reticent, one sensed an emotional resonance. You feel it in all his music (unless you are distracted by the furiousness of some of its sonorities or its reputation for scientific coldness). Like Orphic magic, which, in his case, may not have made trees dance but did often charm animals—besides me. Animals felt it, even those fiercely shy city cats like his "Mr. Black" with the dirty white nose who lived in a refuse cellar on MacDougal Street and would come out purring when Varèse called to him in a tone of voice as tender as though the cat had been a bewitched woman he had been in love with. In Santa Fe in 1936 we used to pass a field where there was a smelly goat that Varèse courted until it would trot over to the fence to be stroked. I was really jealous of that stinking goat.

Varèse's spurt of euphoric improvement did not last. For all his exercising and Dr. Johnson's treatments, by August he was so depressed that he was in a perpetual rage. His depressions (have I said this before?) were never brooding or sullen. They

were fierce and furiously resentful. In prostatic despair he decided to go to Paris to consult the doctor who had treated him
the year before. That was in August, and by that time I was
a landlady.

We had been moving from one unsatisfactory apartment to
another and when I heard that a house on the MacDougal-
Sullivan Gardens was for sale I went to see it. If we owned a
house, I thought, we could make our own rent by renting part
of it, as a friend of mine was successfully doing. The house was
on Sullivan Street and had four stories of which the first and
second constituted a duplex which I coveted the moment I
saw it. There was a large common green between the Sullivan
Street and the MacDougal Street houses and each house had its
own small garden. This purely American bourgeois enclave was
surrounded by a purely popular Italian neighborhood, which I
knew Varèse would like. We had enough in our savings account
for the small down payment—the rest on a large mortgage. As
I wanted the house prodigally, I began making my figures dance
to my desire, a way with my economics. Varèse was entirely opposed, not so much through doubt of my optimistic mathematics
but because he was afraid of being rooted to one spot and of
getting entangled in practical matters. I thereupon solemnly
promised that he should never, never even be consulted on any
of the practices and problems of running a house, and that he
should be free at any time to step out into the wide world without a restraining word from me. As a matter of fact, though he
insisted always on calling it "Pinto Palace" or "Toto Palace,"
188 Sullivan Street soon became his own loved anchorage and
by force of personality his humble workroom became something
in the nature of a shrine visited by curious pilgrims. In the end
it was my mother who made it possible to buy the house by taking a second mortgage, which no sensible person would have
done, and her initial disapproval of my marriage and of my
foreign husband having melted into affection for Varèse, before
long she even waived interest and the mortgage was only paid
off some twenty or so years later after her death, when it was
subtracted from my share of the inheritance.

So 188 Sullivan Street became ours and in May we moved in.

Not into the duplex I coveted, for it was still occupied by tenants who did not move out until the end of August. In the midst of preparations to vacate the third floor for incoming tenants and move downstairs, Varèse took passage for Paris. Of course, under the circumstances I could not go with him and Varèse had the satisfaction of saying, "You see what it is to own a house!" The classic I-told-you-so. I saw him go with a heavy heart although I badly needed a vacation from his exhausting moods. In the first letter written on the *Suffren* he wrote of two days of depression: *"un cafard à engueuler le Bon Dieu."* He continued: "But I have decided to get well—tried to work—nothing doing. But in Paris *it will go (ça marchera,* twice underlined). Then, still contrite about his recent fits of ill humor: "My *belle gosse chérie,* I want to tell you how good and sweet you are—but it isn't easy. If *Arcana* goes well, as it must, it will say thanks to you for me—and better, in sonorous trombone farts." He describes the passengers as *"a pack of peaux de fesse"* (more insulting even than asses, being only the skins), especially seventeen girls from Smith College. "I don't know what that college was like in your time but *Bordel de Dieu* (God's brothel) if the intellectual level was no higher than today, you are a formidable genius to have lived in such a milieu and remained what you are. What a pack of *cons*—pretentious and constipated. It's wonderful, education in your country—New England, the backbone of America!"

After staying for a few days with Bernouard in Paris he moved into a little apartment on the ground floor in the house of a friend on the île Saint-Louis and, as île Saint-Louis is one of the dampest spots on earth and a ground floor the dampest, he soon paid for the beauty of his surroundings with a severe attack of rheumatism added to his other pains.

He wrote me in detail of the doctor's diagnosis, which was appalling. Everything inside him, it seemed, was swimming in pus. He is nevertheless optimistic:

> For the last two weeks I've been under treatment. It will be long but cure is guaranteed. They've made a vaccine of my microbes—I've already had four injections—still 8, besides local

treatments. Three doctors are looking after me. But darling, think of it, I'm going to be cured—and above all my poor head —it's already better. I am gay—Arcanes is singing. It will be for you—I am going to work and do my best so you will be pleased with Arcanes.

It is evident what had been worrying him from the following: "The treatments take a great deal of time but I've decided to get well once and for all. . . . I'm glad it's only physical, not *mental. Merde* for the Freuds."
But again he wrote:

Three times a week treatments, terribly painful (drawing pus— installation of silver nitrate) and afterwards it's bed and complete rest. I'm as though paralyzed—and no head for work. It's not so much the pain as the time they take and the torpor that are depressing—two or three days better, then relapse. I've been lucky the abscess broke below, otherwise it would have meant an operation.

However, of his work he spoke more than of his illness: *Arcanes* (as he called it then) was causing him much joy before causing him the usual torments. On October 9 he sent me a few bars of trumpet fanfares with the following explanation of a dream in which he had dreamed them:

The two Fanfares I dreamed—I was on a boat that was turning around and around—in the middle of the ocean—spinning around in great circles. In the distance I could see a light house, very high—and on the top an angel—and the angel was you— a trumpet in each hand. Alternating projectors of different colors: red, green, yellow, blue—and you were playing Fanfare no. 1, trumpet in right hand. Then suddenly the sky became incandescent—blinding—you raised your left hand to your mouth and the Fanfare 2 blared. And the boat kept turning and spinning—and the alternation of projectors and incandescence became more frequent—intensified—and the fanfares more nervous —impatient . . . and then—*Merde*—I woke up. But anyway they will be in *Arcanes*.

Again about *Arcana* on a postcard:

> *Arcanes*—Never have I written music as solid, as joyous—as full
> of force, of life, of sun. *Arcanes* is developing in a new phase—it
> will take long—and won't be ready for February. I am writing
> now only to tell you that I am happy—something that hasn't
> happened to me for a long time. The idea that I'll be seeing you
> soon helps and stimulates me.

But it wasn't soon. The treatments continued into December,
and in November Varèse asks me to explain to Stokowski why
he cannot leave before the ninth of December. Nor had *Arcana*
continued so joyously. On October 29 he wrote that he had destroyed all that he had written and was beginning all over again.

For the coming season of the Guild a concert for large orchestra in Carnegie Hall conducted by Stokowski was being seriously
considered, with Stravinsky's *Les Noces,* something by Béla Bartók, and *Arcana.* That is what Varèse meant when he said that
he would not be ready by February. However, after much discussion for and against, the idea was dropped and Varèse wrote:

> Unfortunately *Arcanes* will be for large orchestra—not as large
> as *Amériques* but large . . . so I won't be played at the Guild—
> and I don't care. What counts is that I work for myself. Make
> Carlos understand—I know his arguments—that there's no dif-
> ference between writing for a small or a large orchestra. One
> isn't played anyway—and besides I'm fed up with the limitations
> of small combinations—1 execution—then finished—A first class
> funeral—I write as I feel—if I'm played or not is of no impor-
> tance—my time will come—so eliminate *Arcanes* and think of
> something to go with *Noces.*

Referring to a Schoenberg work that was being considered for
the program, Varèse had this to say:

> The Schoenberg rights belong to the League *des cons.* . . . Per-
> sonally I don't care. We've given enough Schoenberg. He is inter-
> esting but dead and his quintette which I have just read is worse
> than *Serenade.*

Varèse: A Looking-Glass Diary

Varèse was always of two minds about Schoenberg; he admired him, considered him an important composer, but liked only a few of his works. He once said of him: "Schoenberg liberated music from tonality but it was as though, frightened by so much freedom, he retreated to the refuge of a system." Varèse did not like closed systems: "Beware the codification of systems and, in spite of all the revolutionary slogans, their latent academicism. There is nothing more deplorable than traditionalists of the left."

The great good news that Stokowski had decided to give *Amériques* (recently published by Curwen) with the Philadelphia Orchestra that season made up for the disappointment Varèse had denied but felt over not having anything for the Guild. *"Amériques* played by Stokowski," he wrote, "will be quite enough for me. . . . I have decided absolutely I must compose and I have no more time to lose with the Guild or things like that."

In a letter in November Varèse discussed another new departure planned for the Guild, a concert of old music to be conducted by Stokowski. He wrote:

> Concert of old music—it must be given. I have some elements— very good—I'll bring them back with me—the Lulli. The rest of the program, Gervaise du Terte, Schütz, etc. I think it is very good for our standing—Carlos' and mine—interested above all to further the cause of really great music.

He asked that Julius Mattfeld, the Guild treasurer, send him a check so that he could pay his friend Charles Borell, a musicologist, for copies of old masters which he had made at the Bibliothèque Nationale and at the Conservatoire.

I have no memory of this concert. Was it ever given? The clipping books for the years 1925–26 and 1926–27 have disappeared. All I can say is that such a concert had been announced on the program of the spring concert of 1925 and that Varèse in November was still counting on it. When Stokowski was appealed to, he seemed to remember that he had conducted this concert of old music and that it also included modern works. Or is he simply remembering, as I do, planning for it?

Varèse had the charming habit, whenever he was away, of sending me round-robin postcards signed by any of the friends he happened to be dining with. One of these cards amused me because Varèse had taken my mother (in Paris for a European trip with friends) to dine with his cronies at a little restaurant, popular with them because of its excellent Viret, which I am sure made my mother a little tipsy, or at least melted some of the starch, for they all liked her and said she was a good sport. The signatures besides Varèse's were: *"Ta mère,* Mary Hurvlut (to me unknown), François Bernouard, A. Dunoyer de Segonzac, *Le Petit Pou."*

His Claude *adorée,* now a girl of fifteen, came to see him. She was at that time living somewhere in Burgundy with her mother and the Vieux Colombier troupe. "Claude came to see me for three days," Varèse wrote. "She is growing up very pretty."

During October and November, he saw many musicians— Ravel, Roussel, Ibert, Lourié, Hoérée, Nadia Boulanger, Florent Schmitt. He mentions painters and sculptors, Brancuşi and his old friends Despiau, Derain, de Segonzac. He also says that Kenneth Curwen and Ursula Greville were on their way to Venice for the concerts of the International Society of Contemporary Music. Varèse was furious with Kenneth, who had "just simply mislaid the manuscript of *Intégrales"* and would have forgotten all about it if Varèse had not mentioned it. The London office, he said, was bedlam and Kenneth should pay more attention to his business and less to "the ribbons and the *Sackbut* of Dame Ursula," referring to Kenneth's hobby, designing hats for Ursula, and Ursula's magazine. As usual, Paris was full of visiting American friends. He had dinner with Mrs. Holmes and the architect of her new triplex Fifth Avenue apartment, Edgar Williams, who was, as Varèse wrote: "the brother of the poet Carlos Williams—you know, the nice doctor we met at Rosenfeld's." Varèse saw more of Carlos Williams later and liked him very much, for how could he not have liked a man who once wrote that he was against the kind of "order that cuts off the crab's feelers to make them fit into the box"! When Edgar Williams returned to New York he came to see me, bringing a letter from Varèse with a book *Le Martyre de L'Obèse* by Varèse's *"vieux copain,"* Béraud.

Varèse finally returned to New York early in December, bringing with him a series of vaccines that his Paris physician had had prepared for him with the further recommendation that he should later have a cystoscopic exploration. He went to Dr. Johnson for the injections.

The fifth season of the ICG got underway. The first concert was on December 27 at Aeolian Hall with Fritz Reiner (conductor at that time of the Cincinnati Orchestra) conducting Hindemith's *Kammermusik* for small orchestra, *Kerob-Shal* for voice and a few instruments by Florent Schmitt, *Moments* for piano by Dane Rudhyar, a *Sonata* for violin and double bass by Lourié, and Casella's *Pupazzetti* for small orchestra. It was not an alarming concert and that is all I can remember about it. From the program notes I learn again that Hindemith at twenty-nine was already a bourgeoning master, described in Riemann's *Musiklexikon* as "the freshest and most full-blooded talent among the younger German composers," and Lawrence Gilman wrote of him: "He has achieved the not inconsiderable feat of delighting the conservatives because he does not yield too much to radical clamor and placating the radicals because he is not hopelessly reactionary." A perspicacious remark. Hindemith's *Kammermusik* had been given the summer before by the International Society for Contemporary Music in Venice. As for Florent Schmitt, he was fifty-five years old, very old for the ICG. One can, however, understand his place quite aside from the quality of his music when one reads P. O. Ferroud's tribute to him in the *Revue Musicale* the year before:

> He is ready for any sacrifices when it is a question of helping someone, especially if it is a young composer in whose gift he believes. With Ravel and Delage he is the firmest defender of

242

Satie and Stravinsky . . . more recently he took up cudgels again over Schoenberg's *Five Orchestra Pieces*. He pursues his battle for the new cause in his vigilant chronicle in *La Revue de France.*

The next concert, on January 24, conducted by Goossens, I remember well, not because it enhanced the "cause" of modern music—so important to us at the time—for, excepting perhaps Ruggles's *Portals,* it did not, but, entirely thanks to a phenomenal young Negro soprano, Florence Mills, for whom William Grant Still had written a song with chamber orchestra accompaniment. The previous spring, Still had brought her to the house and had taken us to hear her sing at the Palace, a vaudeville theater. We also went to Harlem to hear and see her in the Negro musical *Black Birds.* We had both been enchanted by her exquisite small voice and her flowerlike loveliness—the very opposite of the usual blues singer. Now over forty years later I cannot hope to describe her with the immediacy of Paul Rosenfeld's perfect evocation, called "Remembering Florence Mills," a chapter of an article, "Thanks to the International Guild," in his book, *By Way of Art.* Here is Florence Mills:

There she stands, with her fragile pigeon-egg skull, swaying gently, and crooning, warbling, speaking in a voice whose like has not been heard. Larger, stronger, richer, mellower voices have sounded off this platform and off the world's other stages. This one is tiny and delicate. But it has an infinitely relaxed, impersonal bird-like quality: one knows there has been no other voice exquisite exactly like it. A pure instrument, this sensuous, but not a human voice at all. In Noah's ark they said such and such a one sang like a bird, one remembers; remembering that the simile has also been revived from time to time in the course of the world. Still, it is probable that at no time has the application been neater. Here is the very thing, the bird sitting up on a little branch in springtime, caroling; with something of smothered anguish in its tone. One sees two slender legs like lily-stalks, subtly, touchingly intensifying the bird-suggestion with the feeling of fragile, hollow bones.

Varèse: A Looking-Glass Diary

After all these years I still hear the melting tenderness of those labial *b*'s of Florence singing, "Oh, Baby, Baby, Baby . . ."

I don't remember whether it was before or after the concert that we gave a party at our house at which Florence Mills was one of the guests. Alone in a corner away from all the noisy groups Varèse came upon her and was shocked to see that she was crying. He bent over her. "Florence, what is the matter?" he asked. "Has anyone been rude to you?" Negroes, even among artists, were not as generally accepted socially then as they are now. She shook her head and in her soft, small voice said: "It's because I've never been so happy. Everybody treats me like everybody and no one has even asked me to sing."

To get back to the concert: There was Carl Ruggles's *Portals* for string orchestra, with epigraph by Carl's beloved Walt Whitman: "What are those of the Known/ But to ascend and enter the Unknown?" There were Goossens's *Pastoral and Harlequinade* for flute, oboe, piano; Rieti's *Sonata* for piano, flute, oboe, bassoon; and Mme Respighi sang her husband's *Deità Silvane* for voice and small orchestra.

At the last concert of the season, February 14, *Les Noces* was the *pièce de résistance* and by anybody's standards it was an immense success. All Stravinsky's prodigious vitality, brilliance, and rompish sense of fun are in *Les Noces,* besides the charm of Russian folk song. Carlos, as usual, had prepared the work for Stokowski, rehearsing chorus, soloists, and pianists. The four pianists were, all of them, composers: Georges Enesco, Casella, Germaine Taillefere, and Salzedo himself. The text, also by Stravinsky, is as clever and capersome as the music. Witold Gordon said: "It smells of peasant shoe black and as the Russian peasant uses tar, it should be pungent indeed." Too bad it had to be sung in French instead of in its original, more pungent Russian. But even in the literal English translation from the French it is merrily burlesque and retains a Russian flavor.

At last April came and Varèse was to hear *Amériques* in the flesh, so to speak—something he had been longing for and, without daring to hope, had still hoped Stokowski would play. From Paris he had written me before he was certain:

I wish Stokowski would do it—but it's funny. I have never really had any hope. For me it's a work doomed to sleep forever at the bottom of a drawer. If after a few years it's brought out—it will be too late. It will have lost all significance and importance. Anyway, I think that's the fate of my music. Experience has taught me not to give a damn—and if I had to play politics to be performed—it would disgust me with writing music.

That, of course, was Varèse whistling to himself in the dark. He had not learned to *s'en foutre* as he pretended. He cared only too much. He had sent a copy of *Amériques* to Furtwängler, with whom he had become friendly the winter before and added as a postscript in the same letter to me: "Furtwaengler has *Amériques*—am waiting for a letter from him—that is to say—a polite and cordial refusal." And it is exactly what happened.

In another letter the year before he had shown the same kind of musical battle fatigue:

To be played or not played seems to me very futile and a little ridiculous. One of these days we'll go to some sunny country and I'll just write my music—nothing counts but good honest work—*la gloire je l'emmerde* and the "social game" even more.

The *Amériques* that Stokowski was to perform was the first version, for one hundred and forty-two instruments, including nine players in the percussion section and a siren. Varése went to Philadelphia for the final week of rehearsals—in all, Stokowski gave sixteen entire rehearsals to Varèse's score. I joined Varèse two days later for the last rehearsal. We stayed at the hospitable Alexander Liebermans', friends of the Speisers', who like the Speisers were patrons of the arts and had a very fine collection of paintings. I remember particularly some beautiful Vlamincks. "What a commercial desert America would have been," Varèse used to say "without the Jews' patronage of the arts!"

The first performance was Friday afternoon, April 9, and the Friday afternoon audience was notoriously smug and archaic. They hissed and booed and as one paper commented: "It is indeed a powerful piece of music which can cause a Friday afternoon audience to indulge in hisses and catcalls." They quite forgot their genteel manners. A dozen or more left the Academy during the performance and one old lady was heard to protest angrily, "And he dared call it *America!*" Varèse did not take a bow. However, the same reviewer commented: "The Saturday evening audience was more sympathetic and Mr. Stokowski brought Mr. Varèse to the stage three times."

On April 13 Stokowski brought the same program to Carnegie Hall in New York, opening with *Amériques,* followed by *The Swan of Tuonela* by Sibelius, Mozart's *Symphony in C Major,* and Bach's *Passacaglia,* orchestrated by Stokowski. There was laughter during the performance of *Amériques* and booing and hissing after, though excited applauders did their best to compete, and Paul Morris of the *Evening World* had the impression that: "In the end the favorable section won out." Other critics differed. An anonymous reviewer of the *Evening World* mentioned only the opposition:

> A pretty little shindig of boos and hisses broke out last night among the ordinarily self-contained and ultra well-poised ladies and gentlemen who make up the Philadelphia Orchestra's audience in Carnegie Hall, after Mr. Stokowski finished Edgard Varèse's symphonic genuflection to the Fire Department and the Pneumatic Riveters' Union.

Olga Samaroff, in the *Post,* scolded her former husband, saying: "Mr. Stokowski, who has a distinguished record in the matter of introducing important new works could scarcely have done anything more detrimental to the cause of modern music than to produce a composition like *Amériques.*"

Stokowski kept returning to the stage as if there had been only applause and, as one reviewer said, "made his players rise and acknowledge by this action the tribute to their courage and skill." Varèse did not appear with Stokowski and another music critic commented: "Mr. Varèse was wise enough not to let the audience catch sight of the tip of his nose."

Varèse was not in the least chagrined either by the booing or by the hostility and the sarcasms of the critics. He had heard his music and found it good. He had been surrounded after the concert by enthusiastic supporters. Stokowski spoke of *Amériques* in superlative terms, and Varèse believed that this friend of his music would continue to "impose" it with his virtuoso orchestra and that other orchestras would follow.

In his article on *Amériques* in the June *Dial,* Paul Rosenfeld commented: "It is possible that in Edgard Varèse we have another virtuoso genius with the orchestra in his veins." He also gave a pertinent opinion when he said: *"Amériques* is perhaps the transition between the series of tone poems produced by the young Varèse in Europe before the war and those born of the experience of the new world." Varèse may have agreed with this but by destroying *Bourgogne,* the last of the old ones, before any composer or conductor in America had set eyes on it, he chose not to let any of them see for themselves the difference between the old and the new. Only I, with eyes blind to the language of music, saw it. Of *Bourgogne* we knew that Romain Rolland, Hugo von Hofmannsthal, and Richard Strauss put their stamp of approval on it, all of them having been involved, directly or indirectly, in getting it performed in Berlin; we also know that it received the general condemnation of critics and public—someone having been heard to remark that it was even worse than Schoenberg. In other words, men highly qualified to judge (and among them must be included Busoni, who had named Varèse *"illustro Futuro"*) believed in the value of Varèse's pre-American music, and the attitude of Berlin's musical "establishment" is a sure sign that Varèse was already working away from the norm.

Some time that winter Carlos told Varèse that Mr. William Walter, executive director of the Curtis Institute of Music (where Carlos taught harp and Stokowski conducting), was planning a new department of composition and that he and Stokowski had recommended Varèse to be its director and teacher of advanced composition. He advised Varèse to go to Philadelphia to see Mr. Walter, which Varèse did and returned rejoicing; this would be exactly the job he had been hoping for. In March he had an encouraging telephone call from Mr. Walter, but it was followed soon after by this letter:

> My dear Mr. Varèse: When I telephoned you a week ago, I felt certain that it would be possible for me to make a definite proposition to you, looking to next year. But I regret to say that everything is still in the air, and we are quite undecided as to what we shall do. . . . I still hope that we will be able to avail ourselves of your very valuable services in some respect next year, but the matter will have to go over for at least a month before any definite decision can be reached.

The following September Stokowski asked Varèse to take over his class at the Curtis Institute for October. Not having conducted since 1919, Varèse did not feel ready to accept such an offer and in his letter explaining his refusal he wrote: "It would be unfair to the young enthusiasts who form the Curtis Orchestra, after having had the best, to give them anything less than perfect competence at least." Stokowski replied that he understood Varèse's feeling and that he admired him more than ever for his directness; then he added: "As you know I am hoping to have the benefit of your cooperation in the Curtis Institute in some form and I feel that in the future this will realize itself."

It did not. And in spite of the sponsorship of both Stokowski and Salzedo, Varèse never became a faculty member of the Curtis Institute.

That season many musicians—conductors, pianists, violinists—were in New York giving concerts and recitals. There was the giant conductor who did not need a podium, Otto Klemperer, guest of the New York Symphony. He had a passion for Verdi and whenever he came to our house would inevitably at some point sit down at Varèse's piano and interminably play excerpts from the operas. Though he liked Varèse personally, he did not like his music—as how could he with his taste for Verdi! Once, nevertheless, he conducted *Octandre*. That was at the request of Mrs. Alfred Rossin, daughter of Adolph Lewisohn, who gave musicals in her house at 40 East Sixty-eighth Street. The situation was somewhat the same between Varèse and Furtwängler, and though even more friendly, musically their association was just as platonic. Furtwängler had been a guest conductor of the Philharmonic Orchestra the year before and was now its regular conductor. After Toscanini, as a guest conductor in January, had enjoyed phenomenal success, the directors, when it came to renewing Furtwängler's contract, dropped him in favor of Toscanini. Furtwängler was very bitter and Varèse had the pleasure of joining him in flaying Toscanini alive, blood dripping from every word. How long Varèse had known and disparaged Toscanini I have no idea. I only know that after what might be called a brawl which the two of them indulged in during the intermission of the January concert of the ICG, Toscanini became an obsession. The subject of their wrangle was modern music. Like Varèse, Toscanini was notorious for his uncontrollable temper, and when he shouted at Varèse that it was a disgrace to make people listen to the kind of music he not only sponsored but wrote, Varèse met him temper to temper, insult for insult. It was quite a spectacle. From then on, the slightest mention of Toscanini was like the *muleta* to a bull; Varèse charged. Toscanini, in his sweeping invective, excepted only one composer, Respighi, whose guest he had been that evening, whose *Deità Silvane* had been sung by Mme Respighi and whose music Toscanini himself performed. For Furtwängler it must have been soothing syrup to hear Varèse insist that Toscanini was incapable of conducting anything better than Italian opera and that he had the mentality of a coiffeur and looked like one. Salzedo, who was an admirer and a friend of Toscanini, argued with Varèse in vain.

Varèse not being the only person who regretted the change of conductors, Furtwängler's farewell concert, given to a packed house, ended with a tremendous ovation. The last thing on the program was Beethoven's *Fifth Symphony,* and I remember Varèse saying that it was "the most magnificent performance" he had ever heard. Though in Varèse's hierarchy Furtwängler was not a Muck, he was a fine conductor and Toscanini could not be mentioned in the same breath with him.

Walter Gieseking, of the velvet touch, was also giving recitals that winter. He was a phenomenon of placidity among virtuosi. He dined with us before one of his concerts and dawdled over coffee as though he had the whole night before him with nothing to do. Varèse pointed to the clock and said, "Look—you'll be late," to which he replied without looking, "They can't start without me." When he finally decided he would have to go, he picked out an apple from the dish of fruit as he left the table and ate it in the taxi on the way to Carnegie Hall. Varèse—overlooking Gieseking's predilection for Mozart—admired his playing of Debussy more than that of any pianist since Viñes.

Varèse and I did not spend that summer of 1926 on the Mediterranean as planned. Stokowski had scheduled *Arcana* for the following April and his casual inquiry as to the possible date for the termination of the score made Varèse feel harried and consequently sure he would not be ready in time. He could not, he said, afford the voluptuous indulgence of a summer of sea and sun, must not leave the austerity of his worktable. By the time the season began, *Arcana* was still in a state of nerve-racking incompleteness and the ICG, Varèse's once-prized creation, had become a Frankenstein monster. Although Arthur Judson, manager of the Philadelphia Orchestra and of Stokowski, had assumed the management of the Guild, only routine matters were taken care of by his office; and though theoretically the Technical Board was supposed to play an active role, practically they were of no assistance at all to Varèse and Salzedo, exception made for our faithful, irreplaceable Julius Mattfeld. Even indefatigable Carlos—with summers devoted to his harp school in Seal Harbor, winters absent from New York several days a week at the Curtis Institute in Philadelphia, private pupils in New York, and concert engagements—was often forced to leave the brunt of the responsibility of the Guild to Varèse. To Varèse's credit be it said that, in spite of his growing impatience and without the élan of his former enthusiasm, he gave the same scrupulous attention to the preparation of the next three concerts. The supreme worry of all of us—habitual in the ICG but in the fall of 1926 abysmal—was the lack of funds. What was badly needed was *a,* if not *the* Mrs. Reis. A couple of executive secretaries, after kindly offering services they were incapable of performing, had quietly faded away into matrimony. What was *not* needed was a crystal ball to show us a large deficit looming ahead.

On the twenty-eighth of November the first concert of what was to be the last season of the ICG took place in an atmosphere of high expectancy and, as usual, there were in the large audience that filled Aeolian Hall those who came to listen to and possibly to enjoy "modern" music, others for the fun of laughing at it, though by that time the latter was a very small minority.

Goossens was once more the conductor and he is about the only concrete remembrance I have of that concert. For me, as for Varèse, in those last two years intensity of interest centered first in the performance of *Amériques;* then in that of *Arcana*— its slow gestation, delivery, and happy public baptism. Fortunately I have, however, program notes to jog my memory. Observing indelibly only what I observe emotionally, I am a bad reporter and it is my hope that some impersonal music historian will someday write an account of Varèse's pioneer ICG more complete and unbiased than mine.

Varèse's talented pupil, the Canadian pianist and composer Colin McPhee, had a composition of his performed for the first time outside his native country, a sonatina, *Pastorale* and *Rondino.* There was once more a piece, *Darker America,* by William Grant Still. There was a fragment-dance of an unfinished ballet by Carlos Chávez called *H.P.,* meaning horsepower, of which he wrote: "The intention of the work is neither to describe mechanical processes nor to relate the spirit of the work to the aesthetics of machines." Chávez was one of the few composers who were beginning to listen to the sounds around them, interested in writing urban rather than pastoral symphonies."I see in the machine," he further tried to elucidate, "a human process multiple and congealed; in other words a process which is both static and dynamic." The program also included Goossens's latest work, *Three Pagan Poems* for chamber orchestra, played from manuscript. Outstanding—*way out*—was Webern's touching *Fünf geistliche Lieder.* Unfortunately I did not appreciate them at the time as I had appreciated his quartet which two years before had given me such exquisite pleasure. It was that Schoenberg invention, the vaulting voice which goes from the lowest to the highest register in painful leaps and that sounded to my ears—not innocent enough—like the braying of a refined donkey who had had singing lessons.

On January 30 came the second concert, conducted by Otto Klemperer. It opened with the *Symphonische Musik* for nine solo instruments of Ernst Krenek, whose *Concerto Grosso* Klemperer had played the year before with the New York Symphony orchestra. A German critic, Hugo Lichtentritt, quoted in the program notes, wrote of Krenek: "This young Bohemian of 22 years is a typical child of his generation, devoid of sentimentality, greedy for fame, fond of sensation, anarchistic in his aesthetic views, without the least respect for tradition." There was Malipiero's *Ricercari,* which had been commissioned by Mrs. Elizabeth Coolidge, dedicated to her, and performed in Venice and in Brussels at two of the many concerts Mrs. Coolidge organized in Europe at that time. It is for an ensemble of instruments that includes *four* violas. This prodigality of violas coupled with the "seek and seek again" of the *Ricercari* accounts for the epigraph Malipiero chose for his score:

> Cantoni un poco, a recantami tu
> Su la vió
> Su la viola cuccuricu,
> Le cuccuricu
> Su la viola la cuccuricu.

From all I have heard about Malipiero, from the few letters he wrote to Varèse, and from this epigraph, I am sure, quite aside from his musical gift, he must have been a delightful man to know. Varèse always regretted that he had never met him. Casella, whose work *Scarlattiana* Klemperer had also conducted with the New York Symphony, for which it had been composed, was represented for the fourth time on a Guild program by his

L'Adieu à la Vie, written originally for voice and piano, now newly orchestrated for a Guild première. There was a work by Hindemith, *Der Dämon,* or rather some of the dances from that allegorical dance pantomime. But of all the works on the program, the sensuous, "sun-drenched" (as Varèse called them) *Chansons Madécasses* of Ravel were by far the most seductive and were prodigiously applauded. They too had been commissioned by Mrs. Coolidge.

And then *Arcana.*
Stokowski gave Varèse's work on the eighth and ninth of April in Philadelphia and in New York on the twelfth. It is hardly surprising that his performance of *Arcana* failed to come up to the excellence of that of *Amériques.* He had received the score late, he had given it fewer rehearsals, and, an even more valid reason, he was suffering from a very painful bursitis so that with his right arm in a sling he had only his left with which to guide his men through the very great difficulties of the score. After the New York performance he even said to Varèse. "We play the notes—but not yet the music."

Philadelphia was rather less shocked by *Arcana* than it had been by *Amériques,* one critic admitting that he found it "less wild." But the headlines still screamed and the audiences tittered, though I think there were possibly fewer hisses. However, on such occasions I was so tense and apprehensive I was hardly present and whatever impressions I had were not reliable. But even the coolly observant critics never agreed. Some would say that the applause outdinned the boos and the hisses, others the contrary. Happily, Varèse, who was always filled with a beautiful uncritical optimism after his ears had been filled with the long longed-for sounds of his music, believed the former.

In New York, besides those critics I have mentioned who gave Varèse's music the full measure of their approbation if not always total admiration, a few others were becoming at least less sure of their former opinions. One of these was Pitts Sanborn of the *New York Telegram.* It was in February, after he examined some of Varèse's scores, among them *Arcana,* that he wrote an article in *Modern Music* on the changing dramatis personae of the extreme left. After commenting that Stravinsky "had come out for Tchaikovsky, Schoenberg proclaimed his devotion to *Il Trovatore* and various others taken to writing like Bach" (Busoni had started a fashion with his neoclassicism), he names as the radicals of the moment Carl Ruggles, Edgard Varèse, and Henry Cowell. He then declares: "The crown and the sceptre of the left, however, the power that speaks to power, and a big share of the glory are vested in Edgard Varèse."

After the performance of *Arcana* at Carnegie Hall Sanborn touched significantly on the different nature of two audience demonstrations—the one spontaneous and the other, a performance of Antheil's *Ballet Mécanique* the previous Sunday, intentionally contrived:

> New York is a pretty hopeless town when it comes to kicking up what our French friends call a "scandal" at a concert. Sunday night everything was set for pandemonium at the Antheil concert as Carnegie Hall yet nothing much happened. Last night Leopold Stokowski included the latest composition of Edgard Varèse in his program for the season's concluding Carnegie Hall concert of the Philharmonic Orchestra. Now a Varèse piece at a concert is always the signal for a jolly uproar and the contest between the hisses and the applause last night had at least a spontaneity and a meaning that one would be slow to impute to the carefully nurtured affair Sunday.

He then concluded: "However sincere though the hisses may have been, they died away as the applause waxed steadily. It was a very minor 'scandal.' "

Two other critics, Henderson and Gilman, also harked back to the previous Sunday evening fiasco. Henderson commented:

> There was a more spontaneous demonstration than that which fizzled out so dismally Sunday night after the *Ballet Mécanique* of Mr. Antheil. There was an outbreak last night of genuine hissing which could be heard above the resolute applause. Hissing is an honor rarely bestowed upon a composer in this town.

. . . The present writer does not know how to describe such music. It has immense energy. It cannot hesitate a moment to be reflective or tender. . . . There were many persons who were convinced. There were those who refused to give themselves any chance to be. They walked out as soon as they heard the first bar. This is no way to treat a serious composer.

And Gilman: "There is bite and edge to his [Varèse's] music. And there is power. We are far from the blatant emptiness and flatulent longueur of Mr. Antheil's Ballet Mécanique." Then Mr. Gilman ended with one of his characteristic poetic flourishes: "There is portent and mystery in this music and a breaking of bounds, a beating of wings. It is good to hear it and thus to be perturbed."

The *Brooklyn Eagle* man, however, stuck to his guns—and heavy ones they were. For him *Arcana* was "long and infinitely wearying in its revelations of the unspeakably hideous and the appallingly nonsensical . . . an exhibition vulgar and without excuse."

Downes, though not convinced, admitted grudgingly: "There is temperament back of this music if nothing else." Quite a concession for Downes at that time.

Stokowski on the advice of his physician had asked for a year's leave of absence. For the same reason, the painful bursitis that crippled his right arm, it was not Stokowski but his assistant, Artur Rodzinski, who conducted the last concert of the Guild. With this concert on April 17 at Aeolian Hall the ICG came to an end.

Four very different tendencies were represented by the four composers on the program, Alban Berg, Carlos Salzedo, Igor Stravinsky, and Edgard Varèse.

Alban Berg had composed his *Kammermusik* as a testimonial to Arnold Schoenberg for his teacher's seventy-fifth birthday, September 13, 1924, though the score was not completed until several months later. The following is an excerpt from the note Julius Mattfeld wrote for the program:

Varèse: A Looking-Glass Diary

> In this work, Alban Berg has incorporated the aspirations not only of himself and Arnold Schoenberg but also of their fellow worker, Anton Webern. . . . Alban Berg has prefixed to his score a musical motto forming the motives on which the *Kammermusik* is constructed. The motto consists of three themes based on the musical vowels of Arnold Schoenberg, . . . Anton Webern . . . and Alban Berg. . . . In the motto the name of Schoenberg is given out by the piano, that of Webern is heard on the violin and the horn sounds that of Alban Berg. . . . In the composition itself the composer has sought in this tribute to offer its founder an embodiment of his innovations, a fulfillment of his own words: "And thus perhaps the movement will some day return to me (*Und so kehrt vielleicht auch diese Bewegung einmal zu mir zurück*)." How like Yaweh—Schoenberg!

However, instead of returning to its founder, the "movement" has moved further and further away from him. A new generation—Boulez, Stockhausen, Nono, Babbitt, Weber, and so on, and so on—follow not Schoenberg but Webern, who had also turned away from his "master" to follow only himself.

There was Salzedo's Concerto for Harp and Wind Instruments so remarkable in its use of "tone colors" (a possible thirty-seven, Salzedo noted). Most of these he himself discovered and contributed as well as other technical devices that have added a greater expressive richness to his instrument.

Then came Stravinsky's *Octet* with the "Rossinian joviality" of its trombones grunting for a laugh, which it received from the delightedly hilarious audience. When the *Octet* was performed for the first time in Paris at one of the Koussevitzky concerts, Boris de Schloezer (whom I have just quoted) writing in the *Revue Musicale* called it "a natural organic synthesis of many and diverse elements, such as Bach and the 18th century masters, the romantic and sprightly songs of the last century, and the rhythmic frenzy of Negro-American music. This synthesis is our new classical or in other words, objective style"—or in other words, *neoclassicism,* of which Varèse had many scathing things to say, among others: "It is a comfortable tendency—you just lie down in beds that have for centuries been made up. Unfortunately for the timorous and the astute, who take refuge in it and there find comfort and security, it is nothing but a Maginot Line. . . . In neo-classicism, tradition is reduced to the level of a bad habit." Stravinsky, in an article published in *The Arts,* wrote an extensive description of his work in which he said: "My Octuor is an object." I remember Varèse commenting at the time, "But what work of Stravinsky's is not an object?"—Stravinsky's music being so extremely extroverted. A music of boundless energy, compelling charm with innumerable other stimulating qualities—abundance overflows the cornucopia of his tremendous vitality and intelligence—and over all the wings of an enormous ego. It is richly Russian and a little heartless.

The last thing on the program was *Intégrales,* the only work to be given a second hearing by the ICG. For six years the Guild had adhered strictly to its rule of premières only. "Repeated," the program noted, "at the request of over one hundred and fifty members of the International Composers' Guild." I don't know if there were precise statistics to back this statement but it was nevertheless not an exaggeration. When it was learned that this season, as in the previous season, there would be no Varèse work on the program our telephone became more of a nuisance than ever, and we were all of us buttonholed wherever we went by friends and subscribers we did not even know, protesting and demanding that one of Varèse's works be repeated. We would then suggest that they write their request to the Judson office and many did. *Intégrales* received an ovation, and even if the audience had known that this concert celebrated the passing of the ICG, the demonstration could not have been more impressively benedictional.

Winthrop Tryon of the *Christian Science Monitor* wrote: "Perhaps the Guild has never held a more successful session artistically than this one, every piece deserving to be rated as a masterwork and every measure of music masterfully interpreted." And the audience voiced its approval of the Guild's violation of its own rule of premières only by vociferously calling for an encore of *Intégrales* applauding in unison until Rodzinski repeated it.

Varèse: A Looking-Glass Diary

The following summing up on the last page of the program notes might well have suggested a finality:

And on the outside page was a list of the principal works that had been performed.

A year after the Guild's happy euthanasia, appeared Paul Rosenfeld's book of essays, *By Way of Art,* in which there is one entitled, "Thanks to the International Composers' Guild." The following excerpt from his introductory remarks shows him bravely waving the flag of his allegiance:

Edgar Varèse and Carlos Salzedo, operating under the name The International Composers' Guild, maintained a hatchery for musical bacilli where in musical boxes new combinations and voices, aesthetics and world-feelings germinated. . . . A responsiveness to the hour, a spirit of initiative, promptitude and willingness, which we in New York still tend to associate with Parisian circles, combined as it was with an artistic standard of performance, distinguished even the Guild's dullest parties from those of rival organizations. The Society of the Friends of Music declared itself a musical museum beside the Guild. Pro Musica was evidently another depot for modern French work; and the League of Composers, a social function in which the performance of music served the ambitions of mediocres . . . and music a prelude to the apotheosis of personal projections and chicken salad at close quarters.

Rosenfeld further pointed out that the Guild was "cardinal in producing here in New York an audience capable of receiving new impressions."

Musically the ICG ended triumphantly but not its finances. There was a deficit of some six hundred dollars, which may seem like petty cash today but not to us at that time. To appeal to our two principal supporting members would, in the case of Mrs. Whitney, have been infelicitous, since for anyone not interested in music she had done more than music had a right to expect; and our other benefactor was losing interest. The Guild with its emphasis on the composer—that "untouchable of music" as Varèse called him—had not given her the prestige she had enjoyed before coming to New York, in the more glamorous music world of virtuosi conductors and performers. She was, Varèse felt, disappointed. It was Carlos out of his own pocket who paid the deficit.

Now that summer was approaching, Varèse once more felt a longing for sun and sea, and we determined to spend at least three months on or near the Mediterranean. Since Varèse would have to wait for his citizenship papers, it was decided that I should go ahead in order to find a house while there was still the possibility of choice. Having lost my American citizenship by marrying a Frenchman, when we returned Varèse would be an American and I would be a woman without a country. Instead of a passport I was given "traveling papers" that would at least allow me, although a nonentity, to re-enter my native land. The end of May I sailed for France on the S.S. *Savoie*.

Varèse's letters were full of plans. He was trimming *Amériques* for a smaller orchestra and wrote that "the cutting down" was finished except for three places to be recomposed: "So this summer," he wrote, "I'll fix up that old dodo (*vieux rossignol*), write a coda to Arcana and begin 'The One' "—the latter referred to a stage work for mimes, solo voices, chorus, and narrator on an American Indian theme.

The year before, when one day he was lunching with Thomas Patton, the postmaster general, he happened to mention his interest in the American Indian. Not long afterward a case arrived from Washington filled with two dozen or more volumes, the entire set of the Smithsonian Institution's books on American Indians that covered every aspect of their history, folklore, language, music, poetry, and so on. Varèse was particularly fascinated by the legends and their laconic imagist language. He asked me to write a scenario and we chose a myth that was not only dramatic, ritualistic, and spectacular, but also philosophical. The theme: dualism; the title (Indian style): *The One-All-Alone, A Miracle;* the plot: the contest between the evil Arrow-Maker, or Sorcerer, and the mystical hero, who was, in fact, for Varèse, no other than Nietzsche's *Übermensch.* There is no point in going into that rejected project except to say that Varèse later turned the mystical man of the Indian myth into a modern astronomer who exchanges signals with Sirius and when, as in the case of his former hero, the mob turns against him, is drawn up, not into the sun, but to Sirius by what Varèse called *"radiation instantanée."* Varèse wrote his own synopsis for the *Astronomer* and spent years trying to find the right poet to write his text. More of all this later. Of course the Indian idea had been an absurdity for Varèse, an aberration, a positive deflection. Varèse's music was totally unsuited to folklore, to the archaic, his conception of sound too utterly twentieth century. He realized this as soon as he began seriously to consider the music, but for the moment he was all enthusiasm for his Indian myth, and in one of his letters wrote: "Have quite a lot of ideas for 'The One.' More and more I like your libretto."

Then I received a letter in which Varèse's ebulliently anticipatory optimism made the great desideratum of his days—the liberating instrument discussed so many years ago with Busoni

—appear almost imminent. After spending a day talking and working with an electrical engineer of the Bell Telephone Laboratory of Pennsylvania he wrote: "Went to Philadelphia for the whole day yesterday to work. It was wonderful. Sooner or later I'll get what I want. Weyl is extremely knowledgeable and intelligent." That fall Varèse would meet Harvey Fletcher, director of physical research at Western Electric in New York, and for a while his optimism seemed justified.

In many of his letters Varèse referred to the composition classes he counted on organizing in the fall. He had had an announcement printed which included the following endorsement from Stokowski:

> First I knew Varèse as an ultra-modern composer. Later I discovered his profound knowledge of the great composers of the past. He would be an ideal guide for young composers, as his wide knowledge of music of all schools, and his sensitive vibration to them, give an unusual balance to his musical nature.

In March he had sent the circular to Frank Patterson, editor of *Musical Courier,* a music trade paper, and received in reply from Mr. Patterson the very natural suggestion that a better way to reach prospective pupils would be to advertise in the *Courier.* Later came the response of Mr. Sonneck, director of publication at Schirmer's: "I received your announcement. It may interest you to know that I have several times referred budding Bachs and Beethovens to you. Of course I can lead fillies (not filles) and their counterparts to the trough, but I can't make them drink if they aren't thirsty." Facetiously tactless, I thought. This somewhat mocking attitude was not uncommon among men established on the outskirts of music. It is true that Varèse's schemes for making money were rarely practical, because invariably they were deeply embedded in an ideal. When Varèse had an idea, it was to him so indubitably meritorious that success was inevitable and no other point of view tenable. He even repeated himself with the same sort of printed announcement in the following year in Paris, in 1933 an even more ambitious project in Barcelona, and again in 1937 in San Francisco. Varèse was a very impractical bulldog. He was able, however, to inspire with his own unwavering confidence staunch friends. One of these was C. C. Birchard, the Boston music publisher who was bringing out Varèse's songs. Varèse wrote me with pride: "Have just received *Offrandes* contract. Birchard is giving me 15% instead of the usual 10%."

That he would never receive more than a few dollars in royalties from the Birchard edition was for Varèse beside the point. His music had been valued above the ordinary. I have come across an old royalty statement for six months with, intact, a check for seventy-five cents—15 per cent of $5.00 paid for one conductor's score. C. C. Birchard, as its letterhead stated, was the "leading publishers of School, Choral and Community Music." Mr. Birchard, the dear man, must have been bewitched by Varèse and his music to think that such a firm as his could disseminate such a work as *Offrandes*. Varèse's letter continues:

> I am writing him to arrange a rendezvous in order to ask him to look into the possibilities in Boston for master classes—either there—or sending pupils here.

A letter dated the following January shows Mr. Birchard still active on Varèse's behalf. He had appealed to his friend Carl Engel, who was then chief of the music division of the Library of Congress, and wrote Varèse of Mr. Engel's discouraging response:

> Dear Mr. Varèse: Teresa has probably called you to tell you of my result with Mr. Engel. I wrote him that evening and on Sunday morning called him on the telephone. In the meantime he had written me by return. From the letter, more than from the conversation, I definitely conclude it will be imposible for him to become interested in the school. I can tell you more about this when I see you. But the fact is he doesn't grasp the idea as to the importance of teaching with a view to making composers for America. This seems to be one of Carl's present limitations which let us hope he will overcome in time. It may

grow out of the fact that some years ago he gave up composition entirely, and just at a time when his friends were predicting a large future for him. . . . We are sending with your compliments, copies of *Offrandes* to the Paris addresses you have given. We are also sending one dozen copies of the work to your address with our compliments.

Birchard believed in Varèse without question and in the validity of his plan. He was a man of great generosity and simple kindness. He and his future wife, Teresa Armitage, both became charming friends. All his life Varèse had devoted friends but seldom ones who were in a position to further his most cherished projects, or to get his music performed, though not a few, like Mr. Birchard, went to a great deal of trouble to make the attempt. Neither they nor Varèse realized how much time it would take to pull music out of the nineteenth into the twentieth century—more than the efforts of a handful of contemporary composers of whom Varèse was the most impatient.

In the following letter, to the recurring refrain of his classes, Varèse harps on another preoccupation—almost an obsession though here treated jestingly: "I am concentrating all my energy—outside my music—on getting my classes going—I must have money for my pal *GIN*ette (an allusion to my dry martinis of which he disapproved) and hats for Pinto and a beautiful house for Zon Zon and beautiful dresses for *GOB*ette." It shows a surprising modesty in Varèse that he failed to realize how much more he gave me than material things. Just as in a more *mea culpa* mood he had written me in 1925 from Paris—referring again to my passion for houses:

> Yesterday I dined with Slivinsky at our next door neighbors (the very beautiful house at no. 18 quai d'Orléans) Mr. and Mrs. Wilkinson—a wealthy American collector—a friend of Stokowski, she, "Dolores"—you must know the name—She is English, a former Ziegfeld Follies girl. They are very nice, simple and cordial. And what a house!! and what beautiful things!! I disgust myself being poor and not able to give *mon petit amour* the beautiful things she appreciates so much and that would make her so

happy. I'm a poor *con* who clumsily makes a big noise and is a pest to everybody [approximation of *et emmerde les gens*].

Varèse continued in the same letter: "Shall write to Mrs. Rossin in order to be sure to begin my classes in a financially practical way. As for Judson little hope of aid—another windbag. But I don't care—everything is going well. I am canalizing all the energy I spent on the ICG into making some dough. I trot like a regular horse and see a lot of people and morons like . . ." (I omit the names.)

When Varèse heard that Vladimir Golschmann was to conduct his *Octandre* in Paris, he commented to this ungratefully, as it then seemed to me, that Golschmann would not be able to do it. However, his mistrust proved justified, for two years later in Paris a critic reviewing the performance wrote: "Except for a work given at a concern of Pro Musica a few years ago, and whose mediocre execution betrayed its author considerably, we have never heard Varèse in Paris." Then Varèse added: "Besides, my music is not for Paris." Varèse sometimes made assertions contrary to his deepest desire, reminding me of a cat who has tried and failed to catch a fly and walks haughtily away pretending she has never had any such idea.

At last Varèse's letters spoke of departure: "I have my passport—so I am full of pity for the poor little emigrant." Then: "I leave July 1"—with a drawing of a waving Stars and Stripes; finally: "Am packing and Friday it will be my turn to become a Savoyard," for he too was sailing on the S.S. *Savoie*.

Although he had said on one of his up, up, up days that he had never felt better and that "two good months on the Mediterranean and I'll be altogether heroic," he nevertheless, as soon as he arrived in Paris, went to consult Dr. Flandrin, after which he wrote: "Saw Flandrin and Prof. Fisch—I am very ill again and full of pus. . . . I'll tell you more in detail. Your letters are so sweet and I reply to them like an undertaker—But I'll get better. The Drs. tell me my nervous system is completely undermined by this chronic infection which dates from childhood— but I'll get well and *merde* for wine etc." Bob Chanler was in

Paris and they sent me a joint postcard, Bob saying, "Varèse is on the wagon—he looks like a god;" and Varèse, "Bernouard tells me that Mathivet has bought Grandpère's house." So Varèse decided to stop off at Tournus on his way to Antibes to stay overnight with Mathivet in Le Villars. There he found his old sweetheart Ti'ma (little Marthe), now Mme Oudot, who had returned for a visit to her native village. Like Varèse she had tender memories of their youthful friendship when, as she afterward reminisced in a letter to Varèse: "I used to wait impatiently for your arrival at your grandfather's."

Meantime at Antibes I had been living in the delightful house I had rented (Oh, the lovely rents of those days and the heavenly exchange) on the Ramparts—Antibes's last platform, one might say—for Antibes rises, terrace by terrace, from the station square to the cliff road above the Mediterranean. One arrived from the square below, the Place du Marché, through an arch at the top of a flight of steps onto the Place du Barry, where on the right was our house, on the left an old castle which was the same warm sand color of the new blond Paris of today. Picasso has since turned it into a museum, but at that time it was still a quiet, mellow ruin. Varèse had wired me the approximate time of his arrival and I was waiting for him outside the door of our house. I shall never forget the look of joy on his face as he paused under the arch at the top of the stairs, spellbound at the sight of the sun-dazzled white of the Place du Barry. He used to say nostalgically, "I shall never forget that moment."

Being very proud of my find, I at once took him on a tour of our commodious and oddly adorable house with a cellar kitchen hewed out of the solid rock of the cliffside and a bathroom with a laughable tin tub that had a row of gas jets under it to heat the water, which, if I happened to be in it, elicited from Varèse the inevitable. "Ah, *la poule-au-pot!*"

But it was into the great room on top, which covered the entire length and breadth of the house, that I ushered him with a really triumphant flourish. Its many colors glowed in the abundant sunlight and the mosaic floor of yellow, red, and black tiles was a copy of one of Michelangelo's (so the young aesthete who owned the house had told me) and there was a piano. As soon as Varèse saw the piano he hugged me, for he knew then that this gay room of noble proportions was to be his workroom. Finally we climbed a flight of steps to a gallery that opened onto a balcony overlooking Varèse's long longed-for Mediterranean. We stood looking down and away at the variegated sea blues, and Varèse gloated, until Josephine, our little Italian maid, came up to be presented to *le patron*. She then ran down to her rock kitchen and up again with drinks—alas only a lemonade for doctor-ridden Varèse.

The air at the moment being crystalline pure and sea sweet, Varèse could afford to laugh at the account I gave him of the second evening of my stay when, coming out onto the balcony late in the evening, I took a deep anticipatory breath and instead of *l'air de la mer,* the spurious sea breeze blew a large whiff of *l'air de la merde* up my receptive nose. Along the parapet of the Rampart on the wall some distance from our house, to the right and to the left, were picturesque little turrets. These were depositories for the Italians whose houses, back of our seaview row, lacked plumbing and who late evenings brought their *sceaux hygiéniques* up to the turrets to empty them into the sea. Unfortunately the *chasse d'eau,* that is, the flushing equipment was out of repair and as the Mediterranean has little tidal flow, on evenings when the breeze was right—or rather wrong— a decidedly privy odor mingled with the sea air and lingered. Varèse loved Josephine's prompt riposte to my "But Josephine it smells of caca." *"Oui,* Madame," said Josephine, *"mais caca tourné* (curdled caca)." Antibes at that time was as unsanitary as it was beautiful.

Varèse did not look ill—he seldom did when he was—and showed his condition only in a nervous inability to get seriously down to work, though he spent many hours in his beautiful workroom with a copy of *Amériques* open at one of the pages to be re-composed—many of the bars already inked out. Sometimes he sat at the piano fiddling with themes that occured to him for his Arrow-Maker, who was to be played by an acrobat doing somersaults, cartwheels, and grotesque dances and who, more than the rest, for the moment, stirred his musical imagination. He would often call downstairs to ask me to come up and tell him which one of two chords I preferred, but both being to my ears so much alike, it was impossible for me to make a choice, which, of course, he did not really want but only the relaxation of the questioning moment to determine his own— or to discard both. This caesura habit seemed to relieve the tension under which he always worked. In later—in the late last years, however, my heart would sink at the summons, for it came finally to indicate, among other intermittent signs, a slowing up, a fumbling, a nerve jam in the flow. That summer there was a temporary stoppage and he accomplished very little. It worried him. The urge to get his stage work started was very strong in him, his imagination teemed with images, visual and musical, but the élan was lacking—the spring that would bounce him into the midst of it. In August his distress sought relief in a seeming strange, yet characteristic, act: he went secretly to the little church near us and burned a votive candle to Notre Dame du Bon Port, the sailors' particular Vierge Marie. On the date of the twenty-seventh, in his engagement book, is a drawing of a long white candle with a red ink flame, beside it the words: "N.D. du Bon Port," and underneath words written backward, which in the mirror reads: "for the one all alone." For a Catholic-born unbeliever like Varèse there lingers always a special tenderness for Marie (those multiple Maries of Catholicism)—the appeal of the feminine, of the maternal too. Akin to his plea to the sailors' little Virgin was Varèse's fascinated delving at one time into books on occultism, in which he did not believe any more than he believed in the Christian cult; it was also germane to the appeal of myths (where did I read that Aristotle said: "The lover of myths, which are charged with wonders, is by the same token the lover of wisdom"?) and there was also Varèse's love of primitive rites and incantations. He could have said with Baudelaire: *"Je suis un mystique au fond, et je ne crois à rien*—I am a mystic at heart and I believe in nothing." Though myths and religions seem so antagonistic to science (which Varèse held in such high esteem all his life), they are

267

really the poetic expression of the same human need and spiritual thirst for the answer to the unanswerable question—the question that keeps science searching but to which all religions give unbelievable answers. Those answers Varèse's mind was able to ignore because in their poetry he found at times catharsis for his spirit. However, Varèse once wrote: "The emotional dynamic that pushes the composer to write his scores contains the same element of poetry that incites the scientist to his discoveries," and he used to say: "Science is the poetry of today."

Varèse's charming little Virgin lived part of the year in the votive chapel high on the cliff called "La Garoupe," which we could see in the distance from our balcony. It was one of our favorite walks, along the shore under the umbrella palms and up the stony path to the chapel, where we would look at all the touching votive offerings—mostly from sailors saved from the sea, but also the inevitable crutches—then rest awhile on a bench outside in the soft sunny air. Once a year the festively dressed little doll was carried on the shoulders of husky barefoot sailors, down the steep, rocky path, past the stations of the cross, along the road, and into Antibes, where the sailors paused at each little white shrine set up in the streets for the occasion and little girls, also all in white, stepped out to recite something virginal, whose words were lost to my ears in their lisping singsong; then gathering more followers, the procession proceeded to the harbor church where little Marie du Bon Port was established for a prescribed period before being carried back to her chapel high above the sea.

M. and Mme Charles Fontaine, former opera singers, had the house next to ours and it was even odder; besides its kitchen being also scooped out of the solid rock, it was only one room deep and three stories high. We met them very naturally through Varèse's at once making friends with their cat, Pierrot, and their dog, nameless in my memory. With them we used to drive to Juan-les-Pins for a swim, since the beach there was more sanitary than the one near us, much too near those little turrets. We might have gone to bathe at more fashionable Eden Roc, where we had friends staying at the hotel, among them turbaned, earringed, green-eyed Bernardine Zold (whom we had known at Romany Marie's) with her little girl and a distant cousin of mine with her little girl the same age, but Varèse, being a snob *à rebours,* hated any place that was *chic et cher* though we did dine there a couple of times with Bob Chanler, and quite forgetting his prejudice, Varèse enjoyed the beautiful setting and had a very good time. He had, of course, found a little Italian restaurant in Antibes and a very good one, where the proprietor used to offer us liqueurs as an excuse to sit down and relate, interminably, stories of his love affair with a nun, reminiscent of the *Satyricon.* Varèse patiently endured the boredom of his prolixity out of gratitude for his excellent cooking.

On the beach at Juan-les-Pins, Varèse would lie for hours browning in the sun, taking only the briefest dips in the sea, for he no longer liked being the "fish," as he said, he had been as a little boy at Bergeggi. Passing through Juan-les-Pins, Mrs. Rossin, with her son Edgar, during several days joined us and we would have lunch together in the pavilion on the beach, Edgar all the time snapping us in the infuriating way of camera fiends (though today I confess to regretting the loss of those snapshots), while Varèse talked about his school with sympathetic Mrs. Rossin.

Henri Barzun, Varèse's friend of ante-bellum 1914, and his wife were staying in an apartment on the hill in picturesque old Cannes, where we spent the day with them. Mme Barzun was recuperating from a serious illness and they had come to Cannes for the mild air of the Midi to effect a cure, which it finally did. It was an interesting afternoon for me listening to Varèse and Barzun reminiscing and to Barzun describing the adventure of the Abbaye de Créteil and the creation in 1913 of his Orphic Art and Choral Simultaneity, epitomized in one of his books as: *The Voices, Rhythms, Chants of the World in Chorus.* Apollinaire once wrote: "Barzun was so right when he launched his manifesto on Poetic Simultaneity, of which he was the father." Barzun entertained high hopes for the future of this medium, which was rapidly spreading. All his life, writing, teaching, lecturing, he would continue to promote and develop it with an enthusiasm that kept him young into old age and with a conviction of its efficacy that made Henri Peyre in 1961 call him "a mystic and a man of unshakable faith."

That day we did not see their small son, Jacques, who was to grow up to be the distinguished and very versatile Prof. Jacques Barzun of Columbia University, writer, musician, musicologist, historian, translator. When Barzun's bountiful two-volume *Berlioz and the Romantic Century* came out in 1950 it is not surprising that Varèse read it with intense interest and enjoyment, for not only was Berlioz one of the composers he admired most, but besides, the book contained many ideas, those of both Berlioz and Barzun, that corresponded with Varèse's own lifetime articles of musical faith. Varèse's copy is copiously marked, underscored, and annotated. When Barzun writes: "Among Berlioz' teachers, with the possible exception of Reicha, no one could help him," Varèse noted in the margin: "You are *born* an *orchestrator* (and composer)," which is reminiscent of his saying: "Nobody ever taught me anything except d'Indy and Roussel what not to do." That was in 1933 in a letter from Madrid after a disappointing visit to a monk-organist reputed to know everything there was to know about the organ but from whom Varèse learned nothing new. It was also only to be expected that Varèse should give his enthusiastic agreement to another passage in which Barzun points out that the classic composers—Mozart, Handel, J. S. Bach—had a taste for lusty sounds, saying, in the case of Bach, "contrary to the conventional view of him as an austere intellectual"; and doubly marked is Barzun's comment: "The fact is that all great musicians have loved sound full and loud as well as soft and low and they have always been *attacked by the genteel as noisy.*" Again when Barzun writes of the improved instruments of the modern orchestra: "As for increased volume, range and nuances they simply offered opportunities that *composers have always longed for—new meaning through new sensations.*" Varèse underlined all the last part as he did the last two words of the footnote Barzun added: "though the manufacture of musical instruments is still less accurate than that of *cameras* and *bombsights.*"

I could, but I mustn't, go on and on; at any rate, these few examples are enough to show why Varèse in Barzun's *Berlioz* felt a warm fellowship for both Berlioz and Barzun, a feeling which was still rare for him with most musicians in those days. One more quote, however, but this time only because what Barzun said of Berlioz: "Where music was concerned, patience never deserted him," could be said of Varèse.

It was not long after Varèse left Paris that Bob Chanler also came to the Midi to join friends at Saint-Paul, where they all, of course, stayed at the Colombe d'Or, a most attractive inn and favorite resort of Americans in those years—the ones who could afford it. The others found cheaper quarters in the unsanitary old stone houses on the steep streets of the hill town from which vineyards ran down the lower slopes with, in the distance, the sparkle of the sea. No! For a moment memory played me one of those oneiriclike tricks, telescoping Saint-Paul and another nearer hill town, Cagnes-sur-Mer (not on the sea, by the way, but high above), from which it was that beyond the vineyards one caught that bright glint of the Mediterranean—not from Saint-Paul.

Bob often came to Antibes to take us back to Saint-Paul or on longer excursions to Cannes or to Nice. He rode in an ancient automobile hired with chauffeur for the duration of his stay. It was reminiscent of the horse carriages of the Midi with light fringed tops because—or have I dreamed it?—the car had a fringed top too. He always sat in front with the chauffeur looking enormous in an ample white linen suit that gave him the air of one of Conrad's colonial planters.

It was at an alfresco dinner at Saint-Paul that we met Paul Reverdy, one of France's poets most highly esteemed by his peers. Unfortunately, my remembrance of him is only that of a silent, sulky man. Varèse had captured his American girl and got himself seated next to her at the table with the mischievous connivance of our host, Bob Chanler, who believed that no girl could resist Varèse's attentions. It is true that Varèse had a way with girls, and girls with Varèse, that was apt to make possessive males jealous. Luckily for both of us, I did not mind Varèse's gallantries and occasional inconstancies, his urge for erotic variety not being alien to my nature either. As Kahlil Gibran's Prophet advises: "Love one another but make not a bond of love." On that there existed between us a kind of understanding without words—those treacherous things that sometimes take over so disastrously, unless one is Humpty Dumpty, who made words do what he wanted them to.

Every day I gave Varèse an injection of the vaccine he had brought from Paris, but I believe that lying for hours on the sand in the sun and outings with old friends and new acquaintances were even better medicine, at least for his nerves if not for the infection those Paris doctors had diagnosed. He also enjoyed our lovely odd house and having friends in occasionally to eat one of his famous dishes, which he cooked in our rock-cellar-kitchen, or he would invite passing travelers from New York or Paris to lunch on Josephine's excellent Italian "home cooking" (at night she had a husband). Although Varèse did not, as he had predicted, become "altogether heroic" after his "two months on the Mediterranean," he did, in spite of his quarrel with his music, enjoy them with all the intensity he knew so well how to pack into a single moment—an intensity which also unfortunately tended to make the black moments black indeed.

Shortly before we left, Bob Chanler invited us to lunch at a little restaurant in Antibes overlooking the harbor, together with Isadora Duncan, whom he had driven over from Nice. As I remember, the only other person was Mary Destin, Isadora's constant companion—indeed she always made me think of the confidante of classic French drama. While we were drinking coffee on the terrace, Isadora rose and, flinging her long trailing scarf around her neck in that characteristic gesture of hers, floated across the road to where a man was building a boat in one of the recesses of the sea wall. She talked to him with great animation for some time, and, after she had come back across the road, attentive always to her flying scarf, and had sat down with us again, the man was no longer just a boat carpenter but a genius. Varèse used to tease her about her "geniuses," for anyone she chose to take an interest in automatically became one. Less than a week later when Varèse and I arrived in Paris after spending a couple of days in Burgundy, we read in the papers of her strange death in Nice. That trailing scarf, endlessly flung around her neck, had caught in the wheel of the automobile in which she was riding and strangled her. She had died in her gesture.

Our two-day visit to Tournus and Le Villars was for me like a legend which was being realistically staged—not quite reality. It was late when we arrived at Tournus. Varèse's old sculptor friend Desiré Mathivet was at the station to meet us and took us to a hotel on the quiet Saône where he had engaged a room for us. Mathivet was a *"gueule cassée"* of the 1914 war but his terribly mutilated face had been skillfully patched up and he was not too distressingly disfigured. He was an ardent *"Patriote"* and *"Artiste"* given rather to capital letters with two passions: *"Mon Pays et mon Art."* Next morning we went straight to Grandpère's little house in Le Villars, which now belonged to Mathivet. Varèse took me upstairs to the window from which I could see the "view" which, as Grandpère had said, Varèse "loved so much" and where, after his grandson's flying visits, Grandpère used to sit missing his "little Gogo." Varèse standing beside me was very much moved as I could tell by the tense pressure of his hands on my shoulders, and if he had been *me* he would have shed copiously the tears he held back. Then we went over to Varèse's "baby house"—the house of Oncle Joseph and Tante Marie. Cousine Marthe opened the door and after meeting and greeting me, she and Varèse hugged each other. She was handsome and stocky and very much a *maîtresse d'école,* now *Directrice d'Ecoles* at Mâcon (or was it Chalon-sur-Saône?). She had the rich rolling r's of *la Bourgogne* and, as in her letters, her language was somewhat literary. She still treated Varèse as a small boy. She took us to the only restaurant in Le Villars. Varèse was remembered and feted, and the luncheon was a banquet with the best Mâconnais wines. Still in the role of big sister, when Varèse kept fiddling with the grape scissors she gave his fingers a smart slap. After lunch we walked over to the Merle farm, where I met Cousin Joseph and Cousine Berthe Merle and "old Annette"—Joseph's mother and a cousin of Grandpère's. Very old she was and died soon after but her cheeks were like two round red apples. It was she who brought out Grandfather's silver *tâte-vin* (wine-testing cup) and his *couvert* (fork and spoon), which had been kept all these years for Varèse and which she now gave him, as well as a portrait of his mother as a pretty schoolgirl in a black smock—a charming painting by an unknown artist.

Varèse asked me if I was too tired to walk back to Tournus. I wasn't and if I had been I should not have admitted it, for he was, I could see, eager to take me on the path that led along the river, so rich in memories for him. He talked all the way about his childhood, his grandfather, of Ti'ma, his youthful sweetheart, of the gay young companions who used to come with him to Le Villars, and excursions to other towns where there were twelfth-century abbatial churches. The last thing he said that night before we went to sleep: "Tomorrow, wait till you see Saint-Philibert!" Mathivet came over from Villars early next morning to play cicerone, for he knew everything there was to know about the old church, the successive dates of each part—the original dated, he said, from the ninth century, the last, a very small part, Gothic, including one window. I wish I had paid more attention to the historic facts but Varèse's appreciations were more stimulating and it was his enthusiasm that in 1967 took me back to his Saint-Philibert.

After our return to Paris, where we again stayed at the Hotel Jacob, Varèse, on October 9, went to the hospital for that complete cystoscopy that Dr. Flandrin had advised two years before. It was a very unpleasant operation and almost as bad was the result of preoperation stupidity. The head nurse was away and a little ignoramus served Varèse a large meal before, the consequence being, of course, that he was very sick afterward. Hospitals are unhealthy places at best and French hospitals, at least at that time, were not the best.

Before we left Antibes Varèse had received a letter from Simone Ziegler about his classes. Simone and Oscar Ziegler were among our close friends. They were Swiss, and Simone, besides looking like Isadora Duncan when young, was kind, energetic, intelligent, and efficient. In fact she was too generous of herself and died young of a heart attack. Besides doing everything possible to advance her husband's career as a pianist (difficult, because he was), she also, in order to put, as the French say, butter in the spinach, had some kind of a full-time secretarial job and yet also found time to write many letters on behalf of Varèse's problematic classes.

> Stony Creek, Conn.
> August 23, 27
>
> Dear Varèse,
> I am enclosing the copy of Mr. Sharp's answer to my letter to Mr. Meiklejohn. . . . I shall write to him at once and to the other persons he mentions.

She then asks for press notices and I sent her all that I had brought with me. The letter continues:

> We might make up a list of other colleges etc. Haven't you ever thought of doing a series of lectures . . . 5 or 6—what do you think? I am so sure one could interest enough people and at the same time it would be publicity for pupils. (Intimate lectures or lectures with demonstration, Ziegler at the piano) something really good and not so bla as others. Get well and let us know when you are coming back. Francine [her sister] and Ziegler send greetings to you both and friendliest wishes for Louise and you from your
>
> Simone

Mr. Sharp said that in Mr. Meiklejohn's temporary absence he was answering Simone's letter and that he was sending it to Prof. C. H. Mills, director of the University School of Music. He then gave her a list of names of persons to whom she should write saying that he himself was writing to Professor Mills "particularly." His estimation of contemporary music seems to me of period interest:

> I am very much interested in what you say about Mr. Varèse. Two or three years ago I heard Mr. Stokowski conduct one of Mr. Varèse's compositions at the Composers' Guild in New York. The work was received with great enthusiasm. As I am less than an amateur, my opinion is of no value. I can not, however, refrain from saying that it made a great impression on me. A great deal of contemporary music I do not pretend to understand (Honegger's Beer Bottle Solo with orchestra accompaniment, called, I believe, Shipwreck); but people like Stravinsky and Varèse seem to produce new and interesting designs.

In spite of the militant concern of Varèse's friends, there was not sufficient response to form the classes Varèse had envisioned. He had two or three new pupils that winter, but I do not know if they came to him from the institutions Simone wrote to or from other sources. Besides Colin McPhee, there were three or four of Salzedo's young harp pupils, whom Varèse, always ready with nicknames, called *"mes Anges,"* whether because they always flew up the three flights of stairs to the room on the top of our house, where he taught them, or perhaps because they seemed to him so angelic. We were a little cramped in our own quarters that year having, for economic reasons, rented our largest room and one of our bathrooms. Varèse gave one lecture arranged by Simone. I can remember nothing about it, either financially or otherwise, except that he talked about those new instruments he foresaw in the future. His notes have disappeared but as his habit was to repeat and hammer on that same subject in all his lectures (until electronic devices made possible some of the things he had hoped for, however far from the instruments of his imagination), I give the following excerpt from a later lecture in which the wording alone may differ:

> The interpreter will disappear like the storyteller after the invention of printing . . . on these instruments—sound *producing,* not reproducing, the composer in collaboration with the

engineer will one day be able to transfer his work directly. Then anyone will be able to press a button and the music will be released as conceived by the composer. Between the composer and the listener no deforming prism, but the same intimate communion as that existing between writer and reader.

Varèse was to modify this extreme view later on and allow the performer the right to live. At the moment his mind, or rather his whole heart had one yearning, one goal: a means of getting his music heard without the need of performers, orchestras, or virtuosi conductors who now ignored him. Stokowski was the only conductor at the head of a symphony orchestra who had performed his music and after *Arcana* Stokowski performed them no more. In 1930, Varèse wrote to him from Paris that he had finished a new version of *Arcana,* fully expecting Stokowski to play it. But the Maestro replied that his programs were made up for the coming season and without further mention of *Arcana* asked if Varèse's work for the stage would be finished by the coming year so that he could conduct it. If Varèse had been a more prolific composer, Stokowski would have gone on performing each *new* work. A *first performance* then, as Varèse used to say, "a first-class funeral." It was Nicolas Slonimsky who, beginning with *Offrandes* at the second concert of his Chamber Orchestra of Boston, carried on a militant crusade on behalf of Varèse's music. Varèse used affectionately to call him *"mon mécanicien."* He played all Varèse's chamber works, whether in Boston, Los Angeles, Mexico, South America, so that Varèse became a legend in far places. In 1932 he brought *Arcana* to Paris and to Berlin under the auspices of the PAAC. In 1933 he conducted the première of *Ionisation* in New York as well as the first recording which, in spite of its technical imperfections, had a powerful impact on some of the younger composers in Paris as Boulez recalled in his tribute to Varèse at the Domaine Musical, November 1965.

By the time Varèse began to fear that his teaching project would not be realized in New York, he had found a compensation. He had met Harvey Fletcher, director of physical research at Western Electric and by March was spending many hours at their laboratories, in those days on West Street within walking distance of our house. Harvey Fletcher was a man of imagination with an inquiring mind that explored beyond the limited concerns of his own special field, as Edward E. Davies, Jr., has written of him:

> He is one of those rare individuals whose understanding ranges both broadly and deeply. . . . As a pioneer in modern psycho-acoustics, he bridged that forbidding chasm between physics and psychology leaving such permanent spans as the relation between frequency, intensity and loudness (the Fletcher-Munson surves), the subjective loudness (sone) scale, and the concepts of masking.

It may be imagined how Varèse, with his hunger for more and more knowledge of acoustics and his passionate interest in the voyaging of sounds in space, lived for those visits to the laboratory as though he were going to a Socratic banquet. Mr. Davies continues:

> In 1924 he published with M. H. Martin, *High Quality Transmission and Reproduction of Speech and Music,* outlining those factors which both to industry and the hi-fi fraternity have become standard terms of reference.

It is hardly surprising either that Fletcher with his roving curiosity should have been interested in Varèse's outpourings about the music instrument of his imagination and in the quite definite ideas Varèse had for experimenting. Though Varèse was refused the permission which he sought to experiment with an engineer himself, Fletcher did institute experiments and in 1928 Varèse wrote to Salzedo, then in Seal Harbor: "Western Electric is working at top speed on my instrument—it's a go—and you are in on it and will be the first to present it to the public." How Varèse's high expectations raced ahead. It was not "a go" at all, for the experiments were before very long stopped. Why? In the end, the reason is probably to be found in a remark Mr. Fletcher once made to Varèse: "We are here to improve the value of the investor's dollar." Industry saw no return in a problematic musical instrument in which the official music world took no interest.

Varèse that winter did just what he had vowed in 1925 never to do again, he founded another music society, the *Pan American Association of Composers*. I inwardly sighed but tactfully said nothing. To an inquiring journalist Varèse gave the following reasons:

> The Pan American was born because I realized that Europe was drifting back to neo-classicism or rather what is so-called. . . . You can't make a classic; it has to become one with age. What is called classicism is really academicism, the influence we want to combat as an evil thing, for it stifles spontaneous expression. . . . It is not that I believe music should be limited to a passport but rather that today very little music is alive in Europe.

Though one can never be sure that a reporter has reported verbatim, this does have a truthful tinge of the Varèse of the ICG.

Varèse was made president of the Executive Committee with four vice-presidents: Henry Cowell, Carl Ruggles, Emerson Whithorne, and Carlos Chávez.

I remember nothing of the activities of the newly founded organization. Varèse had met the extraordinary founder of the New School for Social Research, Dr. Alvin Johnson, and I know that both Varèse and Henry Cowell arranged concerts for him at the New School, but I have no recollection as to when or whether any of them at this time were under the auspices of the PAAC. I only know that from the beginning, at least after Varèse that autumn went to live for a few years in Paris, the active member of the society was Henry Cowell with the invaluable collaboration of Nicolas Slonimsky, who became its peripatetic conductor, and Charles Ives, an enthusiastic member and generous financial backer. The PAAC concerts which took place several years later I remember very well and shall duly report them in this diary, which is as truthful as the reliability of my memory, some documents at hand, and a very few other memories still alive.

Varèse: A Looking-Glass Diary

There was no Guild that winter to play Varèse and Stokowski, because of his bursitis, was taking a year off—besides, even if Stokowski had been conducting, since there was no *new* Varèse work, there would have been no Varèse on his programs. Happily, however, in March the silence was broken. Georges Barrère, the first flutist of the New York Symphony Orchestra, who every season conducted a series of concerts with his Little Symphony Orchestra, that "gracious harbinger of spring," as Pitts Sanborn called it, played *Offrandes,* and Nina Koshetz sang them. After the regular program Barrère always gave an "ultra-modern" work as an extra, thus described by Pitts Sanborn in the *New York Telegram:* "As is customary when the Little Symphony holds forth, there was an 'after concert,' or concert improper, for which the customers were cordially invited to remain." Barrère always prefaced his "after concert" with a humorous discourse, for he loved to talk, had a quick witty tongue, and was as funny as the best comedians on the stage. Sometimes when the woodwinds were not playing at a New York Symphony concert you might see signs of suppressed laughter on the faces nearest him and you knew that he had given one of his swift witticisms muffled through his beard. Before playing *Offrandes* he told the audience: "You must listen to the music your sons and grandsons will like." The remark proved superfluous, for his listeners applauded so vigorously that Barrère repeated *La Chanson de Là-haut.* A large share, of course, belonged to Nina who, as Pitts Sanborn wrote, "sang with her familiar charm and address and that curious pebbly vibration in her voice." Of the music he commented: "Whether or not these voice parts are wholly persuasive, nobody blessed with hearing could well deny the fascination of the rhythms and the color and balance of the elaborate and ingenious instrumental parts."

Not only did Barrère surround us with laughter whenever we dined at his house or at ours—usually with the Barrères' great friends the Jacquets—but Cecile Barrère was the best cook in or out of France; just to remember her *gigot à l'ail* makes my mouth water. My name being Louise, Barrère called me *"Depuis-le-jour."* *

* An aria from Gustave Charpentier's opera *Louise.*

In spite of the absence of the ICG and of Stokowski, the winter of 1928 was as copiously musical as ever; innumerable concerts, even occasionally opera, often after dinners at Mrs. Rossin's, Irene Lewisohn's, or Mrs. Holmes's, and receptions for visiting musicians; Szigeti and Segovia gave the most triumphant recitals of the season; Beecham arrived from London to conduct the Philharmonic; Nina Koshetz sang with the visiting Cincinnati Orchestra; and at their appointed times Koussevitzky with his Boston players and guest conductor Monteux with Stokowski's Philadelphians came to Carnegie Hall; Béla Bartók had arrived the previous December for a six-week tour and Ravel about the same time with his "twenty pair of pyjamas and fifty shirts" (to quote his biographer, H. H. Stuckenschmidt) and countless "crazy ties" (to quote Stuckenschmidt quoting Ravel). They both gave piano recitals—or at least one each that I heard —Bartók playing superbly, Ravel deplorably by his own estimation. Salzedo told us that the following day when he brought Ravel the press reviews, he found him at the piano conscientiously practicing, but that as soon as he learned of the critics' unqualified approbation, he jumped up, closed the piano with a bang, and said: "Then I don't have to practice!" Ravel was very short and dapper and on the stage made one think of an elegant *petit abbé* of the eighteenth century. He charmed the audience—the critics too, evidently.

A unique personality met that year was the French poet Paul Claudel, at that time ambassador in Washington. Occasionally, when he was in New York with a moment to spare he would come down to Sullivan Street for an hour's conversation with Varèse which he seemed to relish—Varèse was an appreciative listener. Once we took him to a gourmet French restaurant for dinner and, in spite of Claudel's protest that he ate practically nothing in the evening, Varèse had ordered an epicurean meal. Claudel ate every delicious crumb and, it goes without saying, drank deep of the good wines of Varèse's Burgundy. Claudel, who was as devout a Catholic as a medieval monk, had the same robust appetites.

During dinner, conversation ranged very far as well as near and personal. Claudel was a dramatic and colorful raconteur and his tales took us to Japan, where he had been consul, and to Brazil; he talked of the theater and of his own plays, tangling with Varèse on mysticism and the Church until they agreed amicably, raising their glasses, not to agree, going on to poetry, to music and Claudel's collaboration with Darius Milhaud, then finally to Varèse's own work. When Varèse told him about The One-All-Alone, Claudel said he would like very much to see the scenario and would gladly, as Varèse asked, give his opinion if Varèse would send it to him. However, over the last *petit verre*, stretching across the table to grasp Varèse's hand, Claudel cried: "Varèse, let us collaborate, let us write a *Symphonia TERRI-BILIS!*" But it was not to Claudel that Varèse turned when later he was looking for a poet to write a text for his *Astronomer*. Claudel was nineteenth century, that is the past, and Varèse's Astronomer looked with Varèse into the future.

Not long after this Varèse went to Washington for one of Mrs. Coolidge's concerts conducted by Hans Kindler in the hall she had had built next to the Library of Congress and had presented to the government. The next day Varèse lunched at the Claudels' and, learning of Claudel's predilection for Gorgan-zola, sent him from New York one of those huge round black-covered cheeses the French so fittingly call a *"meule,"* or mill-stone. He received this letter in return (I translate):

> Dear Varèse: Thank you for the superb *meule* of Gorganzola—the whole family is sitting down to it. I too was happy talking to you and to continue the conversation I am sending you a collection of my Japanese poems.
>
> I await the scenario.

The poems, in Japanese as well as in French, are in three small, long, slim volumes beautifully bound and boxed in blue cloth—a soft shadowy blue certainly dyed in Japan and not in this country of hard shadowless dyes—written from right to left, the pages accordianned. With them came two typewritten pages of explanation of which let me quote two very Claudelian excerpts:

A thousand secret intentions are hidden in the calligraphy, effected by the poet himself and reproduced lithographically by one of the most skillful artisans in Tokyo. . . . In the disposition of the lines and the words, through the interposition of blanks, the suspension in the empty space of mute consonants, of periods and accents, the collaboration of meditation and the expression of the sense, of the voice, of dream, of memory, of the writing and the thought, it is to be hoped that the intellectual vibration of each word, or essential part of each word, will become perceptible to the patient reader who deciphers each text slowly, one after the other, as one sips a small cup of very hot tea.

Claudel proposed obtaining the Légion d'Honneur for Varèse, but Varèse, who had a mystical horror of decorations, refused Claudel's friendly offer of diplomatic intervention and was to repeat his philosophic rejection in 1939 when Maurice Jacquet did his best to make him change his mind. Varèse used to say, "The only use for a red ribbon in one's buttonhole is to impress one's concierge"; and also, "Today if you don't have a red ribbon in your buttonhole people say, what has he done *not* to have the Légion d'Honneur?" The order was instituted by Bonaparte when he was first consul to reward the military and civilians for services to *La Patrie*—then it was awarded to politicians—then to artists, writers, scientists—then to dressmakers, cinema stars, athletes, crooners—and so on. Perhaps Varèse was an intellectual snob to refuse it!

INDEX

285

Index

Index

Index

Index

Index